MW00830203

FIRSTBORN
GIRLS

FIRST BORN GIRLS

~

A Memoir

Bernice L. McFadden

DUTTON

DUTTON

An imprint of Penguin Random House LLC
1745 Broadway, New York, NY 10019
penguinrandomhouse.com

Photograph on page vii courtesy of the author.

LIBRARY OF CONGRESS CATALOGING-IN-PUBLICATION DATA
Names: McFadden, Bernice L., author.
Title: Firstborn girls : a memoir / Bernice McFadden.
Description: New York : Dutton, 2025.
Identifiers: LCCN 2024040363 (print) | LCCN 2024040364 (ebook) |
ISBN 9780593184974 (hardcover) | ISBN 9780593184998 (ebook)
Subjects: LCSH: McFadden, Bernice L. | African American women authors—Biography. |
Women authors, American—Biography. | LCGFT: Autobiographies.
Classification: LCC PS3563.C3622 Z46 2025 (print) |
LCC PS3563.C3622 (ebook) | DDC 813/.54 [B]—dc23/eng/20241021
LC record available at https://lccn.loc.gov/2024040363
LC ebook record available at https://lccn.loc.gov/2024040364

Printed in the United States of America
1   3   5   7   9   10   8   6   4   2

BOOK DESIGN BY ANGIE BOUTIN

The authorized representative in the EU for product safety and compliance is
Penguin Random House Ireland, Morrison Chambers, 32 Nassau Street,
Dublin D02 YH68, Ireland. https://eu-contact.penguin.ie.

For the firstborn girls who raised me:
Thelma, Gwendolyn, Vivian, and Azsá.
For them and the angelcestors.

AUTHOR'S NOTE

My first maternal ancestor in this country was the descendant of the African ethnic group called the Bamileke.

The Bamileke people lived in the cradle of the world known as Egypt. They fled the land of the pharaohs when Arab Muslims conquered the region, imposing Islam and outlawing the Bamileke spiritual belief system, known as ancestor veneration.

Over a millennium, the Bamileke people traveled southwest across the continent of Africa through deserts and jungles, across rivers and lakes, until they settled in countries that we now know as Nigeria, Cameroon, Congo, Benin, and Togo.

Some of my ancestors built boats that carried them across the ocean to America, where they mixed and mingled and traded and copulated with the indigenous population. Still others were brought here by Europeans, against their will in chains and shackles.

However they arrived, my ancestors planted themselves deep into the soil and soul of this country.

This is a story of my family. This is a story of America.

This is a work of autoethnography.

This is necessary work.

This is love work.

This is legacy literature about me and mine born into a world run by them and theirs.

I am writing with my burnt hand about the nature of fire.

—INGEBORG BACHMANN

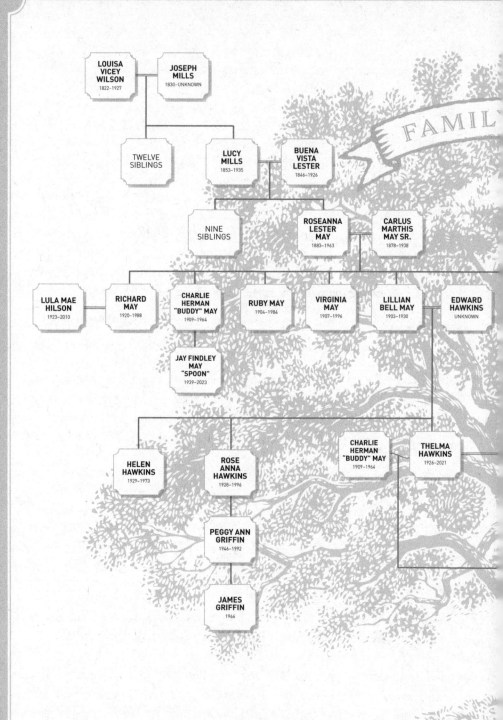

LOUISA VICEY WILSON
1822–1927

JOSEPH MILLS
1830–UNKNOWN

TWELVE SIBLINGS

LUCY MILLS
1853–1935

BUENA VISTA LESTER
1846–1926

NINE SIBLINGS

ROSEANNA LESTER MAY
1883–1963

CARLUS MARTHIS MAY SR.
1878–1938

LULA MAE HILSON
1923–2010

RICHARD MAY
1920–1988

CHARLIE HERMAN "BUDDY" MAY
1909–1964

RUBY MAY
1904–1984

VIRGINIA MAY
1907–1996

LILLIAN BELL MAY
1903–1930

EDWARD HAWKINS
UNKNOWN

JAY FINDLEY MAY "SPOON"
1939–2023

HELEN HAWKINS
1929–1973

ROSE ANNA HAWKINS
1928–1996

CHARLIE HERMAN "BUDDY" MAY
1909–1964

THELMA HAWKINS
1926–2021

PEGGY ANN GRIFFIN
1946–1992

JAMES GRIFFIN
1966

FAMILY

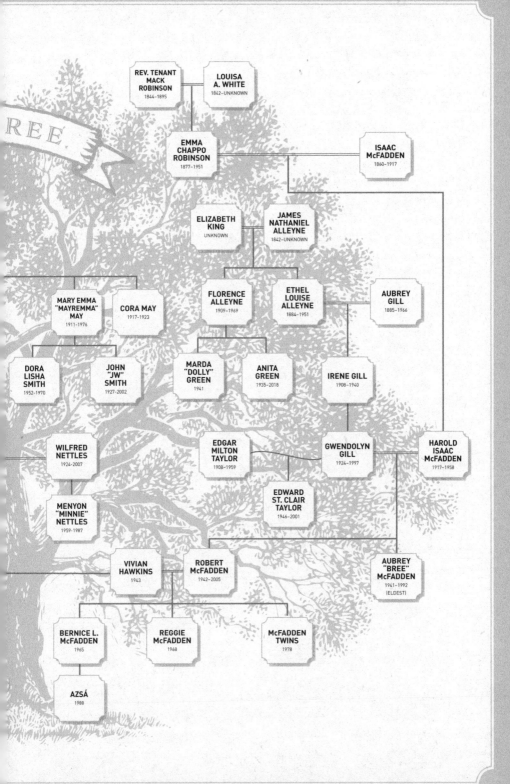

REE

REV. TENANT MACK ROBINSON
1844–1895

LOUISA A. WHITE
1842–UNKNOWN

EMMA CHAPPO ROBINSON
1877–1951

ISAAC McFADDEN
1860–1917

ELIZABETH KING
UNKNOWN

JAMES NATHANIEL ALLEYNE
1842–UNKNOWN

MARY EMMA "MAYREMMA" MAY
1911–1976

CORA MAY
1917–1923

FLORENCE ALLEYNE
1909–1969

ETHEL LOUISE ALLEYNE
1884–1951

AUBREY GILL
1885–1966

DORA LISHA SMITH
1952–1970

JOHN "JW" SMITH
1927–2002

MARDA "DOLLY" GREEN
1941

ANITA GREEN
1935–2018

IRENE GILL
1908–1940

WILFRED NETTLES
1924–2007

EDGAR MILTON TAYLOR
1908–1959

GWENDOLYN GILL
1924–1997

HAROLD ISAAC McFADDEN
1917–1958

MENYON "MINNIE" NETTLES
1959–1987

EDWARD ST. CLAIR TAYLOR
1946–2001

VIVIAN HAWKINS
1943

ROBERT McFADDEN
1942–2005

AUBREY "BREE" McFADDEN
1941–1992
(ELDEST)

BERNICE L. McFADDEN
1965

REGGIE McFADDEN
1968

McFADDEN TWINS
1978

AZSÁ
1988

FIRSTBORN
GIRLS

PRELUDE TO A LIFE

Some women are lost in the fire; some women are built from it.

—MICHELLE K.

The first thing I want to tell you is that on September 27, 1967, I died.

I was two years and one day old.

Two days before my death, my mother, Vivian, and I flew from New York to Cleveland, Ohio, to visit James Forest and his wife, Julia. I was a little bald-headed toddler, and my mother was twenty-four years old with cover-girl good looks.

When Vivian was a child, her mother, Thelma, had been romantically involved in a relationship with James Forest that was as passionate as it was violent. It was a vicious cycle, one that Vivian would relive in her own marriage.

However, by 1967, James and Thelma's turbulent history was like water under the bridge. The former lovers were friendly now, telephoning each other on birthdays and holidays to share news about some person they'd both known who'd hit the number, got married, had a baby, gone to jail, or died. I suppose they stayed connected because they had history. History, if you don't know, is a hard thing to shake because it's as bonding as glue. They'd stayed connected because of their viscid history, but also because James had been like a father to Vivian, who had never had one.

When James learned that Vivian had married and had had a child, he sent for the two of us to come to Cleveland so that he could wrap his arms around us both. "Bring that baby up here so I can smell her head!"

That's how I ended up celebrating my second birthday in Cleveland, Ohio, with Thelma's old flame, his wife, and my mother. On the afternoon of the twenty-sixth, everyone gathered around the white Formica kitchen table. I was seated in Vivian's lap, dressed in a pink frilly dress and colorful party hat. After they sang "Happy Birthday," Vivian held me a safe distance from the flame dancing atop the white candle shaped in the form of the number 2.

"Blow, Bernice, blow!"

The flame buckled and died, and then I plunged my hands into the cake and shoveled the creamy sweetness into my mouth. There was a lot of joy in that room, but there was sadness too. We should have been celebrating at home with my father, Robert, as a family. I suspect that our trip to Cleveland was more than just a visit to catch up with old friends and family. I suspect this was one of my mother's early prison breaks.

JAMES AND HIS WIFE LIVED just a few short hours away from Detroit, Michigan. Vivian hadn't been back to that city since she and Thelma had moved to Brooklyn back in the fifties.

She had planned to take a bus from Cleveland to Detroit to visit her great-uncle Richard, great-aunt Lula Mae, and their children. When James heard her plans, he scoffed. "I can't let you take my grandbaby on no filthy goddamn bus." James's concern was less about the cleanliness of the bus and more about whether Vivian and I would have an easy egress from the city should tempers re-erupt.

∿

TWO MONTHS EARLIER, ON JULY 23, 1967, DETROIT EXPLODED IN ONE of the deadliest and most destructive race rebellions the country had ever seen. Over five days and nights forty-three people were killed, thirty-three of whom were Black. More than 7,200 people were arrested—most of them were Black too.

The last time Detroit tempers flared to that degree was in 1943, the year Vivian was born. During that unrest, nine whites and twenty-five Blacks were killed. Of those twenty-five, seventeen were murdered by the police.

America was and remains a powder keg, and often the match that lights the fuse is racism.

In 1967, Detroit was just one of nearly 160 uprisings that erupted across the nation that summer. The terror disrupted whole families, including my own.

On July 12, John W. Smith, my maternal first cousin, twice removed, was pulled over in his taxicab in Newark, New Jersey, by two white police officers. After some back-and-forth, the officers ripped John from the car, arrested him, and then beat him within an inch of his life.

Residents in the area saw the officers drag his limp body from the cruiser into the police station. The spectators assumed he was dead, and the notion spread like fever. Soon, the police station was surrounded by a mass of angry people chanting, "Show us John Smith! Show us John Smith!"

Police officers dressed in riot gear rushed the crowd with billy clubs. In retaliation, rocks and bottles were pelted, and melee ensued. Over five nights, businesses were looted, fires were set, twenty-six people were killed, and seven hundred people were injured, including a twelve-year-old boy named Joe Bass Jr., whom police shot down in the street for stealing a twelve-pack of beer.

Life magazine put Bass's image on the cover of their July 28 issue.

In the photo, Joe lies crumpled on the blacktop, bleeding from his neck and leg wounds. One arm is folded beneath him, the other bent as if in an embrace. His fingers on both hands are touching. The scene is heartbreaking, hard to shake from my memory, but for some reason I cannot articulate, it's his white Converse sneakers—gray with filth—that dog me.

A week ahead of Joe Bass Jr., my cousin John Smith, called J.W., graced the cover of *Time* magazine. Unkempt Afro, cheeks covered in five-o'clock shadow, mustache and soul patch in need of a trim, he is looking away from the camera, eyes focused on something or someone just out of frame.

When he made the cover, phones jangled in houses and apartments of my family members all across the country.

Hey, y'all know J.W. is on the cover of *Time* magazine?

Mary Emma's boy is on the cover of *Time* magazine!

Rosie May's grandson is on *Time* magazine!

Thelma bought a copy from the newspaper stand outside the Manhattan office building where she worked as a cleaning woman. She made it a point to tell the white man behind the counter that the Black man on the cover was her cousin. In the building, she showed the magazine to her coworkers and the white hedge fund managers who were readying themselves to leave for the evening.

"That there is my cousin," she said, smiling proudly as the magazine passed from one set of hands to the next.

"Really, Thelma?"

"Yep."

In the morning, when she returned home from emptying wastebaskets, scrubbing toilets, and polishing the chrome panel insets of the elevators, she tossed the magazine on the dining room table where her four stepchildren were eating cereal before heading off to school.

"Look," she spat. "*Time* magazine done gone and put the devil on their cover."

She had her reasons for calling him that, reasons I'll get to soon.

THE PREVIOUS YEAR, THE CITY of Cleveland experienced its own bout of civil unrest when a Black customer walked into the Seventy-Niners Café on Hough Avenue, ordered a take-out meal, and, as he waited for his food, asked if he could have a glass of water. When the white waiter refused, hot words were exchanged, and then all hell broke loose.

By September 1967, residents in both Cleveland and Detroit were still simmering with rage, even as icy autumn air swept down from neighboring Canada.

∼

SO, WITH ALL OF THAT IN MIND, JAMES HANDED MY MOTHER THE KEYS to his brand-new 1967 Cadillac. "Go 'head, take my car," he'd said, and then added with a wink and a chuckle, "Make sure you bring it back in one piece."

Famous last words.

On that chilly autumn evening, with his wife, Julia, in the passenger seat and me in the back, Vivian aimed that shiny black Cadillac toward Detroit, and we set off on a journey that would end in smoke and flames.

Infant car seats did not exist in 1967. In 1967, you held your children in your lap, and if they were big enough, you just sat them in the seat like any other grown passenger. And maybe you used the seat belts, but you probably didn't, because although they were provided, you weren't required by law to wear them.

On the dashboard under the glow of the radio was a metal ashtray hidden behind a door with a lip. A light tug to the lip and the silver ashtray popped out like a Murphy bed from a wall. Alongside that ashtray was a cigarette lighter. All one had to do was press the cylinder-shaped lighter into the opening and wait a few seconds. Once it was heated, the lighter would pop up. The smoker could then pluck the lighter from the opening, bring the underside of red-hot coils to the tip of the cigarette, and voilà!

Most cars had ashtrays and lighters in the armrests too. The Cadillac was no exception. It was those ashtrays that got me hauled into the front seat, because I was opening and closing the lids, and the clacking sound was raking Vivian's nerves. Keeping her eyes on the road and hands on the steering wheel, Vivian said to Julia, "Please bring that child up here."

Julia reached back and pulled me into her lap, where I squirmed and squirmed until she finally set me down betwixt the two of them.

Had the car not had ashtrays, I would have been left in that back seat, and I surely would have died on impact.

It was late, the night sky was scattered with clouds, and Interstate 94 was dark. Vivian and Julia bounced their heads to Aretha Franklin's "Respect" flowing out of the speakers. When Vivian approached West Road, she squinted at the sign, unsure if that was the right exit.

"Is this it?" she whispered, easing up on the gas.

"Yeah," Julia confirmed.

Headlights flashed in her sideview mirror as she engaged the turn signal and then *BAM* . . . a car plowed right into the back of the Cadillac. The impact was so hard, the rear end crumpled like paper and then promptly burst into flames.

Vivian has recounted this story as many times as I have asked to hear it. And I have asked many, many times. I ask because I want to remember—I need to remember—this horrible thing that happened to us. I've asked so many times that I know the story backward and forward and inside and out.

The fire was hot. It was like being in an oven. It was like being in hell. Red and yellow flames charged through that ruined Cadillac, roaring like a pride of lions. There was so much thick black smoke. It burned our eyes and seared our throats.

My little ankles were caught in the slither of space that separated the driver and passenger seats. Vivian tugged to free me, but I was stuck as tight as a cork in a bottle.

Meanwhile, the flames had devoured her feet and were making a meal of her calves, licking at her thighs, melting her skin like the waxed candle on my birthday cake.

Unable to take another second of pain, she turned me loose, jumped out of the burning vehicle, and streaked away, desperately trying to outrun the flesh-eating fire. But that made things worse because the wind became an accelerant. She might have run until her entire body was engulfed in flame, but a voice in her head shouted: *Vivian, stop running! Vivian, drop and roll!*

And Vivian did exactly that. She rolled and rolled on that black asphalt until the flames were dead.

I used to wonder who the voice belonged to. But now I believe that the voice my mother heard was not just one voice but a chorus of voices belonging to a legion of ancestors, whom I call angelcestors.

An angelcestor is a divine ancestor who serves as a guide and protector of the living. Mine stretch all the way back to Louisa Vicey Wilson, who is my four-times great-grandmother, but also our Eve, because to date she is the earliest documented woman of my maternal family line.

Flesh smoldering, Vivian limped back to the burning Cadillac, reached in, grabbed hold of me, summoned all of her strength, and yanked me free—tearing the skin around my ankles in the process.

The feat was nothing short of a miracle. Indeed, it was the phenomenon known as hysterical strength, which is a miracle of extreme physical power that occurs in some human beings who find themselves in a life-or-death situation. The part of your brain that is associated with fear releases stress hormones like cortisol, which gives you extra energy and adrenaline, sending more oxygen to your muscles, boosting your strength. Adrenaline also heightens your vision and hearing. As part of the fight-or-flight response, the body releases endorphins. If a person is injured while in fight-or-flight mode, those endorphins will mask the pain.

I still bear the scars from the stitches it took to seal the wounds. I received third-degree burns on my face, stomach, and right hand. Vivian received second-degree burns on her face and third-degree burns on her left thigh, both feet, and ankles. She had to learn how to walk again, and years in the future, on those ruined feet, she would endeavor a foot race with her youngest children and win.

After I was pulled to safety, she tried to coax Julia from the car, but Julia was in shock and would not move. A good Samaritan came along and tugged her from the vehicle just seconds before the second explosion.

"That woman," Vivian says, each time she retells the story, always with a shake of her head. "That woman did not get a scratch on her. Not a burn or a cut, or nothing."

I find it hard to believe that Julia walked away from that inferno unblemished. But this has been Vivian's claim, and she has never wavered from it.

THEY TRANSPORTED VIVIAN AND JULIA by ambulance to Wyandotte Hospital, located in the city of the same name. I was whisked away ahead of them. The first police officers on the scene bundled me in a blanket and sped off to Seaway Hospital in Trenton, Michigan.

It is unclear if my heart stopped beating in the police cruiser or the hospital, but at some point, I was clinically dead for a few seconds or minutes before I was resuscitated and placed on a ventilator.

In the hospital, the doctor, nurses, and the police officers who drove there all circled my bed, silently watching my tiny chest rise and fall with the forced air.

"I don't think she's going to make it," the doctor mumbled. "Where did you say they took the mother?"

The doctor phoned Wyandotte Hospital. "You have a Negro woman there who came in by ambulance who was involved in a car wreck, right? I need to speak to her."

Vivian was in the emergency room, propped up in the bed, staring at her feet, which looked like raw meat.

They'd given her morphine for the pain but couldn't do much about the shock, so when the nurse appeared at her bedside with the black rotary telephone, saying, "It's the doctor in the emergency room at Seaway Hospital calling about your little girl," Vivian just gave her a slow blink.

The nurse pressed the receiver to her ear. "Say hello," she urged.

Vivian's hello was thick and muddy.

The doctor told her that he was going to do all he could do to save her baby girl. He told her to hope for the best but prepare for the worst.

The nurse placed the receiver in the cradle and patted Vivian's shoulder.

But we both survived, and that is a marvel because, according to the National Highway Traffic Safety Administration, in 1967 there were 50,724 motor vehicle fatalities—and we were not among them.

HOURS AFTER THE CAR ACCIDENT, Julia called James Forest from the hospital. When he answered the phone, his voice was groggy with sleep.

"Yeah?"

"J-James, there's been an accident."

After she recounted the evening's events, he muttered, "Fuck. I'll be right there."

James called Thelma, who was sitting at the dining room table, sipping her morning coffee. Dawn was breaking, sparrows were chattering away in the treetops. She already knew it was bad news—people didn't generally call at that hour with good news. She rose from the chair, went into the kitchen, and lifted the handset of the yellow wall phone.

"Hello?"

"Thelma . . . Thelma . . ." He could barely get the words out as he struggled into his trousers.

Her heartbeat climbed.

"James? What's wrong? Is it Vivian?"

After she hung up with James, she went upstairs to the bedroom. Her husband, Wilfred, worked the night shift. He'd be coming home from work soon. Thelma clicked on the lamp, retrieved her phone book from the nightstand, and sat down on the side of the bed. The first call she placed was to Robert, who answered on the first ring.

"W-what hospital are they in?" he stammered nervously.

"I don't know that yet. James is headed to Detroit now; he'll call me when he gets there, and then I'll call you back."

The next call she placed was to her sister, Anna. She was the prayer warrior of the family. After that, she called her aunts, Ruby and Virginia, who shared a brownstone on St. Felix Street in the Fort Greene section of Brooklyn. Ruby had been babysitting me since I was six weeks old, when Vivian went back to work as an attendant at Willowbrook State School on Staten Island. On hearing the news, Ruby whispered into the phone, "Oh my god. Oh my god," and then she called her brother Richard, who lived in Detroit with his wife, Lula Mae, and their twelve children. "Vivian and the baby were in a car wreck."

Just hours after Robert received Thelma's call, he, his brother Bree, and their friend Lonnie climbed into his 1959 four-door Buick LeSabre sedan, and the trio streaked off to Detroit.

I have driven from Brooklyn to Detroit several times, and it has taken me nine hours, not including the hour I give myself for a rest stop.

I don't think Robert stopped for anything other than gas, because within seven hours, they were rushing through the entry doors of Wyandotte Hospital.

A nurse showed them to the room where Vivian was convalescing.

"Stay outside," Robert said to his brother and Lonnie.

Vivian was in a drug-induced slumber. When Robert squeezed her shoulder, her eyes fluttered open.

"I'm here, Vivian," he whispered, choking back his emotions. "I'm h-here."

She thought he was a dream, a premonition brought on by the morphine. By the time she realized Robert was real, he was at Seaway Hospital, staring at me from the opposite side of protective glass.

After that, they went to Uncle Richard's house.

"WE'LL JUST SLEEP IN THE CAR," Robert told Richard after Lula Mae had cleared their empty food plates from the dining room table.

Richard made a face and then laughed and laughed. After he wiped the tears out of his eyes, he lit a cigar and pointed the glowing tip at Robert.

"Boy, where you come from?"

Embarrassed, Robert stammered, "Um, Brooklyn, sir."

"Well, maybe that's how y'all do in Brooklyn, but we from Georgia. We don't live like that."

Bree scratched his head and grinned. Lonnie snickered into his fist.

Richard continued, "We got plenty of room here for you, don't we, Mae?"

"Sure do."

They lived in a sprawling two-level Victorian house with oak wood floors and pocket doors. Sure, the house was packed to the gills with children, but room could always be made.

Richard tilted his head back and blew a cloud of smoke toward the ceiling. Lula Mae disappeared up the back stairs to ready one of the bedrooms. When he heard her slippered feet padding across the floor above his head, his eyes twinkled mischievously.

Leaning over the table, he whispered, "Y'all boys interested in a game of poker before you turn in?"

"Yeah, sure," they chorused, rubbing their palms and gnashing their teeth like sharks. They didn't know that Richard was an orca where poker was concerned.

Richard let them win the first two games, and then he took them for everything they had.

They stayed in Detroit for two days, visiting Vivian and then me and then Vivian again, before heading back to New York, because their employers didn't care nothing about their loved ones.

Robert had been with UPS for only two years, so he hadn't accumulated enough seniority to take time off. The next time he returned to Detroit was to collect us.

In between that, he and Vivian spoke on the phone and exchanged letters.

I have a few of those letters. In one letter, Robert reminded Vivian just how much he loved and missed her, saying:

> *I need you back home with me, as soon as possible. Even if you have to leave Bernice there.*

I have read and reread this particular letter, and it was only recently that I *really* saw the words, and the implications stabbed me in the heart like a knife.

In the letter, it appears that I am of little concern to Robert. He cannot live without *Vivian*, but I am expendable. I am disposable. I am replaceable.

As I read and reread this letter, even though my heart is cracking, I cannot speak to Vivian about this, because I know it will pain her as much as it pains me, and she has endured pain enough for two lifetimes.

So I call my longtime friend in Atlanta and weep my agony over the phone lines for thirty full minutes.

AFTER A FEW WEEKS, I was transferred to the Children's Hospital at 5224 St. Antoine in Detroit, Michigan.

The hospital opened in 1896. It was a stunning redbrick building that looked like a cross between a castle and a fort. When Vivian arrived in Detroit from Sandersville in the late summer of 1952, she wasn't in the city a good two weeks before she was admitted into that very same hospital to have two inguinal hernias removed.

Me being a patient at the same children's hospital fifteen years later wouldn't be worth the mention if we were residents in Detroit in 1967, but we weren't, and that's what makes the event remarkable to me.

This is how our lives touch and blend.

VIVIAN AND I WERE RELEASED from our respective hospitals in late November. By then, fall was but a memory. The trees had shed their vibrant autumn leaves, and the debris was buried under white Michigan snow.

In early December, Robert drove to Detroit alone to collect us. My parents had a time getting me into that car. I screamed and hollered and fought like a wild cat.

Robert was aggravated and annoyed by my behavior, not at all taking into account that this was a normal reaction to the recent trauma I'd suffered. Vivian must have been afraid too. After all, the terror of it was as fresh in her mind as it was in mine.

I imagine that we clung to each other the entire trip. I imagine that she held her breath all the way to Brooklyn.

Robert liked to drive fast. He liked to drag race. It was a habit that he was reluctant to shake, even after he was married with children. If he found himself at a red light, an empty stretch of road before him, and a willing participant on either side of him, then once the light changed from red to green, he'd jam his foot down on the accelerator, shooting the car through the intersection like a rocket.

After the car accident, you'd think he'd change his driving habits to reduce our distress—but he didn't. For years, up until he sold his car in 1984, Vivian would sit in the passenger seat, nervously eyeing the climbing needle of the speedometer.

"Slow down, Robert, please."

But Robert would not slow down. In fact, he increased the speed, barreling down the highway, swerving in and out of traffic like an Indy race car driver. As for me, all I could do was sit in the back seat, helpless and terrified, hyperventilating into my palms. When Vivian's pleas climbed to hysterics, Robert snickered with glee and finally eased up off the gas.

Our terror brought him great joy.

PART ONE

The lion is most handsome when looking for food.

—RUMI

1

My parents met in 1964, dubbed the year of the Negro.
Sidney Poitier became the first Black actor in the thirty-five-year history of the Academy Awards to win an Oscar for best actor for his role as a construction worker in the movie *Lilies of the Field*, and Martin Luther King Jr. was awarded the Nobel Peace Prize. He was only the third Black person to be so honored.

On July 2, President Lyndon B. Johnson signed the Civil Rights Act into law, which is supposed to prohibit discrimination on the basis of race, religion, sex, or country of origin, but says nothing at all of the systematic murder of Black people by civilians or police officers.

On July 16, 1964, fifteen-year-old James Powell, a Black child, was shot and killed by police lieutenant Thomas Gilligan in Harlem, New York. Some accounts claim that Powell slashed Gilligan with a knife, after which Gilligan shot him three times. Other accounts say Powell did not have a knife at all. The shooting set off six consecutive nights of rioting that affected Harlem and Bedford-Stuyvesant, Brooklyn.

The unrest persisted for days. Order was finally restored on July 22, Robert's twenty-third birthday.

A FEW WEEKS LATER, ROBERT SPOTTED VIVIAN STEPPING OFF THE B61 bus, at the corner of Lorraine and Columbia Streets in Red Hook, Brooklyn. Under a teal sky, Vivian strolled toward home in the Red Hook projects, where she shared a crowded one-bedroom apartment with her mother; stepfather, Wilfred; and his four children from a previous marriage. Robert stood alongside his delivery truck, gawking, helplessly struck by Vivian's shapely, thick legs, fall of shiny black hair, soaring cheekbones, and bedroom eyes.

She was a knockout.

He hurried to catch up, trampling over a freshly chalked hopscotch diagram. Oblivious to the kiss-teeth annoyance of the little girls, he tried and failed to dance out of the reach of water shooting from an open fire hydrant. The wet moved like a shadow down the left leg of his Levi's jeans. A teenaged boy transporting a pig-tailed, chubby girl propped on the handlebars of his Schwinn, swung wildly to avoid Robert. The sudden shift toppled the girl to the pavement, where she bounced like a ball before flipping Robert the bird.

Reaching Vivian, he brushed his fingers against her bare arm. "Hey, hello."

Startled, she turned around and glared into his smiling face. Before she could admonish him for touching her, he dropped a pickup line so tired—*Can I walk with you?*—it yawned.

She eyed him, brought a lit Newport cigarette to her lips, and sucked. On the exhale, she announced that he could walk anywhere he chose, because the sidewalk was free and open to the public. He trailed her all the way to the entrance of the projects, but she refused to give him her telephone number, and finally he turned and walked back to his delivery truck.

But Robert was persistent. Every day she stepped off that bus, he was there waiting. Nowadays, that behavior is called stalking. Back then, though, a woman was supposed to feel flattered when relentlessly pursued by a man.

Vivian was polite but firm in her disinterest, but he was as insistent as a toddler determined to get his way. Annoyed, she took to exiting the bus a stop earlier, walking a few blocks out of her way, accessing the projects through a different entrance. It didn't take long before Robert became hip to her scheme, and days later, when she stepped off the bus, there he was.

LONG STORY SHORT, SHE GAVE him her telephone number.

I wonder, when she took the time to study his face—the shape of his nose and neatly trimmed mustache—what it was she saw when she finally looked into his eyes. Did she see the hurt standing in them like puddles after a hard rain? Did the puddles mirror her own?

After all, being raised by Thelma hadn't always been a bed of roses, because when crossed, disobeyed, or challenged, Thelma's retribution could be vindictive and cruel. Once, when Vivian was fourteen years old, she'd started seeing a young man who claimed he was eighteen, but Thelma suspected that he was twenty years old if he was a day.

"That boy is too old for you, Vivian," Thelma said. "And I don't want you seeing him. You better stay away from him, you hear me?"

Vivian had heard, but she did not obey, and when the man-boy gifted her a pair of expensive cashmere sweaters, Vivian snuck them in the house and hid them in the bottom of her trunk, underneath her everyday clothes. A few days later, when she came home from school, Thelma was standing at the stove wearing those sweaters—both of them. Vivian was shocked but didn't say a word, and neither did Thelma. Over dinner they spoke about everything but those sweaters, even though all Vivian could think of was how Thelma's oversized bust was stretching the knit to ruin. Afterward, Vivian washed the dishes, went into the bedroom, and cried. She never saw those sweaters again.

Thelma didn't physically punish Vivian, but she would rail on for days about the tiniest of infractions: the tub wasn't clean enough, the carpet hadn't been swept properly. It seemed to Vivian that Thelma just enjoyed making her miserable. It was that badgering that drove Vivian to run away in the summer of 1958. She was fifteen at the time—same age I was when I first ran away—same age as my daughter when she ran away.

The day her life changed, Vivian had been away from home for two days. Her aunt Anna had spotted her in a neighborhood bar and reported the sighting back to Thelma.

"Sis, I seen Vivian. She's safe, don't worry. I'm going to get her and bring her back home."

Back then, teenagers went to bars and were served if they looked eighteen. Vivian presented mature for her fifteen years, which was probably why she attracted older men. Hours after Anna called Thelma, two men dressed in suits walked into the bar, straight up to Vivian, flashed gold badges, identified themselves as NYC detectives, and asked her name. She gave it, and then they arrested her for larceny. They handcuffed Vivian in front of her astonished friends, read her Miranda rights, and hauled her away in the back of an unmarked police car.

A day later, Thelma stood up in court and accused Vivian of stealing money and jewelry from her. Vivian contends, to this day, that she did not steal one piece of jewelry or one red cent from Thelma. Vivian was sentenced to a year at Westfield State Farm, a women's detention facility in Bedford Hills, New York.

Every weekend, Thelma took the hours-long bus ride up to Westfield State Farm to spend time with Vivian. She went to visit as if Vivian was at summer camp and not a detention center, bringing cigarettes, candy, sanitary napkins, and magazines but never an explanation, and Vivian didn't ask for one.

Vivian had her stories, and Robert had his, and maybe they swapped tales about their heartless mothers, absentee fathers, and the festering wounds they carried behind their rib cages, next to their hearts.

Vivian was already dating someone when they met, but Robert moved hard, and he moved fast. That's what toxic people do. They sweep you off your feet, dazzle you with sweet words, gifts, and promises. In short, they love-bomb the shit out of you. I imagined he future-faked her, told her all the things she'd ever longed to hear, made promises that no other man ever had.

The man Vivian met in 1964 was quiet and affable, kind and thoughtful, handy, helpful, and good with her stepsiblings. It didn't take long before he'd charmed her completely, and in no time the man in whom she previously had zero interest was now crowding her thoughts.

BY EARLY SEPTEMBER 1964, MY PARENTS WERE OFFICIALLY A COUPLE when Robert helped Vivian's family move from the tiny Red Hook apartment into a green-and-white three-bedroom clapboard house on 143rd Street in South Ozone Park, Queens.

In '64, South Ozone Park still had the look and feel of a small country town, with its honeysuckle-fragrant air, peach trees, and trailing vines drooping plump fruit. Rockaway Avenue, the main throughfare and shopping district, was paved, but many of the side streets and avenues—including 143rd Street—were not.

Until the early sixties, South Ozone Park and her sister neighborhoods had been predominantly white from their inception. Which is to say, since the land was taken from the First Nations people by white Europeans.

When Vivian and the family moved into the area, most of the

residents were descendants of the Italian immigrants who began pouring into America in 1880 and numbered in the millions by 1924. Before they became white, Italians suffered under the same discriminatory abuses in America as Black people. In an 1882 *New York Times* editorial that appeared under the headline "Our Future Citizens," the editors wrote:

"There has never been since New York was founded so low and ignorant a class among the immigrants who poured in here as the Southern Italians who have been crowding our docks during the past year."

The Italians weren't just a problem in New York, they were a problem in the Deep South too, specifically New Orleans, Louisiana, which had more Italian immigrants than any other Southern state.

"Lately the Italian element with bleared faces, unattended hair, careless dress, suspecting and dark, have formed picturesque additions to the criminal line," the *Times-Picayune* reported.

In New Orleans on March 14, 1891, a mob numbering in the thousands stormed the New Orleans prison and abducted and lynched eleven Italian men who had been accused of killing police chief David Hennessy in 1890.

It has been labeled as the largest single mass lynching in American history. But I disagree.

Lynching, by definition, is the public killing of an individual who has not received any due process. The word is most often associated with death by hanging, but a public killing of any type is still a lynching. The year before the mob murdered those eleven Italian men in New Orleans, US soldiers slaughtered three hundred Lakota men, women, and children in Wounded Knee Creek in South Dakota, this because their "ghost dancing" was making white people nervous.

"The savages swoon from exhaustion and then see Christ," read one headline in the *Salt Lake Tribune*.

It would come to be known as the Wounded Knee Massacre.

Future president Teddy Roosevelt said that the mass lynching of the Italians was "a rather good thing." John Parker, who was elected as governor of Louisiana in 1920, described Italians as "just a little worse than the Negro, being if anything filthier in their habits, lawless, and treacherous."

To Americanize themselves, Italians, like the Irish, aligned themselves with their Anglo-Saxon Protestant oppressors and projected all the hateful bigotry and violence they had experienced onto Black people.

In America, if people can't beat their oppressors, they join them.

BY THE SEVENTIES, THE BLACK population in South Ozone Park had grown exponentially. White people were complaining to their city council members about their safety and the dip in property value.

When they saw that the politicians weren't doing anything to stop the Negroes from moving into their neighborhood, they took matters into their own hands and began firebombing the homes of Black residents.

In the summer of 1975, when I was nine years old, a group of Black children were riding their bicycles around Rosedale, a community eleven minutes by car from South Ozone Park, when they saw what they thought was a parade. Excited, they pedaled toward the American flag–toting crowd and realized much too late that they had ridden into a lion's den. The parade was, in fact, a mass of protesters demanding that Black people be banished from the neighborhood.

Before the children could turn and flee, they were set upon by a band of angry, slur-hurling, rock-pelting white children.

The first time I was called a nigger by a white person was in Queens.

∾

I DON'T KNOW IF ROBERT AND VIVIAN DISCUSSED MARRIAGE IN THOSE early weeks of the courtship, or if pregnancy is what hurried them to the altar, but on March 27, 1965, just eight months after Robert first spotted Vivian walking down Columbia Street, they tied the knot in a small ceremony held in my grandparents' home.

In their wedding photo, Vivian is glowing in a light blue semi-formal dress, her baby bump on show. Robert, dressed in a neat black suit, is gazing at her. The expression on his face dangles somewhere between a smirk and a smile. I don't see love and happiness in his eyes, I see satisfaction, like the looks I've seen on the faces of hunters posing over the corpses of slain animals.

Vivian was three months pregnant with me when they stood in the dining room surrounded by friends and family and vowed to love each other in sickness and health till death do they part.

I was conceived in that house, in the bedroom just a few feet away from where they said "I do" and kissed. Here is my origin story:

It was Old Year's Night 1964. Robert had joined the family for a meal of fried chicken, corn bread, collard greens, and black-eyed peas. There was liquor. There was always liquor. The weather turned foul. Heavy snow plummeted from the dark sky, and soon there were snowdrifts, some as high as molehills, covering those country-like roads, rendering them undrivable. Even so, Robert insisted on heading back home to Brooklyn, but my grandparents would hear none of it.

"Okay, I'll just sleep on the couch."

Thelma, never one to bite her tongue, jumped at the opportunity to make him blush. "The couch?" she huffed. "Why you acting like y'all not fucking? You'll sleep right in the room with Vivian."

THELMA WAS A STRONG PROPONENT of sex. She enjoyed having sex and talking about sex. The act and its consequences were demystified for me at a very young age, when she set a large medical book on the dining room table and opened it up to a page that depicted anatomically precise drawings of a man and a woman.

"You see here, Bernice," she said, pointing at the penis. "That is the dick." She tapped her finger on the illustration.

"The man climbs on top of the woman," she continued, stacking one hand on top of the other, "and then he sticks his dick in there." She unstacked her hands and pointed at the vagina on the drawing of the woman. "And that's sex. Do you understand?"

I bounced my six-year-old head. "Yes, Grandma."

Wilfred, who was seated in the living room, within earshot, turned away from the television and looked over at Thelma. "Baby, c'mon now."

They'd been together long enough for him to know that she loved crass language and that there was nothing he could do or say to change that. But he never stopped trying.

"What?" she said, throwing her hands into the air. "Would you rather her learn about this in the street?"

Wilfred gave his head a slow, pitiful shake, before returning his attention to the television. What was he going to do with her?

SO, IT WAS IN VIVIAN's tiny bedroom, on the first floor of that two-story house, in the soft dark snowy morning of the New Year, that I first came to be.

2

B loody '68.
    Vivian didn't even know she was pregnant again when she learned Martin Luther King Jr. had been assassinated. When she heard the news, a wave of nausea rolled through her chest, and she went running into the bathroom to puke.

Afterward, she went into the bedroom and shook Robert awake. "King is dead," she sobbed when his blurry eyes fixed on hers.

"What?"

"They killed Martin Luther King!"

Robert threw an arm over his forehead and groaned.

Then Vivian called Thelma's sister Anna. The news had reached Anna ahead of Vivian, and upon hearing it, Anna had gone to the living room to stand before the wall where she'd mounted framed photos of Martin, John F. Kennedy, and a painting of a white, long-haired Jesus. When the phone rang in Anna's apartment, she was sitting on her sofa, with the photo of King clutched to her bosom, crying her eyes out. She'd done the same when John F. Kennedy was murdered in '63.

"He was a good white man," she'd declared through a deluge of tears. "Not many of those in the world."

In their little house in Queens, Thelma stared at the thin-lipped news anchor on the television. "What a downright shame," she murmured pitifully.

Wilfred, who was standing in the doorway, balled his fists, huffing. "I knew they were going to kill 'im when he started talking about poor people."

After King's murder, people all across America emptied into the streets, wailing and screaming for change. And then two months later, on June 6, an assassin's bullet snatched away JFK's younger brother, Robert.

"These crackers done gone and lost their motherfucking minds," Thelma whispered to her Black coworkers.

That October, Tommie Smith and John Carlos, Black Olympic sprinters, stood on the dais in black socks to bring attention to the plight of the many Black people who lived below the poverty line. They donned beaded necklaces around their necks to protest lynching—the uniquely American pastime that had killed more than four thousand Black people between 1882 and 1968. After they received their gold and bronze medals, Tommie and John bowed their heads and raised their Black gloved fists into the air.

The powers that be did not take kindly to their expression of Black solidarity. For months, Tommie and John were bombarded with death threats from white people both known and anonymous.

It had been one helluva year by the time my brother Reggie came wailing into the world on November 30, which just happened to be Barbados Independence Day, which made Robert twice as happy.

MY MEMORIES TRULY BEGIN TO crystallize in the fall of 1970, the year I turned five years old.

I was in my bedroom with its glossy snap-pea-colored walls and beige curtains splattered in decals of colorful fruit and vegetables. There was a little blue child's table with two matching chairs, a closet with sliding doors, a crib, and a built-in bookshelf on the wall near the bedroom door. The room smelled of baby talc and the cocoa butter Vivian slathered on my scarred hand and face in the morning after I washed my face and brushed my teeth and then again at night, after my bath.

Before the baby, Vivian read to me from the Mother Goose nursery rhyme books that lined the bookshelf. As she read, she traced the tip of her index finger beneath the words, so that when she said them, I knew which word it was, and I repeated after her.

But with the new baby, she didn't always have time to read to me, so she bought me a red Kenner Close 'n Play phonograph, on which I could listen to the vinyl Disney records and read along with the narrator from the corresponding books.

Vivian was thrilled that her children had so many reading options, because when she was a little girl growing up in Sandersville, Georgia, the only reading material they had access to was *Little Black Sambo*, the Bible, and the Sears catalog, which was placed in the outhouse because it was free and toilet paper wasn't.

Reading was my favorite thing to do. I loved it more than playing with dolls, watching television, jumping rope, Simon says, hide-and-go-seek and tag, and hot peas and butter. I loved it because reading offered me an escape into another world, because the world I lived in was often scary and violent.

On that day in September 1970, when I first began to form the memories that will trail me into adulthood, I was seated on the top bunk bed, listening to *Snow White and the Seven Dwarfs*, when the telephone rang. The volume on my Kenner Close 'n Play was low enough for me to hear Vivian's hello from the kitchen.

"What?" she uttered, astonished. "How did that happen?"

When I heard the kitchen chair scrape across the linoleum floor, I lowered the volume on the Kenner another notch. I was a curious child. I was always listening. I was an observant child. I noticed things that other people did not notice. Like the way sunlight glints off a shard of broken glass or the familiar shapes clouds morph into and the faces like silhouettes hiding in tree bark.

In that moment, I heard the change in Vivian's voice, and I knew that it was disturbing news.

For most of the call, Vivian was silent, save for a few soft, sad moans. "That's a damn shame. I'm so sorry to hear that, Mama. I'll give Aunt Mayremma a call."

Her goodbye was followed by the clicking sound of the pilot light on the stove before the apartment filled with the scent of her Newport cigarette.

THE PHONE CALL WAS ABOUT our cousin Dora Lisha, the daughter of Mary Emma Smith, called Aunt Mayremma—sister to my great-grandmother, Lillian. Dora Lisha had been rushed to North Carolina Baptist Hospital in Winston-Salem after having suffered burns over 70 percent of her body. She lingered between life and death for five and a half days before finally succumbing to her injuries.

On Dora Lisha's death certificate, under *Describe How Injury Occurred*, it states: *Burned lighting stove.* She was seventeen years old.

Mayremma had lost her sister Cora to fire in 1923, when the barn on the family land in Sandersville, Georgia, went up in flames. Some say Cora had taken a box of matches into the barn. That it was a dangerous pastime of hers, one that her mother, Rosie May, had reprimanded her about incessantly. But children will be children. Cora was just five years old. They didn't know she was even in the barn until the fire was completely doused. When her father, Carlus, and his sons went into the smoldering barn to inspect the damage, they found her little charred remains.

Fire, it seems, is a running theme in my family's history.

The only photo I've ever seen of Dora Lisha is a school photo, which was used on her funeral program. Her face is round and chubby, and her shiny bangs sit a bit lopsided on her forehead. The smile on her face is guarded.

Burned lighting stove.

1n 1963, seven years before Dora Lisha died, a Vietnamese Mahayana Buddhist monk named Thich Quang Duc set himself aflame at a busy intersection in Saigon in response to the South Vietnamese Diem discriminatory Buddhist laws. The act of setting oneself on fire and burning to death is called self-immolation, and it is considered the most extreme nonviolent protest known to man. The scene, which was captured by photographer Malcolm Browne, shows Thich Quang Duc sitting calmly as the fire consumes him. There is little emotion on the faces of the onlookers. They watch as if a man aflame is a common occurrence.

Dora Lisha would have been ten years old when Thich Quang Duc sacrificed himself. I doubt she missed seeing the image because it circumvented the globe, appearing in newspapers and on network TV news programs. When most people saw that photo, they pulled their eyes away and covered their mouths in horror, but not Dora Lisha. I imagine Dora Lisha leaned in for a closer look.

It was rumored that her big brother, John "J.W." Smith, was interfering with her.

People in my family tend to use phrases like *interfering* or *messing with* in place of exact words like *molesting* and *raping*.

The accusation had been passed from one family member to the next, traveling all the way up from North Carolina to New York, which is why Thelma had referred to him as the devil.

When Dora Lisha told her mother about the violation, Mayremma narrowed her eyes and snarled, *"Chile, get out of my face with that nonsense. You been lying since you could talk!"*

She said this even though she knew that her own brother, one Charlie Herman May Sr., called Buddy, had *interfered* with his nieces, one of which was my grandmother Thelma.

Maybe too, before the nieces came along, he had practiced on

Mayremma and his other sisters. I don't know that part to be true, but I do know that where there is smoke, there is fire.

I don't believe that Dora Lisha suffered her injuries from lighting the stove.

I believe Dora Lisha smeared her body in Crisco oil, lit a match, and intentionally set herself aflame. Maybe she just wanted to make herself undesirable. Perhaps she thought if she was repulsive to look at J.W. would leave her be.

Maybe death wasn't the end goal, maybe it was peace.

AFTER VIVIAN FINISHED HER CIGARETTE, she came into my bedroom and set two baby bottles on the dresser. Reggie was sound asleep, mouth open, leaking slobber. He had a plush teddy bear locked between his fat thighs.

"This one is filled with milk," Vivian said, pointing to the green bottle. "And this one is filled with water." She aimed her finger at the blue bottle. "If he wakes up, give him the milk first, and if he's still hungry, then give him the water."

Vivian spent Saturday and Sunday evenings playing bingo at the bingo hall on Empire Boulevard, which was just two blocks away from where we lived. I know it was a Saturday because Robert was in the bedroom snoring after coming in from work that morning and polishing off a six-pack of Rheingold Beer.

It was still just beer then.

She went into their bedroom, and when she returned, she was carrying the red leather purse where she kept her bingo blotters and chips. She kept that purse for years, and by the time she finally let it go, the cracked and flaking leather was blotchy with purple ink.

My eyes bounced from the purse to her face.

"Okay, I'll see you later. Be good."

"Bye, Mommy," I said, smiling, even though my stomach was

already tying up in knots. I hated when she left us alone with Robert, and had, at that tender age, begun catastrophizing—worrying that something terrible would befall her and we would be left to be raised by Robert. She wasn't out the door good before dread settled around me like a fog.

VIVIAN TELLS ME STORIES OF me as a toddler. One favorite story is about when I began walking. *You liked to play with the pots and pans. So I let you play with the pots and pans. You were in the kitchen, and I was in the living room, watching television and folding laundry. A few minutes passed, and I looked up and you were wobbling toward me. I was so surprised that I screamed. The sound startled you, and you plopped down on your butt and cried. You were seven months old.*

That is a happy story. I will tell that story to my own daughter, who herself started walking at eight months old.

The next story Vivian likes to tell is not so happy: *Whenever I'd leave you with your father to go play bingo and return, you'd be in the closet. I'd come in, say, "Where's the baby, Robert? Where's Bernice?" And he'd point at the closet.*

For years, I thought the second memory was as precious as the first. But as I grew older and began to question things, it seemed a curious choice for a child of that age. After all, the closet was small and dark, and wasn't that where the monsters lived? There and underneath the bed? If a child didn't know anything else, they knew that.

The thought nagged me, and one day when Vivian began recounting the story for the umpteenth time, I interrupted her. I was well into my thirties by then.

"Mommy, did I ever go in the closet when you were home?"

Vivian twisted her lips in thought. "No, no you didn't."

"So, Daddy told you that I went in the closet all on my own?"

"Yeah."

I stared at her for a second, hoping she was getting what I was putting down, but the look on her face told me otherwise. "How can you be sure that *he* didn't put me in the closet?"

The amused expression on her face melted into confusion. "Oh, Bernice," she sighed. "Why would he have done something like that?"

He did so many horrible things, I don't know why this horrible thing was such a stretch of her imagination.

FOR NOW, HOWEVER, ROBERT WAS snoring in the next room, Reggie was sleeping peacefully, and I was enjoying *The Jungle Book* in solace.

I'd fallen asleep, the needle of my Kenner Close 'n Play tracking the dead wax of the runout area. The sound gently tugged me awake, and when I opened my eyes, I saw Reggie standing in his crib, staring at me. As soon as he saw me move, he began to whine.

I raised the cover of the record player and climbed down from the bed. The only light in the apartment was the one in our bedroom. Beyond that was the living room, which looked to me like a dark cave. As I stared into the abyss, my mind erupted with images of fanged creatures hiding in wait for the moment they could gobble me up.

I backed away from the doorway, reached for the bottle of milk, and gave it to Reggie, who quickly snatched it from my hands, pushed the nipple between his ravenous lips, and emptied it in a blink. He tossed the bottle to the floor and continued his hollering. I gave him the bottle filled with water, which he drained just as quickly. We stared at each other.

"I don't have anything else to give you."

Lips trembling, he flung his head back on his neck and howled. I tried to hush him, I tried to lift him out of the crib, but the railing was too high, and he was too heavy. He raged and raged, violently jumping like a monkey in a cage. I didn't know what to do. I was only five years old. Then the phone rang. It rang and rang and rang.

I wasn't allowed to answer the phone, and between Reggie's shrieking and the blaring telephone, I thought I would fall apart.

Helpless, my lips quivered with my own impending sobs. I climbed into the bottom bunk, clapped my hands over my ears, and let the rush of tears come. Suddenly, the mattress in the crib crashed to the floor, taking Reggie with it. Splayed and wide-eyed, the shock of it turned him mute.

I was just as stunned as he was. Neither of us moved a muscle. We remained as still as statues, bracing for the moment when Robert would come charging into the room to yell at us. But he never did.

Eventually we fell asleep. When my eyes opened again, it was morning. Reggie was gone, the mattress of the crib was back in place, and Ray Charles's "Hit the Road Jack" was blaring from the stereo in the sunlit living room.

THE OTHER THING THAT SURFACED IN MY MEMORY FROM THAT YEAR of being five was my first trip to Sandersville. Thelma had taken me down to Sandersville, Georgia, to visit the birthplace of her mother, Lillian, and the place where she was raised. We arrived in Augusta on a sweltering summer day in 1970.

The river city was still convalescing from an uprising instigated when sixteen-year-old Charles Oatman died in the county jail under mysterious circumstances. Barely one hundred pounds and mentally disabled, Charles Oatman was arrested by police after fatally shooting his five-year-old niece. Detained without bond, he was tortured and abused while awaiting his day in court. His family implored the powers that be to have Charles relocated to a facility that best served his needs, but their pleas were ignored, and he was dead in six weeks.

According to Carrie Mays, the undertaker at Mays Mortuary,

"He had three long gashes across his back, about a half an inch deep and about a foot long. . . . The back of his skull was busted out. He had cigarette burns all over his body." Charles's jailers claimed that he had fallen off his bunk bed after playing cards, but the autopsy revealed that Charles had died by drowning, because his lungs were filled with fluid.

When the word got out about Charles's death, three hundred people gathered outside the county jail, demanding answers. When none came, protestors ripped the state flag from the pole and set it ablaze, lighting the fuse that burned for two days. When the protests were over, six Black people were dead, ten wounded, and more than thirty businesses destroyed.

The jailers were never convicted of the murder of Charles Oatman; instead, the blame was heaved onto the shoulders of Oatman's cellmates: sixteen-year-old Lloyd Brown and seventeen-year-old Sammy Lee Parks.

Lloyd Brown speaks:
(Make sure to read this in a robot-like voice. Emotionless. Read these words as if they have been spoon-fed into your mouth. Read these words like your life, your mama's life, and the lives of anyone you love depend on it.)

"Oatman was beaten by Parks every day. . . . Oatman was then tied in a crucifix position to a top bunk in the cell and beaten and kicked until he was bleeding from the mouth. . . . He was placed on the floor and Parks jumped on him, placing his knees into Oatman's stomach. . . . I could usually see Oatman's heart pounding as he was so thin but the pulsating motion was not visible after the final beating.

"Parks and his partner then placed Oatman on the lower bunk and played cards for about fifteen minutes.

"He was unconscious, and Parks tried to revive him by pouring salt into his eyes and hot water on his chest and in his mouth, but Oatman did not react."

Sammy Lee Parks was convicted of voluntary manslaughter and received ten years for the death of Charles Oatman. Lloyd Brown was trialed separately and received the same ten-year sentence.

Ten years later, Lloyd Brown speaks:
(Read this part like there is a rage simmering beneath your skin. Read this part through clenched teeth. Read this part with wild eyes. Read this part with clenched fists.)

"The deputies took Oatman out for whippings. That's all I know," he said, adding, "This took half my life away, especially for not having done nothing."

THELMA HAD LEFT SANDERSVILLE FOR Detroit in 1947, and then a few years later, her sister Anna left Sandersville for Brooklyn, but their baby sister, Helen, remained behind, living her entire life in Sandersville, Georgia. Helen got pregnant at fifteen, and sixteen-year-old George Braddy, who lived down the road with his family, was named as the father. But that is highly unlikely, because George Braddy died in January 1946, and Helen's son, Cecil, was born in December of that year. I don't know many things, but I do know that a dead man cannot inseminate a woman.

Eventually though, Helen married a man named Jimmy Lee Cummings, and they started a family. It was Jimmy Lee and Helen who collected Thelma and me from the airport in Augusta, Georgia, on that sweltering summer day.

"Lawd." Helen laughed when she first set eyes on me. "That chile needs some meat on her bones!" She was right; I was scrawny.

She tugged my skinny arm, exclaiming, "We gonna fatten you right on up!"

In the car to Sandersville, we traveled with the windows down; Thelma rested her arm on the side, drumming her fingers on the door and moving her lips to the lyrics of "Stoned Love" by the Supremes. The conversation jumped around before landing on the tragic death of the Oatman boy and the violence that followed.

"White people," Jimmy Lee crowed, shaking his head. The broken statement dangled in the air like a dead Black body from a lynch rope. He glanced in the rearview mirror. "Hey, Thelma, how da white folks up in New Yaawk?"

Thelma smirked. "Same as down here."

"Did Helen tell you 'bout da trouble we had in Sandersville?"

Thelma gazed out the window. "Yeah, she told me."

That January, a carload of white men carrying shotguns had been spotted riding around the Negro section of town. A concerned citizen phoned Eloise Turner, the wife of Richard Turner, who was what the papers called a "Negro leader."

Turner, a plumber and carpenter by trade, who believed he was "tapped by destiny to lead Sandersville Blacks," had petitioned the city council to make improvements in the Black community. He wanted Black people to be hired onto the all-white police and in local government, and he wanted fully integrated schools.

Eloise was at the back of the house when shotgun blasts rang through the air. Luckily she was uninjured, but the same couldn't be said for the couple's home and station wagon.

"All we are asking," Richard Turner had said to the council, "is a little piece of the pie."

IN 1970, WHEN I FINALLY arrived in the land of my foremothers, little had changed in Sandersville since 1943, when Vivian was born; or 1929, when Thelma and her sisters arrived there from Philadelphia;

or 1903, when Lillian was born; or 1864, when General George Sherman and his troops came through Sandersville on their March to the Sea and burned down the jailhouse and the courthouse. There were still cotton fields that stretched for miles, and clay-colored dirt roads, pecan trees, and watermelon patches. Kerosene lamps were still in use, as were outhouses and chamber pots, and many residents still fetched water from the spring. Luckily for us, Helen's water was piped into her house.

I was the latest female envoi in a procession of women stretching back an entire century, to my four-times great-grandmother Louisa Vicey Wilson—our family's first documented ancestor. Louisa Vicey Wilson made her appearance on the 1870 census. She was listed as thirty-seven years old, female, Black, married, illiterate, and mother of ten children, ranging in age from two to nineteen.

Thelma and I spent a week in the sun-splattered rooms of that little wooden house, which boiled with heat even after the sun set. Every night after that wonderous ball of fire disappeared, the sky transformed into a velvety black blanket stitched with twinkling stars, signaling the opera of the katydids, tree frogs, crickets, and loons that chorused until daybreak.

HELEN WAS A SLIM, DARK, timid-looking woman, who Vivian remembers as one of the hardest-working women she'd ever known. "She picked more cotton than anyone—even the men." I can see her now in a threadbare gown, cradling her elbows, scarfed head tilted to one side, amusement glowing on her face as she listens to Thelma recount some outrageous story. She looks like the subject of a Gordon Parks photograph.

Thelma is lying in the bed on her back, one arm folded beneath her head and naked save for cotton bloomers, radiant in the steady yellow light of the kerosene lamp. With every chuckle, her enormous breasts inch apart, gliding until they come to rest in the coves of her hairy underarms. I am lying beside her, in a similar state of partial nudity, playing itsy-bitsy spider with my fingers. There are only so many times a spider can be washed away before a four-and-a-half-year-old is driven to boredom.

I sat up in the bed, crossed my skinny legs pretzel-style, and reached for Thelma's tits. They looked to me like fleshy shoelaces, and I was still learning to tie knots. Vivian had told me that practice made perfect, and so I grabbed Thelma's tits and proceeded to practice.

"Hey, hey!" Thelma cried, swatting me upside my head. "You crazy?"

Both she and Helen had a good hard laugh at the expense of my childishness.

"All right." Helen yawned into her fist. "I'm going to bed. Good night."

"Good night," Thelma said, and then looked at me. "Bernice, you need to pee?"

I had to do more than pee. There was a chamber pot under the bed, but number two would require me to go out into the dreaded outhouse. That stinky wooden box was scary enough in daylight, and so I certainly did not want to experience it at night.

"No, I don't have to go," I piped.

Thelma yawned, turned over, and reached for the lamp.

"Grandma, I gotta go," I whispered.

"God dammit," Thelma muttered. She sucked her teeth, sat up, and swung her legs over the side of the bed. Fussing under her breath, she padded across the floor, snatched her robe from the hook on the door, and wrapped herself into it. "C'mon, you."

Outside, by the side of the house, Thelma raised the lamp high over my head. As soon as I tugged my bloomers down and squatted in the circle of light, my bowels locked.

After a few seconds, Thelma said, "Well, go on."

Her patience was thinning, and I didn't want to be popped a second time that evening, so I straightened myself, poked out my lips, and announced, "I can't."

Thelma huffed, yanked my bloomers up around my waist, grabbed my hand, and led me back into the house. In bed, I curled up against her warm body and rested my head on her tit. Thelma turned the knob of the kerosene lamp, shrinking the flame until it was a tiny puff of smoke.

3

I grew up in Crown Heights, Brooklyn, on 300 Sullivan Place in apartment A5.

It was a picturesque neighborhood with tree-lined streets and flower beds that burst with color in the spring. During my childhood, Crown Heights felt like a hamlet. Everything we needed was within walking distance: supermarket, gas station, vegetable and fruit stand, Chinese restaurant, butcher shop, bakery, laundromat, millinery, and several clothing boutiques and shoe stores.

In its previous life, Crown Heights was Crow Hill, a neighborhood settled by formerly enslaved people. Photos from that era depict wooden shacks and dirt roads. Some claim the neighborhood got its name from the considerable number of crows cawing away in the trees. However, others peg the reference squarely on the formerly enslaved.

In 1854, the city erected the Kings County Penitentiary, which was also known as the Crow Hill Penitentiary and Crow Hill Castle. The prison was a massive fortresslike structure and occupied a square that encompassed President Street, Crown Street, Nostrand Avenue, and Rogers Avenue. Had it not been torn down in 1907, it would have cast a shadow over Sullivan Place.

As we crept toward the new decade, Crown Heights began to change again. The old-world European residents died off or moved away, leaving the area to Hasidic Jews, Black Americans, and the fresh influx of Caribbean immigrants.

Robert, Vivian, and I were the first Black family to move into 300 Sullivan Place, and the white residents weren't a least bit welcoming. They didn't return Vivian's smile or hello and routinely let the door close in her face, even if her arms were ladened with groceries or she was pushing me in the carriage.

After we moved in, the white tenants began moving out in succession. One family after the next left in the dead of night, leaving the doors to their vacated apartments sitting wide-open on their hinges.

When I was growing up on Sullivan Place, there were dozens and dozens of children living there, and when the weather was nice, we filled the streets with our beautiful Blackness. On the weekends, we zipped up and down the block in games of tag and hide-and-go-seek. We made music with our hand-clapping games, chorusing:

Miss Mary Mack, Mack, Mack
All dressed in black, black, black
With silver buttons, buttons, buttons
All down her back, back, back.

Down, down baby, down, down the roller coaster,
Sweet, sweet baby, I'll never let you go,
Shimmy, shimmy ko-ko-bop
Shimmy, shimmy pow!

Pedestrians trampled over our brightly chalked hopscotch courts and walked wide half circles around double-Dutchers, narrowly avoiding the swiftly turning clotheslines or PVC cables we used as jump ropes. We spent the nickels, dimes, and quarters our parents gave us on candy from Henry's Fruit and Vegetable market. Hopped-up on sugar, we raced 'round and 'round the block on our bicycles, pedaling for our lives, sometimes towing our friends along on their metal roller skates that fit over their sneakers and locked in place with a key. We whooped and hollered, ripped, and ran until the streetlamps came on, which was our notice that it was time to go home.

IN SEPTEMBER 1970, I ENTERED kindergarten at Junior Academy on Quincy Street in Bedford-Stuyvesant. Junior Academy was co-founded in 1965 by the Black sports journalist Joe Bostic. In 1971, I returned to Crown Heights for first grade at P.S. 161, located on Crown Street, just a few blocks away from where I lived.

P.S. 161 opened in 1924, when the neighborhood was still predominantly Jewish. Both Pulitzer Prize–winning author Norman Mailer and music mogul Clive Davis attended the school when they were children. Back in the 1920s and '30s, the school was so overcrowded that some students were placed in the cafeteria, which was below the first floor in the part of the building that we called the basement, which is where my tenure there began.

When Vivian dropped me off on that first day of school, the intake person took one look at the scar on my face and determined that I was learning disabled and so placed me in a class with learning-disabled children. That classroom was in the bowels of the school, across from the cafeteria. We were placed out of sight, lest the sight of us disturb the *normal* students and their parents.

There was a student with dwarfism, who also had epilepsy, so he wore a helmet to protect his head from injury should he suffer an episode. Another classmate was legally blind, her eyes appeared as big as globes behind her thick glasses. There was another girl with cerebral palsy, who had forearm crutches; a boy named Jeffrey

(I remember his name only because he tried to date me when I was thirteen years old) who was insolent and misbehaved—the teacher spent most of the day yelling at him in betwixt trying to silence a boy with Tourette's syndrome, whose tics were a mixture of snorts, cuss words, and names of fruits.

Indeed, we were a sight to behold . . . or a sight to hide, as it were.

From 1867 to 1974, various cities across America enacted ordinances that outlawed the public appearance of people who were unsightly, diseased, mutilated, or deformed. Coined Ugly Laws— New York drafted its own version in 1895, but lucky for us, it was never enacted.

For the next few weeks, I spent my days seated at my desk, staring silently out the window, lost in my daydreams, inhaling the aromas of whatever lunch the cooks were preparing. Our teacher was a petite white woman in her early thirties. She had green eyes and skin so thin it looked translucent. She smelled like Jean Nate and cigarettes. She was nice enough, but unqualified to deal with children with special needs or behavioral problems.

Snort, snort. Bitch. Fuck. Olives.

Donald, those are bad words. Well, olives *is fine, but the other words are—*

Bitch. Fuck. Olives. Snort. Snort.

Retard! Retard! Donald is a retard!

You're the retard, Jeffrey. Now, get your retarded butt down off of that desk and go stand in the corner!

No, you go stand in the corner.

The teacher's face turned as red as a maraschino cherry. She balled her fists in frustration, released a shuddering gasp, and stormed out of the classroom before we could see her tears. Cheering, Jeffrey jumped from one desk to the next, kicking our books, crayons, and pencils onto the floor. A few other students jumped up and joined in the melee, writing on the board and running around the room. The meek and obedient remained in our seats, watching in quiet terror, until the door swung open, and the principal of the school, Mr. Epstein, charged into the room.

All the children hurried back to their seats, except Jeffrey, who was obstinate. He met the principal's glare with his own. It was a standoff, until Mr. Epstein touched his hand to his belt buckle. We all knew what that meant. All the bluster whistled out of Jeffrey. He dropped his head, ashamed, climbed down from the desk, and shuffled over to Mr. Epstein.

Mr. Epstein grunted triumphantly, caught Jeffrey by the ear, and dragged him from the room.

Snort, snort. Bitch. Fuck. Olives.

IT TOOK A WHILE BEFORE Vivian realized that I never had homework or that the pages of my black-and-white composition notebook were mostly bare. When she went to the school to investigate, she learned that I had been placed in a class filled with children the administration had for one reason or another deemed unteachable, misfits, and throwaways. Vivian was outraged.

"Bernice reads very well for her age, and she can count to twenty without using her fingers or her toes!"

After she threatened to call the board of education, I was transferred to a class on one of the upper floors.

Because my scars were beacons for bullies, my grade school years were miserable.

I hadn't suffered too much torment in the misfit class, but in this new class, my scars became a fresh source of anguish for me. The friends I'd grown up with on Sullivan Place had always known me, and if the way I looked troubled them, they never let on. I don't remember a time when any of my playmates ridiculed, harassed, or taunted me about my scars. To them I was simply Bernice, but at P.S. 161 I was burnt-face Bernice.

Burnt-face Bernice, burnt-face Bernice, burnt-face, burnt-face Bernice! There were days when the entire class chanted that awful hymn.

Recess was a dangerous time for me. In that big schoolyard, I was as vulnerable as an injured animal in the African savanna. I tried to make myself small and invisible, but the bullies always found me. One, two, sometimes three would chase me around the schoolyard, catch me and pummel me until some teacher came to my rescue.

I remember my first-grade teacher was a short, stout white woman with silver hair. She reminded me of Mrs. Claus and was just as kind. After a few weeks of my mistreatment at the hands of my classmates, she charged herself as my lunchtime guardian, and from that day until the end of the school year, I joined her in a booth at the luncheonette down the street. There, she'd order a tuna fish on rye, a cup of chicken soup, and coffee, and I would have whatever my mother had packed in my lunchbox for the day. I wish I could remember her name so that I could exalt it here on the page, because I am so very, very grateful for her kindness.

Unfortunately, at three o'clock, when it was time for me to head home, she could not save me from my tormentors, who were always hiding in wait. Those tiny tyrants would follow me all the way home, shoving and kicking and spitting on me all in full view of adults who rarely, if ever, intervened on my behalf.

As far as I was concerned, the adults weren't much better. I'd seen grown men and women recoil at the sight of me or, worse, point and laugh. To me, the eyeballing felt as bad as the battering and name-calling, and whenever I found myself caught in the glow of a stranger's hot gaze, I melted under the heat.

Sometimes I would walk home with two of my friends, Annette and Deborah, who also lived at 300 Sullivan Place. Annette was my age and as petite as I was, but Deborah was two years older than us and tall. We'd all seen Deborah whip the brakes off fifth-grade boys—so my first-grade tormentors knew not to come up against her. But that didn't keep them from trailing us like a pack of jackals, hurling insults and chanting my hurtful nickname.

Now, as an adult when I'm faced with an unsettling or traumatic event, I can turn to meditation or a deep-breathing coping strategy, but when I was a child, all I had to soothe myself was my imagination, so I created a story, which I recited in my head whenever I found myself the subject of unwanted fascination:

> *Once upon a time there was a little girl named Bridgette who was born to the king and queen of Africa. Bridgette was a princess who was destined to assume the throne, but the wicked witch set the family castle on fire. The inferno killed Bridgette's parents and left Bridgette's face scarred.*
>
> *The wicked witch bundled Princess Bridgette onto her broom, flew her across the oceans to America, and left her on the doormat of Vivian and Robert McFadden's apartment. They took her in, renamed her Bernice, and raised her as their own.*
>
> *After the fire, and the death of their queen and king, the followers fled the Kingdom of Africa and spread around the world. Some of those people came to live in America, in Brooklyn specifically. Sometimes when those people were going about their daily lives, they came upon Bernice and immediately recognized her as Princess Bridgette of the Kingdom of Africa—that's why they could not stop gazing at her.*
>
> *The end.*

Once I made it home, I should have felt some sense of relief. After all, home should be a safe place, a sanctuary. But mine wasn't.

"Did your mother have anyone in the apartment last night?"

The interrogation from Robert began as soon as I walked through the door.

"No, sir."

"Are you lying?"

"No, sir."

Robert was constantly accusing Vivian of sneaking men into the apartment after he left for work as an overnight driver for United Parcel Service.

"Someone told me they saw you talking to a man on the subway. They said you two looked very cozy." He'd sling the accusation and watch Vivian's face to see if there was any truth in the lie he'd created.

The first several times he used this tactic, she defended herself. But after some years, she finally caught on. "Oh yeah, Robert? Well, whoever *they* are, tell *them* to come over here and tell me what they saw to my face."

Once, when I was about ten years old, Thelma gave us all handheld cassette recorders. Vivian threw hers in her bureau drawer and forgot about it. I used mine to record my made-up stories and the songs I sang along to from the radio, and Robert used his for surveillance.

We learned this one Friday night after he'd gone off to work and Vivian was in their bedroom, stretched across the bed, watching television, waiting for the egg whites she'd slathered onto her face to dry.

She'd gotten up to check for something in the closet, and that's when she saw it from the corner of her eye. On top of the armoire, where Robert kept his underclothes, socks, and T-shirts, was a small wooden chest, like the ones you see in cartoons, filled with treasure. Behind the chest was the silver recorder.

Vivian frowned. It seemed an odd place to store the recorder. Her intention was to place it in the wooden chest, but when she picked it up, it was warm to the touch. She held it up to her face and saw the black spindles whirling behind the glass window.

He had been secretly recording her, and who knows for how long.

I heard what I thought was crying and jumped out of my bed to see why. Heart in my stomach, I shot into her room and almost screamed when I saw the cracked and scabby dried egg white on her face. I quickly realized that she wasn't crying but laughing. When Vivian saw me, she was chortling so hard, she could barely speak.

She raised the cassette recorder above her head, pressed her free hand onto her stomach and, still quaking with amusement, flopped down onto the bed.

Even though I saw that she was laughing and not crying, I was still concerned. "Mommy?"

She tossed the recorder down to the bed, opened her mouth to explain, but before she could, a fresh wave of laughter gripped her, setting her eyes to watering. Pointing at the recorder, she gathered herself long enough to say, "That stupid motherfucker was recording me!"

My eyes swung to the recorder and then back to her face. The corner of my lips twitched with a smile, even though I was unsure what was humorous.

Vivian snatched the recorder up, brought it to her lips, and yelled, "You stupid motherfucker!"

The following morning, when Robert came home, Reggie and I were sitting in our bedroom, watching cartoons.

"Good morning, sir," we chimed.

Robert grunted, went into his bedroom, stripped off his work clothes, and reappeared in his shorts, white T-shirt, and slippers. He went into the kitchen, made himself a ham sandwich, washed it down with a glass of Kool-Aid, and then poured himself a finger of Hennessy.

"Y'all get dressed so we can go to the park," Vivian called to us.

We were out the door in forty minutes, and when we returned home late that afternoon, Robert was in bed, snoring. The recorder, which Vivian had placed back where she'd found it, was gone. He never brought it up and neither did Vivian, and the recorder was never seen again.

OF COURSE, HE STILL CONTINUED to accuse her of imaginary amoral activity, but she just dismissed him with a side-eye or a suck-teeth and went about her business. But I was a child. I did not have that power, and I believed his was omniscient.

"Did you come straight home from school?"

"Yes, sir."

"Are you sure?"

"Yes, sir."

"Don't lie to me. I told you; I have eyes everywhere."

4

At least you got a father," my friend Annette countered one day when I was complaining about Robert.

She said it like having a father was a prize or a gift that she'd been deprived of. Before Vivian learned the truth about her own absentee father, she had expressed the same type of yearning. I was the only one of my close friends who lived in a two-parent household, everyone else was being raised by single mothers. I secretly envied my fatherless friends. I was sure with Robert out of the picture, Vivian, Reggie, and I would be so happy.

Of course I was just a child, unaware of the financial impact Robert's absence would have on our lives. As it were, we did not want for anything. In fact, there was little we asked for that we did not receive, and our telephone, light, and gas utilities had never been disconnected due to lack of payment. Not all my friends could make the same claim. So many of them were living hand to mouth, and one missed paycheck away from losing their homes.

Another friend being raised by her single mother was Sharon—a year younger than me, and her brother, Milton, was the same age as Reggie.

Sharon and Milton lived in the courtyard apartment with their mother, Pinky. That apartment could be accessed only through the backyard. In the building's early days, that's where the superintendent lived. It was a two-bedroom apartment, with small windows that let in very little light, so it felt like a cave.

Pinky was Panamanian. She had a gold tooth and a head full of thick hair that she dyed a reddish-brown. She was good-looking, and she dressed in a manner that complemented her killer curves. Once, when I was walking down the street with her, a man pointed at her behind, saying, "Jesus, girl, that must be jelly 'cause jam don't shake like that!"

It didn't sound like a compliment to me, but Pinky gushed, threw her head back and laughed in that wide-mouthed, raucous way that made women who didn't have Pinky's confidence and good looks feel small.

Those women called her wild behind her back, as well as loose and wanton, because she dressed the way she dressed, and she laughed the way she laughed, and had two children by two different men.

Does she even know who the fathers are?

I doubt it.

Seems to me she changes men as frequently as I change the sheets on my bed.

As often as I change my drawers!

If she keeps carrying on like that, she'll look around and find herself with baby number three.

Whore.

Floozy.

But I liked Pinky. She felt more like a big sister than a parental figure.

It was with her that I had my first sip of hard liquor and crab meat, straight from the shell. She had gathered Sharon, Milton, Reggie, and me at the kitchen sink, which was filled with a dozen or so live crabs, clawing at the porcelain sides. Reggie and I leaped back in surprise. We'd never seen a crab outside of a television cartoon.

"Don't be afraid." Pinky laughed. "They can't get to you."

We inched a bit closer. Reggie, ever curious and fearless, stretched his hand out toward the crustaceans.

"Hey," Pinky cried, quickly slapping his hand away. "You'll get pinched."

"What are you going to do with them?" I asked.

"Eat them," Sharon stated matter-of-factly.

Reggie and I exchanged unsure glances.

"You've never had crab before?" Pinky asked with surprise glinting in her brown eyes.

I shook my head. "No."

Pinky set a huge pot of water on the stove and turned the burner on before going into the living room and squatting down beside the metal milk crate of vinyl records. Soon, the apartment filled with salsa music. There was always music in her home. She twirled back into the kitchen with an imaginary dance partner. Hips rolling to the syncopated rhythm of congas, maracas, and claves, Pinky danced around the kitchen, sprinkling bottles filled with herbs and spices into the boiling pot of water. We twirled and swayed along with her.

"¡Wepa!" she cried, as she grabbed her metal tongs, seized one of the crabs, and dropped it into the water.

My mouth dropped open, and my dancing feet came to a halt.

In the hot water, the crab battled for a few seconds before it went still. Cooked alive.

I was still in the grip of astonishment, when Pinky dropped the second, third, and fourth crab into the cauldron. The fifth victim slipped free, hitting the floor with a clatter before skittering for its life across the brown linoleum. Terrified, we kids bolted from the kitchen screaming. Pinky's raucous laughter pressed into our backs.

Later, we sat around the dining table covered in newspaper, staring at the platter of cooked crabs, bowls of fried plantains, yuca, and corn on the cob.

"This is how you do it, okay?" Pinky instructed as she plucked a crab from the tower, yanked a leg, and snapped it in half.

"See?" she said.

I gazed at the white flesh and nodded uncertainly. Then, Pinky pinched the flesh, pulled it clean from the shell, and shoved it into her mouth.

"Mmm."

Sharon and Milton eagerly followed suit. But Reggie and I were hesitant.

"Go 'head," Pinky encouraged, snatching up crabs and tossing them on the table before us. It took some goading, but finally my brother and I dove in and found that we really enjoyed it.

I was still trying to sweep the image of the scrambling crabs aside, when Pinky filled her water glass with Coca-Cola and then topped it off with two splashes of white rum. She swirled the glass around and then raised it to her lips and drank. Gratified, she bounced her shoulders in sweet satisfaction before reaching for another boiled crab. When she saw me looking, Pinky whispered, "Do you want a sip?"

Reggie, Milton, and Sharon were busy ripping apart their crabs and singing the Spider-Man cartoon theme song. When Robert wasn't looking, I'd snuck sips of the Rheingold Beer he used to drink before he switched to Hennessy. It was a little bitter, but I liked it because the bubbles reminded me of soda. I shrugged, neither offering a yes or a no.

Pinky thrust her glass at me. "Here," she said. "Take a sip, it won't hurt you."

I glanced at Reggie. He wasn't paying me any attention. He'd hooked the crab claw to his bottom lip and was pretending that it was eating him alive. Milton and Sharon snorted with laughter.

"Just a sip," Pinky warned.

As soon as the concoction hit my tongue, I frowned. I wasn't fond of the taste of Coca-Cola to begin with—I preferred 7UP or Sprite—so I wasn't sure if the bad taste was the rum, the cola, or both.

"Yuck," I spat, handing the glass back to her.

Pinky laughed, took a large gulp of the cocktail, and then leaped up from the table. "¡Wepa!" she cried, dancing off into the kitchen to retrieve the last few crabs left in the pot.

BEING WELCOMED HOME BY PINKY'S joyful music and generous food was so different to going to my own apartment. Robert didn't want Vivian to give us keys, which meant that when we came home after school we'd have to ring the bell to get into the building, nine times out of ten he was already in a drunken sleep and couldn't hear the bell. But maybe he did hear it and just laid in bed giggling to himself.

Whatever the case, in order to gain entry, Reggie and I would have to wait until someone entered or exited the building. At our apartment door, I'd press the tiny black buzzer until my finger hurt, and still the sound didn't wake him. Sometimes, we'd go across the hall to Mr. and Mrs. Marshall's apartment, the grandparents of my first love interest, Garfield. I'd use their phone to call Robert, but he never answered. The phone would ring and ring until it clicked off and sounded a busy signal.

The Marshalls were always very nice to us. They'd allow us to sit in the apartment until Vivian came home. But most days, the Marshalls weren't home, and Reggie and I would settle ourselves on the floor in front of the apartment door and work on our homework until Vivian came home at six o'clock in the evening. When she rounded the corner and saw us sitting on the floor with our notebooks and textbooks open in our laps, she kissed her teeth and rolled her eyes before angrily shoving her key into the lock.

One day, Vivian got so fed up that she had keys cut for me.

"Here," she said. Dangling from the silver chain were two shiny keys, one silver and one copper-colored. "The silver one is for the outside door and the brown one is for the apartment door." She handed me the keys. "Put it around your neck."

I did as commanded.

"Don't lose them, you hear me?"

I nodded.

Most of my friends were latchkey children and wore keys strung around their necks. I wasn't really a latchkey child in the true sense of the word because, unlike my friends, there was a parent in my home when I got out of school.

"When you get in the house, you make sure to lock the door behind you, go into your room, do your homework, and be very, very quiet." She pressed her index finger to her lips.

I understood that Robert did not know about the keys, and it would be about a week before he became aware of them. He was always asleep, snoring loudly, until Vivian went into the bedroom to shake him awake for work. But one afternoon, when we let ourselves into the apartment, he was coming out of the bathroom. His head whipped around in surprise when he heard the door creak open.

"What the hell!" he growled at us. "Where did you get that goddamn key?"

Now we were all in trouble, all three of us.

"M-mommy," I stammered.

Robert walked toward us with his hand out. "Give it to me."

As punishment, he forbade us to play with our toys, and he took the television out of our room. "Read a book," he tossed at us as he carried the television into his bedroom. That order might have felt like a punishment to Reggie, but reading was my favorite thing to do, so it didn't bother me at all.

Of course, when Vivian came home, they argued about the key. When Robert refused to return it to me, she went out and got another set cut. So began a cycle of Robert confiscating the keys and

Vivian replacing them. The circus went on for weeks before Robert installed a chain lock on the door. Which meant that I could unlock the door and Reggie was small enough to slip through the narrow opening and let me in. But that solution was short-lived because he was growing as fast as a weed.

"I'll show him," Vivian grumbled as she marched us to Bedford Avenue and enrolled us in the YMCA, where we could spend the hours after school swimming in the pool. But then, Reggie, being the rambunctious boy he was, continuously violated the top two cardinal rules of the YMCA pool etiquette:

NO Diving
NO Running
NO Food
NO Glass

Our memberships were revoked, and we found ourselves hall rats once again.

The bright fall days were turning crisp, which signaled the impending winter. The hallway was drafty, and the porcelain-tiled floor was cold under our behinds.

"Mommy, can't we just go to the library?"

Vivian's eyebrows rose. "The library at school?"

"No, the one on Eastern Parkway." The Central Library at Grand Army Plaza is a looming structure with many rooms, housing more than five million books. I'd visited the library on school trips, and Vivian had taken us there a few times.

"Hmmm," she sounded as she considered the idea.

"Pleeeeease."

"You know you're supposed to be quiet in the library, right?" She looked over at Reggie, who was sitting on the floor, running his match cars across the carpet. "You hear me, boy?"

He gave her a sheepish look. "Yes."

"Okay, then," she said.

Those afternoons were the best. I spent hours roaming the stacks, randomly choosing a book from the shelves, reading a few paragraphs before gently replacing it. I did this over and over again. I loved the smell of the books, loved how books felt in my hands, especially the old leather-bound copies. The library was nirvana to me.

"One day, I'm going to have my own library of books," I'd whisper to myself as I walked through the aisles, sweeping my fingers across the book spines.

Sometimes though, Reggie and I went to the museum, which was adjacent to the library, and we'd roam through the exhibit rooms, gaping at art and artifacts from all around the globe. But my favorite installations were those that spotlighted Africa and indigenous cultures.

Ultimately, like most things that brought us joy, Robert put an end to it. "You two better bring your asses straight home after school or else." The *or else* could mean any number of things: a pop upside the head, a twisted ear, or two lashes across our backsides with the belt. The upside, I suppose if I had to find one, was that he stopped putting the chain link on the door.

THAT SAID, ROBERT'S CONTROLLING BEHAVIOR continued.

During the Vietnam War, a seventeen-year-old Robert had enlisted in the army and spent three years in the Philippines, driving transport. I have a photo of him with his brigade. He looks like a goofy kid. The way he's cheesing into the camera, you'd think he'd just won a five-day, four-night stay to Disneyland. I don't know who he was before he went into the military, but I don't think he was the same person who returned home.

Robert thought of himself as a brigadier general, and he treated Reggie and me like his lowly recruits.

For a short time, my aunt Laura, a firstborn girl of a firstborn girl, was married to Robert's baby brother, Eddie. As a young man,

Eddie strongly resembled the crooner Smokey Robinson. He didn't have Smokey's light-colored eyes, but his skin was as fair as Smokey's and he'd conka-lined his hair so it would lie down like Smokey's hair.

You can imagine the effect he had on women. Laura tells me that long before she became acquainted with Eddie, she was aware of Robert.

"You know that color Robert would turn in the summertime? Like a red penny. Like a bronzy-copper complexion. Pretty. Pretty-prettyprettypretty. I liked to sit in the window and people watch. Robert was hard to miss with that prettyprettypretty complexion and those army fatigues."

Army fatigues?

"Oh yes, he wore those fatigues a lot! He'd parade up and down the street, with his hat pulled down low over his eyes. Up and down, up and down. The women would stop and stare. Even on the hottest days, when it felt like God had turned on an oven, Robert had on that damn uniform. I think he liked the attention. And he got a lot of attention, but I never did see him speak to any of those women.

"When I started dating Eddie and he took me 'round the family and introduced me to Robert and Bree, I was shocked. I said, this is your brother? He wasn't active duty then. But he was in the reserves, I believe.

"Eddie was with me, and Bree with Audrey, and they already had two kids, but your father didn't have anyone, and I thought that was odd because he was such a good-looking man with that pretty-prettypretty color. But what did I know, I was just fifteen.

"Then you know I got pregnant, and me and Eddie got married, because that's what you did back then. What a mistake that was. I left Eddie because he was sleeping around, and when I confronted him about it, he'd run home to his mother. Mrs. Taylor ruined those boys. A Black mother ain't always the best thing for a Black son. I'm sure glad I had a daughter."

5

"What do you wanna be when you grow up, Bernice?"
This was a common question asked of me by the adults in my life.

I'd visited the United Nations on a school trip, and the homework assignment was to write a report and read it in front of the class. I wrote that I was going to become an ambassador when I grew up.

The teacher flashed a patronizing smile at me and said, "That was a very nice report, Bernice, but it takes a lot of years of college, and you have to learn several languages to become an ambassador."

I laid my report on her desk and went back to my seat. She hadn't come right out and said that my dream of becoming an ambassador was out of reach for a little Black girl like me, but her statement and haughty tone implied it. She made me feel embarrassed and ashamed of dreaming big.

So, going forward, I was careful of what I shared with adults when they asked me about the hopes and dreams I had for my future self.

"I want to be a librarian."

I didn't really want to be a librarian; I just liked the idea of spending time around books. My favorite part of the school week was the day the class went to the library. I was into my mystery phase at the time, reading all things Hardy Boys and Nancy Drew.

Secretly, though, I really wanted to write books, but I wasn't sure if that was a thing that I could aspire to. After all, as far as I was aware, most, if not all, writers were white, and I wasn't.

The only person I knew of who shared the same desire as I did was the fictional television character John-Boy Walton from the TV series *The Waltons*. John-Boy Walton was a white man who lived with his family in rural Virginia. He was the eldest son and an aspiring writer. He worked part-time as a librarian and was taking creative writing courses in the hopes of one day publishing a novel. Every night before bed, John-Boy opened his journal and set about writing about his experiences and his family. The Waltons aired in 1972, when I was seven years old and already a bookworm. I tuned in every week just for John-Boy's storyline. Had he received another rejection letter, or had he finally found publishing success?

I modeled John-Boy's behavior, religiously journaling my thoughts, desires, and hatred of Robert in a green hardcover ledger book Vivian had taken from her office and given me.

Finally, after several seasons and years of determination, John-Boy sold his novel to a big-city publisher. I was so moved by his victory that I wept. I knew then how much I wanted that success for myself.

After some months of pouring my heart onto the pages of my journal, Robert found it hidden on the closet shelf beneath the boxed board games of Monopoly, Candy Land, Perfection, and Operation.

When I came home from school that afternoon, it was sitting

open on the kitchen table, next to the ashtray with a Camel ciga-rette smoldering. Robert was standing in front of the window, arms folded across his chest, gazing out at the backyard.

I didn't immediately recognize the book as mine.

"Good afternoon, sir," I said.

When he turned to look at me, the fury on his face looked like a storm cloud.

"So, you hate me?" he snarled.

I was confused for a second, and then my eyes dropped to the open book. I saw my jagged and uneven script and instantly under-stood.

My heart began to race.

Fresh tears stung my eyes as I stammered out my defense. "N-no, sir."

He glared at me for another minute before walking to the table, snatching up the ledger, and slowly stripping the pages from the binding. He tore the pages crosswise and lengthwise until they looked like strips of confetti.

By the time he was finished destroying my journal, I was sobbing.

"You better never write anything like that again or I'll tear your little ass up," Robert warned as he shoved the carnage into a brown A&P paper bag and pushed it at me. "Now, go and throw it in the incinerator."

Later, in my bedroom, while Robert snored in the next room, I pressed my pillow over my face and cried.

When Vivian came home, with Reggie in tow, she saw my puffy eyes and asked, "What happened, Bernice?"

She knew it was either one of two things: a bully at school or the bully at home.

"Daddy ripped up my diary and . . . and . . ."

Reggie, who was just about four years old at the time, aimed his finger at me and asked, "Why you crying, Bernice?"

I was so distraught I couldn't even finish the sentence. Vivian closed her eyes and took a deep breath. "Calm down, and tell me what happened."

When I was finished, she took another deep breath.

"I'm sorry he did that, Bernice, but let this be a lesson to you. You should never write down anything that you don't want people to know, okay?"

I nodded.

"Keep those things in your head. You understand?"

I nodded again.

MAYBE ROBERT WAS STILL FUMING about the unkind things I'd written about him, because that night, he and Vivian had one of the worst fights I'd ever witnessed.

Monday through Friday, Robert left the apartment at nine o'clock at night to head to his job as a truck driver for UPS. Nightly, he drove an 18-wheeler from Manhattan to different drop-off points in cities in the surrounding states. He usually arrived home between ten and eleven the following morning, drank himself to sleep, and then got up to do it all over again. Sometimes though, he'd get dressed in his brown UPS uniform, leave the house as usual, and return home before midnight.

Those nights he'd either called in sick from a pay phone on the street or arrived at work only to be sent back home by his supervisor, who had smelled the liquor lingering on his breath beneath the scent of the mint Life Savers or Doublemint chewing gum Robert used to mask the odor.

"Go home, Mac. I can't let you drive under the influence."

When Robert came home, he'd ease the apartment door open and softly close it before tiptoeing in, hoping to catch Vivian doing something she had no business doing. But he never caught her doing anything other than relaxing in front of the television, talking on the phone, or simply curled up in bed asleep. She always kept her bedroom door open so she could hear us in the next room. That particular night when Robert crept in and flicked on the bedroom light, Vivian was staring dead at him.

"Why are you sneaking in here like a snake?"

Her open eyes startled him, her accusation infuriated him.

"I'm not sneaking!" he barked defensively, even as his eyes darted around the room. He resisted the urge to swing open the closet door or drop to his knees to peer under the bed. Instead, he said, "Someone told me that they saw a man coming into the apartment tonight."

Vivian sucked her teeth. "That might work on the kids, but it don't work on me. Now turn off the light, I have to get up early for work."

And with that, she turned onto her side and gave him her back.

Robert stood there for a few seconds, glowering. Without switching off the light, he turned and walked away. A second later, Vivian climbed out of the bed, stomped across the floor, flicked off the light, and slammed the bedroom door shut.

In the kitchen, Robert retrieved the half-empty bottle of Hennessy from the cabinet, poured himself a drink, and gulped it down in one swallow. He took the bottle and the glass to the kitchen table, poured a second drink, and lit a cigarette. By 2:00 a.m., the bottle was empty, there were eight cigarette butts in the ashtray, and Robert was fuming. He was tired of being disrespected by his idiot supervisor and his slut of a wife. He saw how men looked at her. She liked the attention, even encouraged it. The previous week, she'd gone to the hairdresser and gotten her hair dyed red.

Red!

"You like it?"

He absolutely did not like it.

"You look ridiculous," he said. "You look like a tramp."

"Your mama looks like a tramp," Vivian had tossed back.

Robert balled his fist and charged at her, growling, "Don't talk about my mother."

Remembering the incident, Robert got angry all over again.

———

FROM THE OTHER SIDE OF the wall that separated my bedroom from theirs, I could hear my parents scuffling and grunting like boars. Then the wall shook, sending the little tin skirts around the light sconces teetering.

Between the wallops I could hear Vivian's muffled, agonized cries, and then, suddenly, their bedroom door flew open and Vivian raced out of the room, wailing, "I hate you; I hate you; I fucking hate you!"

I was trembling when I slipped from my bed and tiptoed to my closed bedroom door. They were warring in the kitchen now, bumping up against the washing machine, the dinette set, and the tall brown metal cabinet that held the plates, coffee cups, saucers, and silverware.

I creaked open the door. "Mommy, Mommy?" I whispered into the darkness.

There was a loud thud, and the floor beneath my feet shuddered as if a hundred-pound bag of wet cement had been dropped onto it. Vivian's agonizing moans echoed through the darkness.

"Mommy?"

Then I saw the scene I have never been able to scrub from my memory.

I saw Robert's white boxers before I saw his face. They glowed like a night-light in the dusky darkness. And then he emerged from the shadows; bare-chested, perspiration glistening on his forehead and streaming in rivulets down the sides of his face, his breath laboring with the effort it took to drag Vivian across the floor by her hair.

At the sight of her, my bladder sprung a leak, dripping urine down my thighs. My eyes rose to meet Robert's, and I saw that they were as black as oil beetles.

"Get back in bed," he snarled, before hauling his kill into his lair and slamming the door.

An hour or so later, Vivian came into my bedroom and turned on the light. I was still wide awake, because my terror and wet underwear wouldn't permit me to fall asleep.

My wide, terrified eyes clamped on to her haggard face.

She swept her hair out of her puffy eyes and said, "Get up and get dressed, we're leaving."

Vivian got us dressed, threw some clothes in a suitcase, and we fled to Thelma and Wilfred's house in Queens.

"Just leave the motherfucker," Thelma snapped when she opened her front door and found us huddled together on her stoop shivering in the predawn darkness. She knew from her own experience that leaving a violent relationship was easier said than done, but she said it anyway.

I've read that it takes at least seven times for a woman to leave her abuser for good. Vivian must have left Robert twice as many times, but she always went back.

6

Thelma was a beauty. Butterscotch-complexioned, long black hair, and ample bosom. She stood just four feet, eleven inches tall but carried herself like she was twice that height. She cussed like a sailor and had fingers as sticky as molasses. Which is to say, she was a thief. And she was a riveting storyteller, which is a nice way of saying that she was a liar.

She was born in Philadelphia, Pennsylvania, in 1926 to Lillian Bell May and Edward Hawkins. The family lore is that Edward was a minister who was afflicted with anisomelia, also known as short-leg syndrome. It's uncertain whether the pair were legally married, or if Edward was also the father of Rose Anna, born in 1928, and Helen in 1929. When Lillian died in March 1930 at the young age of twenty-seven, her death certificate stated that she was a widow. After her death, the three sisters went to live with their grandparents, Carlus and Rosie May, in Sandersville, Georgia.

Carlus passed away in 1938, and his son, Charlie Herman,

a.k.a. Buddy, became head of the household. In 1942, Thelma became pregnant at the age of fifteen. She gave birth to Vivian in March 1943. In 1947, Thelma left Vivian in the care of Grandma Rosie and joined the great migration. She went to Detroit, where her uncles Lee and Richard had settled.

It didn't take long for her to shake off the red clay dust of Sandersville, and before anyone could say boo, she was citified and as polished as one of the shiny sedans rolling off Henry Ford's assembly line.

She met James Forest in Detroit—a handsome brown-skinned man of medium height and build. A roofer by day, musician at night, and a card shark and pimp on the side. Thelma first met him at one of the nightclubs she frequented.

James approached her after a set one night. She was sitting at a table with a group of girlfriends, fanning her damp neck with a napkin when he approached.

"I saw you out there dancing," he said. "You got moves. You thirsty? Can I get you a drink?"

Thelma studied his neatly trimmed mustache and dark glittering eyes while the other women at the table smirked and looked away. She wasn't a drinker, but she said, "Sure. I'll have a rum and Coke."

He looked at her friends. "Can I get y'all something?"

"Nah, we're good," they chorused.

"Rum and Coke," he said, aiming the middle and forefingers of his right hand at her like a pistol and then strutting off to the bartender.

He was barely out of earshot when the women huddled over the table.

"Be careful, Thelma, that one has a reputation."

"Oh? What type of reputation?"

"I hear he's a pimp."

The information wasn't the deterrent they'd hoped it would be. Thelma's eyes gleamed with interest. "Is that right?" she cooed.

JAMES AND THELMA HAD BEEN together for a few years by the time Thelma sent for Vivian to come live with them in September 1952. She was nine years old and had never received any formal schooling. Under the guidance of Grandma Rosie in Sandersville, two or three times a week, Vivian, along with the other children in the community, gathered in the pews of the Minton Spring AME Church to learn adding, subtraction, and the alphabet.

Poor Black children required only enough schooling to understand and follow the directions of their future white employers. Opportunities in that town were limited to working on a farm, in the chalk mines, or as a domestic.

When Thelma enrolled Vivian into the Detroit public school system, they placed her in a first-grade class filled with six-year-olds. Vivian was nine and menstruating.

The trio lived in a tiny one-bedroom apartment above a newsstand in a two-story brick building that hugged the corner of a wide, tree-lined street. One of the houses on that block was a rooming house for homosexual men. In warm weather, the men congregated on the porch to play cards, drink, or just people watch.

"Heeeeeeyyyyyy, Thelma!" one of them would drawl when he spotted her coming up the street from her job as a domestic in one of those grand homes in Indian Village.

"Hey, baby," Thelma returned.

She'd always stop and talk with them for a spell, exchanging neighborhood gossip or lamenting about the number none of them had hit that day.

Before moving to Detroit, Vivian had never seen an effeminate man, and she'd certainly never seen a man in makeup, so the first time she and Thelma passed the house with its crowded porch, her mouth fell open like a broken hatch door. The front door and windows of the house were open, and Lloyd Price's song "Lawdy Miss Clawdy" could be heard out on the sidewalk. Some of the men leaned up against the clapboard walls, swigging from cold bottles of beer and pop; others were sitting on the stoop, smoking cigarettes, bouncing their heads along to the melody.

One didn't have to look too hard to glimpse the foundation on their faces and charcoal-colored eyeliner.

"Pooh, baby, close your mouth 'fore a fly flies down your throat!" one of the men cried when they saw the astonishment on Vivian's face.

Thelma popped her upside the head. "Now, Vivian, you know better than that," she admonished. Vivian's mouth snapped shut, but her eyes continued to bulge.

"Who's that, Thelma?" asked a thin man with slanted eyes and conked hair the color of cooked carrots.

"This is my daughter, Vivian."

"Daughter? Daughter?" The man's eyes stretched. "Well, I'll be a monkey's ass!" he cackled. "I would have pegged her for your sister!"

The compliment made Thelma smile.

JAMES WAS A WOMANIZER, AND Thelma was a jealous woman. Vivian was witness to many of their brawls, most of which, according to her, were incited by Thelma, who could not keep her mouth shut or her hands to herself.

More often than not, to keep from killing her, James would punch a wall, storm out of the apartment, jump into his Cadillac, and speed off. Sometimes he was gone for hours, other times he didn't come home for days. He'd return with a peace offering: a bouquet of flowers, or one of those Chinese collared silk dresses Thelma was fond of.

And things would be fine and dandy again, until he came home smelling like some other woman or Thelma walked into a club and found a woman up in his face or sitting in his lap, and the cussing and fighting would start all over again.

Vivian wasn't used to this type of chaos. Grandma Rosie had been a widow for a long time by the time Vivian came along. She'd heard stories though, stories that painted Carlus as a whoremonger, which was true because he had sired a boatload of children with a woman who lived less than a mile away from him. He was also a preacher, fond of spouting scriptures as he thrashed his wife.

When Carlus died in 1938, Thelma was eleven years old. No telling what she'd seen transpire between her grandparents, and maybe that's why the chaos in her romantic life didn't seem abnormal.

Vivian thought of Thelma as juvenile, in need of protection. She told me, "Even though I was the child, I always felt like I was the mother."

ONE NIGHT IN A RAGE, Thelma took a hammer to James's safe, which was filled with money and guns. She had spent an hour or so fumbling through several combinations, but none of them worked.

"Fucking motherfucker!" Thelma raged, smashing the dial to bits before turning the weapon on the handle. The racket was deafening.

"Mama, please stop. Please!" Vivian wailed, frantically trying to tug her away from the safe.

Thelma turned on her and raised the hammer into the air. The look on her face frightened Vivian almost as much as the threat. She cowered and backed away. Moments later, James walked through the door, whistling. When he saw Thelma in mid-swing, the tune fell dead. He blinked unbelievingly, and then his face turned into a storm.

"You little bitch, I'm gonna kill you!"

Thelma swung the hammer at him. "Come on with it, motherfucker!"

Because he was bigger and stronger, he easily disarmed her and tossed the hammer to the floor. Then he caught her by the throat, lifted her into the air, and flung her across the room like a rag doll. When she hit the wall, three curlers popped off her head and scattered across the floor.

"Leave my mother alone!" Vivian shrieked. She leaped on James like a cat, pounding on his head with her fists until he shook her off and she hit the floor with a thud.

Thelma jabbed him in the eye with her finger; James hollered and finally released her from his death grip. Cussing, he walked in a circle with the palm of his hand over his injured eye. Moving his free hand behind him, he pulled a pistol from the waistband of his trousers.

Vivian gasped. She knew if she didn't get Thelma out of that apartment, they might both end up dead. She grabbed Thelma by the hand, and the two ran out of the apartment, down the stairs, and into the frigid Detroit night. Gowns billowing, bare feet clapping against the cold pavement, mother and daughter fled for their lives.

James followed them out of the building, jumped into his Cadillac, and sped after them. In no time he was upon them, the chrome bumper just inches away from their calves. He leaned out the car window, aimed, and fired. Maybe he was a poor shot, or maybe he just wanted to scare the shit out of her; either way the bullet missed and went whistling off into the night.

Detroit is a city of alleyways. On that night, Thelma and Vivian used them as an escape route, taking them all the way to Uncle Richard and Aunt Lula Mae's house. Uncle Richard had guns too.

THELMA AND VIVIAN STAYED OVERNIGHT, which was just long enough for James's temper to cool. By the next afternoon, they were back in the apartment and there was a new safe in place of the one Thelma had damaged.

"You better keep your hands off this one," James warned.

Sometime after that incident, James decided he wanted to pull up roots in the Motor City and replant in the Windy City, and Thelma followed with Vivian in tow. But Chicago was short-lived. The fussing and fighting continued, and when James pulled a gun on Thelma and pressed the nozzle to her lips, she knew it was time for them to part ways. She thought about going back to Detroit, but her sister Anna in Brooklyn said, "Sis, come on down here. I got room enough for you and Vivian, and anyway"—she sighed—"I miss you."

It made sense, because not only was Thelma's sister living in Brooklyn, so were her maternal aunts, Ruby and Virginia, the women who had mothered her after her own mother died. She needed that mothering again, for herself and for her daughter. So they packed up the few rags they owned and boarded the Greyhound bus headed for the Big Apple, and that's where they both would live for the rest of their days.

Little did Vivian know, when she and Thelma moved to Brooklyn, that in the years to come, she would find herself in a relationship just as violent or worse than Thelma had endured with James.

7

Me, on the other hand, I desperately wanted out of New York, out of Brooklyn, out of apartment A5, and out of my life. Bluntly put: I wanted to die.

I couldn't have been more than six or seven, but the turmoil in my home life and the constant bullying at school had taken a toll on my mental and physical health. I was plagued with headaches and tummy aches. I was a chronic fingernail biter, gnawing away at them until I drew blood.

"Keep it up and I'm going to put hot sauce on your fingers," Robert threatened.

I was a leg bouncer too.

"Can't you stay still? You got ants in your pants, and you need to dance?" Vivian laughed.

Later in life, I discovered that these conditions and behaviors were all referenced symptoms of anxiety disorder. What I learned as I was writing this book was that people with anxiety disorders are more likely to have suicidal thoughts. Risk factors for children include but are not limited to bullying and conflict in the home. The dark idea formed in my mind after a particularly rough day at school when a boy shoved me to the ground during recess. He was reprimanded by the teacher and sent to stand in the corner of the classroom as punishment. After school let out, he caught me on the street and pounded on me until my nose bled. My world was one big ball of horror, and I was coming apart at the seams. I couldn't take it anymore; I wanted out and began to plan my exit.

1. Death by electrocution

I understood that people had ended their lives by placing toasters into their evening baths, but the thought of frying myself to death was terrifying.

2. Death by jumping

We lived in a six-story apartment building. I'd seen the photo of Evelyn Francis McHale, who in 1947 leaped off the Empire State Building to her death. She landed on a parked car. In the photo, Evelyn did not look dead. She looked like she was in a peaceful sleep. I wanted that type of peace for myself. But I was petrified of heights.

3. Death by overdose

Maybe I saw it on one of the old black-and-white movies on television or heard it spoken about among the adults in my life, but I was well aware that sometimes unhappy people took a handful of sleeping pills to put an end to their miserable lives.

The only medication my parents kept in the bathroom medicine cabinet was baby aspirin. To me, the peach-colored pills tasted like candy, and I treated them as such. If I wanted something sweet and I didn't have a pack of Now and Laters or Bazooka bubble gum in my room, I'd go into the bathroom and sneak a tablet or two from the bottle.

I wasn't sure whether baby aspirin could end my life, because Vivian gave it to me to make me well. That said, I did not strike it from the list.

Even as I planned my demise, I worried about leaving Vivian and Reggie alone with Robert. I felt a responsibility to protect them. I couldn't fight Robert off, but the occasional fainting spell, or hysterics, did seem to curtail his bad behavior. If I were dead, there would be no one to intervene on their behalf, and then what would happen to them? It was a conundrum that added another layer to my stressful existence.

But the day I found Robert's gun, my thoughts turned from suicide to murder.

Patricide is the deliberate act of killing one's father. It is the rarest form of murder, accounting for less than 2 percent of homicides in this country. It is predominately carried out by middle-class white males and is an act that is rare among women.

Studies show that daughters who kill their fathers are less likely to be psychotic as is seen in cases where sons kill their fathers. But in both instances, the fathers were aggressive, domineering, and tyrannical.

SOMEONE HAD GIVEN THELMA A pair of Persian cats. She kept the boy and gave me the girl, which I named Priscilla.

It had been sometime since I had a pet. When I was very little, I had a blue-and-white parakeet named Paul, who lived in a white cage in my bedroom. I was afraid of him, because periodically Robert let Paul out of his cage, and he would flit frantically around the room, chirping, swooping, diving, and flying into walls. I don't know why Paul flying terrified me so, but Robert would stand in the doorway of the room with his arms folded over his chest and laugh until water ran out of his nose. Eventually, he would capture Paul and throw him back into the cage. Paul would sit on his perch, still chirping, clearly frazzled, his little feathered breast rapidly rising and falling.

One day, I came home from school and found that Paul and the metal cage were gone.

When I asked Vivian where the bird was, she shook her head and mumbled, "Your father."

No further explanation was needed.

But Priscilla was still at home, a beautiful black-and-white Persian mix. Even-tempered and sweet. At night, she would climb into bed with me and sleep at my feet. I loved her fiercely, and so she was added to the roster of living things that I sought to protect from Robert.

He made Priscilla's life as miserable as ours. He enjoyed mistreating her, often hanging her upside down by her hind paws and laughing at her terrified mews. On more than one occasion, he shoved her outside the window, where she clung to the window screen by her claws for dear life.

She hated him as much as I did, and whenever he was in the apartment, she vanished from sight. I empathized with her. I wished I could disappear too. It took months before I found her hiding place, and the gun, which I was not looking for.

One day, as I was exiting my bedroom, I saw Priscilla scurry beneath my father's record player console. It was a handsome piece of furniture. The radio, turntable, and speakers were inset in a long wooden casing that looked very much like the wooden linen chest that sat at the foot of my parents' bed.

"Aha," I cried, dashing after her. Reaching the console, I dropped to my knees and peered into the shadowy darkness. Priscilla wasn't there. In fact, there was nothing, save for a few dust bunnies. I thought that my eyes were playing tricks on me because I was sure I saw Priscilla slither under the console.

As a response to my confusion, my imagination sparked to life. Maybe there was a secret panel in the wall! I ran my hand along the baseboard, stopping every few inches to pat and push the ornamental molding, but it didn't open, shift, or buckle. Baffled, I pulled myself up from the floor and went about my day, turning the vision of Priscilla slithering under the console over and over in my head.

Later, when Priscilla still had not reappeared, I rechecked all the other hiding places: under my bed, under the kitchen table, my bedroom closet, and the bathtub, but she was nowhere to be found.

As I searched, I called her name. "Priscilla . . . pssss . . . pssss . . . pssss . . . Priscilla."

Finally, she responded with a soft meow. I froze. Had I heard right?

"Priscilla?"

Once again she meowed.

I realized that the sound was coming from the console, so I lowered myself to the floor, shoved my hand underneath it, and ran my palm along the rough plywood underside.

My hand hit empty space. Surprise, surprise, there was an opening. Slowly, carefully, I slid my hand into the pocket until my fingertips brushed fur.

"Priscillaaaaaaa," I sang, happy to have found her.

She purred in response and brushed her wet nose across my knuckles. I pushed my hand deeper still until it was buried under her warm, furry belly.

"C'mon, Priscilla," I urged.

When I wrapped my hand beneath her belly, my fingers brushed a hard, metal object. As I puzzled over what I was touching, Priscilla scrambled out of the hiding space, squeezed past my arm, and shot off to my bedroom.

I grabbed hold of the object and pulled it from the shelf, out into the open.

In my palm was a pewter-colored small-caliber gun.

I squeaked with fright and almost dropped it. The shaking started in my fingertips, scurried to my fingers, and spread up my arm. I didn't know much about guns, other than they killed people.

Afraid it would fire in my shaking hand, I mustered all the composure I could and very gently placed it back into its hiding place.

I didn't tell a soul about that gun, not Vivian and not my friends. I kept the discovery all to myself and the secret grew and grew until it nearly consumed me.

I didn't know that there was such a thing as intimate partner violence, or that four in ten Black women experience physical violence from their partners in their lifetimes, or that the presence of a gun in a home afflicted by domestic violence increases the likelihood of homicide by 500 percent.

Even without knowing those statistics, I knew deep down in my soul that one day soon my father would use that gun to kill my mother, so I decided that I would have to kill him first.

∿

I WHOLEHEARTEDLY BELIEVE THAT I WOULD HAVE KILLED ROBERT HAD his mother, Gwen, not stepped in, saving both our lives.

Gwendolyn was an enigma to me, even though I'd known her from the day I was born until her death in 1997, at the age of seventy-two. By the time Robert and Vivian got married, her once-slim dancer's body was a memory, her face had rounded and inflated with age and alcohol. She was still smoking and drinking and just a few years away from the first in a series of heart attacks that would render the organ so weak, she needed a pacemaker to keep it beating.

Gwen was a reluctant grandmother, because she had been a reluctant mother, the role having been thrust upon her because she enjoyed sex, and pregnancy was usually the consequence of such pleasure. She existed on the perimeter of my life, even though for many years, she lived right across the street from us at 245 Sullivan Place in an apartment that overlooked the park where me and the other neighborhood children played. Gwen was certainly one of the watching eyes my father had warned me about.

By the time her grandchildren came along, her nerves were frayed. Our youthful energy rattled her, and those rare visits she made to our apartment often ended with her snatching up her purse and fleeing as though a fire alarm had sounded.

GWENDOLYN DOROTHY GILL WAS THE daughter of Aubrey and Ethel Gill, immigrants from Barbados who, like so many before them and many more since, came to America for a better life. Aubrey had worked on the construction of the Panama Canal alongside white men from America and Europe, who were paid in gold, while Aubrey and the other Black workers were paid in silver.

He saved his coins and made his way to Cape Breton in Nova Scotia, where he found work at the Sydney Plant and knew cold weather for the first time. No matter how many layers he put on, the chill found its way under his skin and clamped its frigid jaws around his muscles and joints. He almost returned home to Barbados, but the money he was making had a hold on him, so he toughed it out and soon set his sights on the USA. From Nova Scotia, he crossed the border into Michigan and hitched a ride with some other men to Detroit, where there were jobs available for a few good men at Olds Motor Works.

Aubrey was nearly seven feet tall, dark, and handsome, and his Bajan lilt only added to his exoticism. Black women, mostly transplants from the Southern states, knee-buckled and swooned when Aubrey parted his lips and that pretty talk tumbled out of his mouth. Because he was a man, and men had needs, he dabbled with the women but did not commit to one, because he had a wife and daughter back in Barbados, whom he loved dearly and was working hard to bring to America so they could be a family again.

Aubrey left Detroit for New York to live with his younger sister, Aletha Jenette, who had been residing in Brooklyn since 1919. She and her Grenadian husband owned a two-story brick house on Herkimer Street in Bedford-Stuyvesant. Aubrey wasn't with his sister long before he was hired as a superintendent for a luxury apartment building on Eastern Parkway. He was reunited with his family on May 30, 1922, when Ethel and their fourteen-year-old daughter, Irene, arrived at Ellis Island.

Gwendolyn was born two years later, and she was raised with the belief that Aubrey and Ethel were her parents, and Irene, her big sister. She'd learn as an adult, when all parties involved in the con were gone, that Irene was in fact her mother and not her sister. The fib was invented because Irene had been just sixteen and unmarried when she gave birth to Gwendolyn.

Like mother, like daughter. Ethel too had a child out of wedlock at a young age. A boy named Jerrold, who was a grown man by the time she and Irene left Barbados to join Aubrey in America.

History is repetitive.

When Gwen came of age, Ethel enrolled her in the Mary Bruce school of dance in Harlem. And when Mary Bruce was approached by Mike Todd, American theater and movie producer and onetime husband of Elizabeth Taylor, to procure a few of her dancers to perform at the Gay New Orleans–themed dance program he was arranging for the 1940 World's Fair, Gwendolyn was one of the lucky chosen. It was at the fair that sixteen-year-old Gwen met the twenty-three-year-old ex-convict Harold McFadden.

Harold was born in Louisville, Kentucky, but spent his formative years in Harlem. He was a smooth-talking guitarist, who at the age of sixteen was convicted on a second-degree assault charge that landed him in Auburn Prison for eighteen months. "A new speed record," reported the *Daily News*. "The jury deliberated half an hour and returned a verdict of guilty of second-degree assault, carrying a penalty of two and one-half to five years in prison."

Not his criminal past, weekly Sunday service under the watchful eyes of the Lord and Savior Jesus Christ, nor Ethel's threats were any match for Harold's silver tongue, which he used to talk Gwen right out of her brassiere, garter belt, stockings, and cotton panties.

On October 11, 1940, two months before Harold and Gwen got engaged, Irene passed away at Kings County Hospital, having lost her battle with fecal fistula from sigmoid pelvic abscess and bronchopneumonia. Both Ethel and Gwen were still in the throes of grief when they went to pick out Gwen's wedding invitations at the same stationery store that had printed Irene's funeral program. They'd return there again, after the baby was born, to mill over the books of birth and christening announcements.

That December, Gwen and Harold exchanged vows in a small ceremony at the Church of the Black Virgin in Harlem. Afterward, they returned to the spacious apartment at 1452 Bedford Avenue, in Brooklyn, where the newly married couple would live with Gwen's parents.

Ethel didn't like Harold one bit. The fact that he was Black American was a strike against him that he didn't have any control over. She didn't like that she had to continuously remind him to take his shoes off at the door. "Stop tracking dirt into my house, young man!"

She didn't like that Harold spoke to her like she was one of his friends and not his mother-in-law. "Hi? Hi? We say good morning, good afternoon, and good night in this house!" Ethel stripped her teeth, then added, "I don't know what Gwen sees in you, because you are very unmanly!" *Unmanly* is Bajan speak for "rude."

Harold didn't like Ethel either, because she treated him like a bother and Gwen like a little girl, even though she was his wife and just months away from becoming a mother.

AUBREY "BREE" ISAAC MCFADDEN WAS born on July 22, 1941. Harold couldn't stop staring at that little, brown, precious life he and Gwen had made. From the beginning, his son was an accessory, an ornament he presented to the world like a badge of distinction. Fatherhood, he would never learn, was more than just proclaiming that he had a son.

But within weeks, the novelty of fatherhood faded. Harold didn't like the stinky diapers, the spitting up, and the crying. He hated the crying most of all, and little Aubrey wailed day and night.

"Dem bubbies not making enough milk to fill his belly," said Ethel. "Put a little pet milk and water in the bottle and give him."

And, to make things worse, Harold wanted sex and Gwen was refusing his advances.

"The doctor said I have to wait six weeks."

"Why?"

There was no shortage of women willing to sleep with him. They were in the audience at the clubs he played, on the train he rode to the clubs, at bars and music halls, and in the department stores where he shopped for suits and shirts, ties and hats.

Gwen was willing at the sixth-week mark, but then her period was back on, and so they would have to wait for at least another five days. And then five days turned into seven and then ten and then Harold went out of town with the orchestra to play venues in New Hampshire, Maine, and Massachusetts. When he returned, it was the middle of October. The New York air was cool and crisp, the trees were dressed in vibrant orange, yellow, and purple leaves, and the radiators in the apartment were rattling and hissing. But the racket still wasn't loud enough to drown out the sounds of their urgent lovemaking.

That November, Gwen announced her pregnancy during Thanksgiving dinner. The only person who lit up with the news was Aubrey.

"Another baby?" he said, clapping his hands and grinning.

Harold shook his head in disbelief, forced a lopsided smile, and then after a beat, leaned over and planted a stiff kiss on Gwen's soft cheek.

"That's—that's real nice, honey." The words came out as flat as cardboard.

Ethel, never one to hide her pleasure or disappointment, loudly sucked her teeth, rose from the table, stalked off to her bedroom, and slammed the door.

"Oh, she'll be okay," Aubrey said, as he used the fork to scrape at the grains of rice on his plate.

The three sat there in uncomfortable silence until Harold glanced at his watch, pulled the cloth napkin from his collar, and said, "Uh, I'm late." He sprang up from the table.

Gwen looked up at him. "Late for what?"

Aubrey set his fork down. "Yes, late for what?"

"I-I-I'm playing the Savoy tonight," Harold stammered. He looked down at Gwen. "I told you, Gwennie, didn't I?"

Gwen slowly shook her head. "No, no you didn't."

Harold flicked his temple with his thumb and middle finger. "Aah, I must have forgot. I must be getting old." He laughed.

In their bedroom, Bree was stirring in his crib. Harold went to the hall closet and retrieved his hat, overcoat, and guitar, sheathed in a black case.

Gwen turned around in her chair. "Will you be late?"

"Yes, I think so. Don't wait up." He plopped his hat on his head and wrenched open the door. He was already in the hallway when he threw "See you later, Mr. Gill" and "Bye, honey" over his shoulder.

He pulled the door shut behind him, and Aubrey and Gwen listened to the sound of his leather shoes dash down the marble stairwell.

Aubrey shook his head and rose from his chair. He knew what a man on the run looked like when he saw one. But he kept that to himself. It was Thanksgiving after all, and he wasn't always right.

HAROLD DIDN'T COME BACK THAT night or the next, or the one after that.

Gwen called his mother, who claimed that she hadn't heard from him but would call around, before they started checking the hospitals and the morgues. Gwen waited a day before she called Harold's mother again, but the operator said that the number had been disconnected.

"The man gone. Men leave. It's not the end of the world," Ethel said when Gwen came crying to her. "Life will go on and so will you."

On July 22, 1942, one year to the day when Bree was born, Gwen gave birth to her second son, my father, Robert Lewis Mc-Fadden.

And Ethel was right; the world didn't end. Life went on and so did Gwen.

In 1972, thirty years after Ethel had given Gwen that sage advice, she was still single and, now, a grandmother to eight.

The night before Gwen would make the announcement that irrevocably changed my life, Vivian, Reggie, and I had sat around the kitchen table dunking hard-boiled eggs into bowls of liquid food coloring. After Reggie and I went off to bed, Vivian hid the colored eggs around the apartment for our annual Easter egg hunt.

When Gwen arrived at the apartment the next day, Reggie and I were scampering around the living room in our pajamas, in search of the hidden eggs. "Take Five" by the Dave Brubeck Quartet filled the apartment. Robert played that song every Sunday morning. Saturday night had been an uneventful one. Robert drank less than usual because he was fighting a cold.

For years, Sundays had been a peaceful day in our apartment, because the liquor stores were closed, and, for some reason—thank God—Robert never thought to buy two bottles of Hennessy on Saturday instead of one. Without his liquid courage, Robert was mouse quiet, spending most Sundays in front of the television watching old Westerns or in the kitchen cooking pig feet or beef stew. In time, however, those serene Sundays came to an end when someone introduced him to a bootlegger who never closed.

But for now, all was well. The window shades were up, and the apartment was so bright with sunshine that I could see dust particles swirling in the rays. We were so consumed with our scavenging that we didn't hear the doorbell. When we looked up, there was Gwen, standing in the doorway, dressed in her fur-collared tweed coat and patent leather slingbacks.

"Good morning, Grandma," Reggie and I pealed in unison.

Gwen flinched as if we'd flicked something at her.

Vivian was standing alongside her. "Can I take your coat, Mrs. Taylor?"

"No, no, I'm not staying long," Gwen said, sweeping the oversized, smoky-lensed sunglasses from her face.

Robert came out of the bedroom, wrapped in his brown velvet samurai-warrior-styled bathrobe. Gwen smirked.

"My goodness, Robert, you're still in bed?"

"Hello to you too, Mother."

He always called her Mother, which I found very formal and lacking in affection. He folded his arms across his chest and smirked back at her.

Annoyed, Gwen grunted, sat down on the couch, and crossed her thick legs at the ankles. Vivian joined her there, grinning like a cat with a canary in her mouth. Something was happening, but I didn't know what that something was. Gwen looked at Robert, and he nodded for her to begin.

"Well, children, this summer I will be taking you to Barbados with me."

I was only familiar with the place because it often peppered Gwen and Robert's conversations.

"Where is that?" I asked.

Gwen gave me an incredulous look.

"In the West Indies," she balked as if I should have known this information without her having to tell me. "Where the *other* side of your family is from."

Other sounded in my mother's ear like *better*. Everyone knew that Gwen was disappointed that all three of her sons had married Black American women, and worse yet, not a one of them was fair-skinned.

Reggie and I sat on the floor, cross-legged, silently and obediently listening as Gwen prattled on. My mind swung between the words spilling out of her mouth and the yellow cellophane-wrapped wicker Easter baskets, filled with jelly beans and chocolate eggs, sitting on the kitchen table. I had no idea where the West Indies were or what type of people inhabited such a place. Did they all look like my grandmother or like the American Indians in the Westerns my father so loved?

"How are we getting there? Covered wagon?" I asked.

"Oh, Bernice." Vivian laughed.

Robert frowned, and Gwen's face clouded with disgust.

She did not take kindly to disrespectful children. But I was only pulling from the information I had gleaned from watching Westerns.

"No, we're going to fly."

"On a plane?" I bubbled excitedly.

"How else would we get there, Bernice?" she said dryly.

8

Visit Barbados today and you'll see luxury limestone villas and beach resorts crowding the sandy shoreline, but in 1536, when Portuguese explorer Pedro a Campos, en route to Brazil, came upon the triangular-shaped coral island, the perimeter was chock-full of fifty-foot-tall, centuries-old fig trees dripping with aerial roots. Those trees looked like bearded sentries, and so Pedro a Campos dubbed the island Los Barbados, which means "the bearded ones." The Spanish followed in the 1500s, renamed the island Isla de Barbados (Isle of the Bearded Men), and pillaged it of most of the indigenous population to use as slave labor in Spain.

England was at war with itself when Sir William Courten, a wealthy merchant, financed the colonization of Barbados. He employed Captain John Powell, who arrived on the island in May 1627 with ten enslaved Africans and eighty white settlers, most of whom were criminals and seditionists. Initially, Barbados was claimed under the English crown, but William Courten acquired the title rendering him the sole owner until 1639. In the beginning, the primary export crop was tobacco, but it was quickly replaced with sugar, which the English called white gold because it generated more money in trade than all the other English colonial products combined. It is estimated that between 1627 and 1807, approximately 387,000 enslaved Africans were sent to work on Barbados's sugar plantations.

In the fall of 1751, a nineteen-year-old George Washington, who would go on to become the first president of the United States, traveled by ship from Virginia to Barbados with his brother Lawrence. It would be the first and last time George Washington ever left the continental United States. He wrote in his journal that "the island was also densely populated, so everywhere furnished with inhabitants." A contemporary observed that "it resembles a scattered village in the midst of a garden."

FOLLOWING GWEN'S EASTER SUNDAY ANNOUNCEMENT, I sat in my bedroom shoveling jelly beans into my mouth with my six-and-a-half-year-old imagination churning out visions of the West Indies that were rife with images of teepees and war paint.

I was excited about flying in a plane. The memories of the flight from New York to Cleveland in 1967 and the one from New York to Augusta in 1970 were lost to me, so this trip felt like the first time. It also gave me something else to obsess over other than my miserable life.

We flew on Pan American Airlines, which back then was the premier American airline, boasting a fleet of 747s that flew from every major city in America to nearly every country in the world. Pan Am's flight attendants (called stewardesses back then) were pretty and thin and mostly white. It was an era in air travel when checked bags were free, as were cocktails, blankets, headphones, and hot tasty meals served with real silverware. Smoking was allowed in the terminal and on the airplane.

In the seventies, people dressed up to fly. Passengers put as much thought into their flight attire as they did into their Easter and wedding outfits. I remember I wore a pale purple sleeveless dress with a Peter Pan collar, patent leather shoes, and white lace cuffed ankle socks. Reggie had on a pair of Bermuda shorts the color of pea soup, leather shoes, and a green-and-white-striped crew-neck shirt. Vivian had slathered us both in Vaseline, and we boarded that flight looking as shiny as new minted pennies.

On the plane, Gwen sat on the aisle, Reggie in the middle, and me at the window.

Gwen rested her hand on Reggie's thigh. "You ready?" she said as the plane sped down the runway.

We both nodded, not knowing what to expect, and then suddenly we were airborne. Reggie and I both yelped with excitement as we soared into the clouds.

What a wonder it was to be so high up in the sky. I wasn't afraid at all, just intrigued. The airport, apartment buildings, and houses beneath us shrank to the size of my dollhouse furniture and then evaporated from sight, and then there was just the shadow of the plane skating across the dark Atlantic Ocean. Soon, the ocean disappeared, and there was nothing to see but blue sky.

TWO HUNDRED TWENTY YEARS AFTER George Washington ascended the gangplank of the brigantine *Success* and planted his feet on the sandy beach of Barbados, I arrived on the island and inhaled the warm air, saturated with scents of sea salt, sugarcane, and golden apple. There were still plenty of bearded fig trees, and the native people still lived simply and contently. The beaches were mostly deserted save for the smattering of vacationers from England and America, and there were only a few peddlers hawking everything from fresh aloe to handmade jewelry fashioned from coconut shells, shark teeth, coral, and driftwood. It was 1972, Barbados's popularity with tourists was still in its infancy.

From my meal, I'd saved the square of plastic-wrapped pineapple sponge cake, tucking it safely into my little yellow purse when Gwen wasn't looking. It would be my offering to the great chief of the West Indians that I believed was greeting us at the airport. Instead, we were met outside the terminal by Gwen's first cousin Anita.

Short and plump, with smooth skin that was dark as a soursop seed, Anita wrapped her fat arms around my brother and me, exclaiming, "Aww, these are Robert's children!" When Gwen had seen that Robert, as a teenager, was following in his older brother's footsteps—getting mixed up in bad company and emulating the walk and talk of the neighborhood hoodlums—she sent him to live with Anita, and her sister Dolly, for a whole year.

He had left an indelible impression on them, and so Anita was thrilled to have his offspring there with them.

After a few seconds, I broke the embrace, pulled the cake out of my purse, and presented it to her. Her face beamed with delight. "For me?" she sang, plucking the sponge cake from my hand. "Thank you, sweet girl!"

We followed her through the small parking lot to a 1956 brown-and-cream Ford Fairlane. Sitting behind the steering wheel was a family friend named Emerson. When he spotted us, he pulled his six-foot frame out of the car. The panels of his brown-and-yellow-flowered shirt flapped open, revealing a dark muscled chest covered in tightly coiled hair. He smiled at us, and the gold incisor in his mouth winked in the sunlight. Cheeks burning, I lowered my eyes and mumbled hello when he greeted me.

Anita climbed into the front passenger seat, and Gwen, Reggie, and me in the back. With calypso music pumping through the speakers, we bumped along the uneven dirt road that cut through acres upon acres of sugarcane. The proximity of the plants to the sea created a salty-sweet fragrance in the air. I thought that if happiness had a scent, this would be it. I took a deep breath and held the air in for as long as my lungs would allow.

Soon, the landscape changed. The sugarcane disappeared,

replaced now with cliffs dripping pink and white fragrant bougain-villea, banana and coconut trees, rambling limestone villas, and tiny wooden houses painted in all the colors of the rainbow.

Anita turned around and threw her fat arm over the back of her seat. "Gwen, do you know that Chisholm woman running for president?"

"Yeah." Gwen nodded.

She didn't know her personally, but Gwen did know someone who knew someone who knew Shirley Chisholm, the first Black woman ever elected to Congress. In January 1972, she became the first Black candidate to run for president. She was a source of pride for the West Indian community because she was the daughter of a Guyanese father and Barbadian mother.

"You know, she mother is a Hill. She family to Patsy Hill and dem," Anita continued.

Gwen frowned. "The one that went mad?"

"Nooo, not she. You thinking 'bout Fred Hill bandy-leg sister Patsy. Not that one, I talking 'bout the one who had a child from a white English man."

Gwen nodded, moaning, "Ooh, her."

"So, you gonna vote for the Chisholm woman, Gwennie?"

Gwen made a face. "You mad or what? I ain't wasting my vote on her. What a woman know 'bout running a country, anyway, huh? And a Black woman at that! If you think dem white people are going to vote for her, you just as mad as that Patsy Hill girl!"

At the time Gwen made that statement, Mia Amor Mottley, who is now the current prime minster of Barbados, was six years old.

A goat shot out from the brush into the road. Emerson quickly turned the wheel, wildly swerving the car. Gwen and Anita shrieked, me and Reggie squealed, "Whoooaaaa," as if we were on a carnival ride. Straightening the car, we traveled a few miles without incident, until Emerson pointed out the window. "Look there, children. You see that?"

I whipped my head around and saw the most unbelievable thing.

There was an entire house sitting in the middle of the road. Behind the house was a line of cars, and ours was the latest addition.

"Why is it in the street?" I asked, blinking in astonishment.

Emerson addressed me from the rearview mirror. "It's not in the middle of the road; it's on a flatbed truck. Dey moving it."

I knew houses were built, bought, sold, and torn down—but moved? How could that be? I leaned over the front seat to get a better look.

"See there," he said, pointing. "See the wheels underneath the flatbed?"

I angled my head until I spotted the tires. "Ohhh," I moaned. This place was filled with surprises.

Just then, the truck shuddered to life and began its slow trundle up the road with the string of automobiles trailing cautiously behind. These movable wooden houses, I would learn later, are called chattel houses and date back to slavery days.

We arrived in Paynes Bay in the parish of Saint James, located on the west coast of the island. Back then it was a sleepy little village, where people didn't lock their doors or windows. But now, it's known as the Platinum Coast and is chock-full of private luxury homes and high-end restaurants, owned and operated by wealthy foreigners. Now there are gates on the windows, and everyone locks their doors.

ANITA LIVED IN A MODEST chattel house with her younger sister, Dolly, and Dolly's two children, Fay and Carlo. Anita had been married once, but the union was fruitless. Her husband loved rum, and Anita loved the Lord, and their devotions mixed about as well as oil and water. After a few years, they parted ways. So now the sisters raised the children collectively. Fay slept in the room with Anita, and Carlo slept in Dolly's room.

The house was brown and trimmed white with the customary steep gable roof constructed of corrugated iron. There were three bedrooms, a kitchen, dining room, and a front parlor used for formal visitors. It sat directly across the road from the beach and had an obstructed view of the beautiful aqua Caribbean Sea. The backyard was enclosed by sheets of galvanized panels, some rusty, some shiny, that bucked and writhed noisily in high wind. There was a lime tree and a coconut tree and free-roaming chickens and ducks and a sizable sow, secured away in a pen constructed of cement blocks. The closest I had ever been to chickens and ducks and livestock was at the petting zoo in Prospect Park and even then, there was a separating fence. When I saw the outhouse and an open-air shower, my mind immediately galloped back to Sandersville, Georgia, and shivers went down my spine. But what was more unsettling than having to do my business in that wooden box was the thought of bathing out in the open.

I tugged at Gwen's skirt.

"What, child?"

I pointed at the shower, whispering, "But everyone will see me."

"What you got to look at?"

BOTH ANITA AND DOLLY WORKED as domestics. Anita was a housekeeper, cook, and nanny for a wealthy white family from Massachusetts who owned a villa on a former four-hundred-acre plantation, turned the world-famous Sandy Lane hotel, estates, and golf club, and Dolly was a chambermaid at a local hotel. The sisters had little formal education, and Dolly even less so, having had to leave school at a young age to help care for the children of her elder sister, Thelma, who was employed as a personal cook for a white family who owned an international cosmetics company and had residences all around the world.

I DIDN'T MISS ROBERT AT all, and within a week or two, I stopped pining for Vivian. As I adjusted to this new life, I missed Brooklyn, and everyone and everything I'd left behind, less and less. I'd been quickly accepted by my cousins and their friends. Of course I still had to answer the usual questions about my scars.

"What happened to your face and hand?"

"I got burned."

"How you do dat?"

"I was in a car accident."

I was not the only one of the neighborhood children with scars. There was a girl named Micky who had been chased down and mauled by a neighbor's vicious German shepherd. The flesh of her right arm and leg looked like pulp. Another kid had lost the thumb on his left hand and an index and forefinger on his right—the consequences of blast fishing, a form of fishing that uses dynamite. And there was a boy named Carlson, who was deaf and mute. We were all imperfect in our own small ways.

In a very short time, I became comfortable with barefoot living—we put on shoes only to go to church—and the green lizards that watched me curiously from the windowsills and walls. I loved being lulled to sleep by whistling frogs and awaking to the symphony of wood doves and roosters. Back then, there weren't many streetlamps, and moonless nights swathed the island in darkness so deep that the stars looked like diamonds. But those evenings when the moon was in bloom, it shone like a thousand-watt light bulb.

Summer was the rainy season, and there were plenty of days when the skies dumped water enough to flood the roads, keeping us cloistered in the house until the deluge subsided. It was on one of those water-drenched days that I was reminded of a memory that I had left behind in Brooklyn.

Dolly was at work, Reggie was down for a nap, and Fay was in the kitchen with Anita, watching her make coconut bread. Carlo and I were in the front room pitching marbles across the rug, humming along to the tunes sailing off the radio. When "Conrad" by the Merrymen came on, we broke into song. The catchy melody was about a man named Conrad who was causing confusion in Paynes Bay because he was a duppy.

After the song ended, and a commercial for Banks beer came on, Carlo asked over the salesman's pitch, "Have you ever seen a duppy?"

I was familiar with the word, because of the song, and I'd heard it sprinkled in conversation, but my ears were still becoming used to the melodic language, and so I didn't always fully grasp what was being discussed or sang.

I shrugged. "I don't know," I said, and then added, "Maybe?"

"Maybe?" Carlo echoed, mocking my American accent. "You would know if you saw one."

I was too embarrassed to admit that I didn't know what a duppy was. I thought it might be an animal of some kind. An animal that wasn't found in America. Like a mongoose. I didn't know such a thing existed until I came to Barbados. Maybe a duppy was like that?

"What's it look like?" I asked.

Carlo tossed a marble into the air and caught it in the palm of his hand. "They look like dead people."

"Huh?" I was confused. "Dead people? Like zombies?"

I'd seen *Night of the Living Dead*, and that movie had given me nightmares for weeks.

"They come out at night and haunt you," he continued.

"Ghosts?"

"Yeah," Carlo said, tossing the marble back into the air. "Duppies."

I had seen one or at least I thought I'd seen one.

I was six going on seven, and Vivian and a few of her girlfriends were in the kitchen, playing spades. I was supposed to be asleep, but I was lying there in the dark, my eyes fixed on the light beneath the door, listening to their muffled conversation and raucous laughter.

When I sensed something next to me, I thought it was Reggie, because sometimes he crept up the ladder to my top bunk. When I whipped my head around, instead of seeing Reggie's mischievous grin, I saw a white man dressed like a cowboy—hat, spurs, bolo tie, and all.

Even though the room was as dark as a broom closet, I could see the man quite clearly, because he was sheathed in light. I stared, frozen, wanting to look away but unable to. The seconds ticked, my bladder let loose, and then he smiled, a big toothy cartoon grin, and I closed my eyes and screamed louder than I have ever screamed before or since.

The door swung open, the light flicked on, and Vivian and her friends rushed into the room. I was inconsolable. All I could manage was, "White man, white man!"

They checked the windows, looked under the bed and in the closet, but there was no one there.

"I think you just had a bad dream," Vivian said as she stripped the soiled sheets from the bed. "That's why I don't like you watching those scary movies," she added.

I didn't think it was a dream then, and I don't think it was a dream now.

"Well?" Carlo pressed.

"Nope."

I hadn't seen that ghost again, but after that night, I placed it on the list of things that I was afraid of:

Robert

Ghosts

Roaches

Monsters under my bed

Fire

Monsters in my closet

Robert

Fire

Robert

My mother dying

Robert

Zombies

Robert

There was something else I kept from Carlo. I didn't tell him about the fragrance that sometimes filled the room I happened to be in. It would just materialize in the air, as strong as smoke as potent as the perfumery section in the department stores.

"Mommy, do you smell that?"

"Smell what?"

After five or ten minutes, the scent would fade away. I didn't feel afraid whenever I smelled it, in fact it made me feel happy and light and loved. Could that be a duppy?

Of course, now whenever I smell that scent, I understand that I am being visited by an ancestor or angelcestors, as I have come to refer to them.

THE RAIN STOPPED JUST BEFORE sunset and we children excitedly streamed out of our homes as if we'd been caged for weeks. We gathered in the gap, which is a street as wide as a driveway, that snakes from the main road up through the interior of the neighborhood.

There, under a sky streaked in gold and red, we rushed to the Bico Ice Cream truck to buy our favorite treats. The frost still biting our throats, the boys went off to kick a soccer ball around while we girls formed a circle to play hand-clapping games.

Brown girl in the ring
Tra la la la la
There's a brown girl in the ring
Tra la la la la la
Brown girl in the ring
Tra la la la la
She looks like a sugar in a plum
Plum plum

One girl after the next broke the circle, hands planted firmly on their hips, they entered the center and began to *wuk up bad* . . . which is Bajan speak for the stirring, sometimes sensual, sometimes frenzied, gyrating, thrusting, and bumping of one's hips and groin.

Those two months in Barbados were the happiest I had ever been because I was not expected to be a surrogate mother to Reggie or referee fights between adults. And while my scars still drew stares and whispers, I was not harassed and tormented. My time there was peaceful. And I mostly attributed that tranquility to the absence of men.

That said, there was one male who was a constant in my life that summer. A relation by marriage, Irving Chesterfield Morris—called B. Irving by some, Sharky by others, and Grandfather by me and my cousins—was a tall, sinewy man, with strong tobacco-stained teeth and skin sun-baked the color of mahogany. He'd been a fisherman for his entire life and claimed to have seawater flowing through his veins. He lived next door to Anita and Dolly in a shack of a house that he shared with a family of feral cats. When he wasn't out in his boat, he was on the beach, sitting on a bog in the cool shade of a manchineel tree, puffing on cigarettes and mending his cast nets while keeping a watchful eye on us children.

One day, as Reggie and I were dashing in and out of the surf, Grandfather decided that it was time that we learned how to swim. Of all the children in the community, we were the only ones who did not know how.

We followed Grandfather to his wooden rowboat.

"Get in."

He was a strong seventy-one-year-old man. So strong, he had no problem lugging that boat with us in it across the sand and into the sea. With each stroke of the oars, we were pulled farther and farther away from the shore, until we were so far out, the people on the beach looked like miniatures. We stopped when we reached the bobbing white buoy. Adjusting his battered straw hat on his head, Grandfather lowered his gaze to our expectant faces.

"Wunna ready?"

Reggie and I exchanged unsure glances, and even though we didn't know what we were supposed to be ready for, we dipped our heads like seals. With that, Grandfather stood, wrapped one long arm around Reggie and the other around me, raised us up and over the side of the boat, counted off backward from three, and dropped us into the water.

We sank like stones.

As we sank, Grandfather's body blurred, and everything under the sea—the colorful schools of fish, a passing turtle, black sea urchins—all crystallized.

Panic struck, but before we could drown, instinct kicked in. We kicked and paddled and kicked and paddled until our heads erupted through the surface. Grandfather was standing, hands on his hips, peering down at us. His eyes were cloaked in the shadow of the straw brim of his hat, but I could see his open-lipped smile.

"Yuh good?"

We nodded uncertainly, frantically treading water to keep from sinking again.

"Yeah, yuh good," he said, and then sat down, grabbed the oars, and started rowing back to shore.

"C'mon," he barked over his shoulder.

My mouth dropped open and was instantly filled with seawater. I gagged, coughed, spat out the salty liquid, and set off behind the rowboat. Reggie was already a length ahead of me, dog-paddling for his life. I followed, trying and failing to push images of sharks out of my mind. I'd seen fishermen haul sharks in on their boats, then toss them onto the beach, thrashing and gnashing their sharp teeth, until the oxygen left their bodies and they died. Fried shark meat was a staple of our diet, and I very much enjoyed eating it. But now, as I swam for my life, I was terrified that I would become the meal.

Don't look down. Don't look back. Don't look down. Don't look back.

When we finally reached shallow water and planted our feet in the soft white sand, our cousins and friends, who had been watching from the beach, cheered.

Grandfather hauled the wooden boat through the surf, across the sand, and dropped it in the shade of a young coconut tree. He pulled a red-and-white-checkered kerchief from his swim trunks and swabbed the perspiration from his face. After gazing thoughtfully at the cloth, he aimed his crooked index finger at me and Reggie. "Wunna were either going to sink or swim," he said. "And yuh swam, so you good." And with that, he strode off.

I understood that that swimming lesson was also a lesson about life.

9

At the end of the summer, I arrived back in New York five shades darker, with a shiny pair of silver bangles on my left wrist and a Bajan lilt that made my friends wince every time I opened my mouth.

"Why are you talking like that?" they jeered.

The accent lingered for a few weeks but was completely gone by the time the temperature dropped and autumn dragged her paintbrush over the trees.

Things at school were still the same and things at home were worse because when I returned, I learned that Robert had thrown out all of my books.

"Mommy!"

Vivian rushed into the room. "What's wrong?" Her eyes followed mine to the empty bookshelves. "Oh." She sighed. "Your father."

And that said it all. He'd gotten rid of my entire collection of Dr. Seuss, two boxed sets of Little Golden Books, all my Hans

Christian Andersens, Disney vinyl records, and my absolute favorites: *Charlotte's Web* and *Where the Wild Things Are*.

They were all gone. I was crying so hard, my chest hurt.

Vivian placed her hands on my jumping shoulders. "Bernice, they're just books. We can get you some more," she'd said.

They weren't *just* books, they were my friends, my security blankets, my pacifiers, and my safety nets.

Sniveling, I looked around the room for Priscilla for comfort. When Vivian saw me searching, she sighed, "Sorry, Bernice, he got rid of Priscilla too."

Although my eyes were filled with tears, behind those tears was blood. That night, when Vivian was at bingo and Robert was in bed, snoring like a hog, I went to the stereo console, lowered myself to my stomach, and shoved my hand up into the opening. I patted around the shelf, but my hand never touched the cold steel of the gun. He'd moved it. All that remained were balls of cat hair. Once again, the angelcestors intervened, saving my life and Robert's.

Eventually, I did get more books, and in the summer of 1973 and again in '74, Reggie and I returned to Barbados.

I looked forward to those trips more than my birthday or Christmas. Those two months away a year worked like a salve that mended me just enough to get through the ten months that separated my torturous life in New York and my joyful existence in Barbados.

But then in the winter of 1974, I went into the bathroom, pulled down my underwear, sat down on the toilet to pee, and saw in the seat of my panties a streak of blood as red as the color lipstick Gwen claimed only cock-rats wore. *Cock-rats* is Bajan-speak for "whores."

GWEN HADN'T ALWAYS FELT THAT way about red lipstick; in fact, in her younger days she'd adored the color, and while she didn't wear it to her government job, she did apply it when she was going to the theater or to the cabaret shows she so loved.

She wouldn't have had it on the day she met Edgar Milton

Taylor, an elevator operator at Howard Clothes on Jay Street in downtown Brooklyn.

Like Gwen, Edgar's parents had also emigrated from the Caribbean, having sailed from Saint Kitts to Ellis Island in 1901. That first year in America was a chaotic one. The stock market crashed for the first time since its inception in 1792, and William McKinley became the third US president in the history of the United States of America to be assassinated.

Damn near white in color, with wavy hair and dreamy brown eyes, Edgar had inherited his complexion from his mixed-race mother. He was old enough to be Gwen's father. Eighteen years older to be exact, and married with children. Six of them. Gwen was a twenty-one-year-old abandoned wife and mother of two, living under her parents' roof, slowly suffocating under her mother's thumb. And she was lonely, because potential suitors lost interest once she revealed that she had not one but two small children at home.

Gwen had had a trying day at work and was lamenting going home to her nagging mother and needy children, so when she stepped into Edgar's elevator at Howard Clothes, Edgar's smile and his "Lawd have mercy, if you're not the most beautiful thing I've seen in all my days!" felt less like a pickup line and more like a life buoy.

She'd blushed, did not say thank you or meet his eyes. Instead, she requested the floor. "Three, please."

Edgar pulled the gate closed and turned the brass crank. As the elevator climbed, they stood silently gazing at the arrow clicking over the raised numbers above the door. When they reached the third floor, Edgar turned the crank again.

"Third floor, men's hats, slacks, and dress shirts," he announced ceremoniously.

"Have a good day," he piped, tipping his hat.

Howard Clothes was a men's store with an in-house clothing factory. It was as good a place as any to meet a potential husband. Gwen knew of two women who'd met their current boyfriends there, and one who'd just accepted a proposal of marriage.

FOR SOME REASON SHE COULDN'T put her finger on, Edgar lingered in her mind. Three days later, Gwen was back at the store. She stood in front of one elevator door and then another until finally, the panels parted and there he was.

"Aah, the beauty has returned. God has answered my prayers."

Gwen stepped in. "Three, please."

"You smell nice," Edgar whispered above the creaking of the elevator.

A week later, when he looked up and saw Gwen for the third time, he said, "I get off at seven. We can go to Nedick's for an egg cream or maybe a coffee at Chock full o'Nuts?"

Maybe Edgar confessed early on that he was married, but that things were bad at home, that he'd fallen out of love with his wife, and had stayed with her that long only because of the children. Maybe he even lied about the number of children, because hearing that he had six might have given Gwen pause. Or maybe she did know and it didn't matter, because of how whenever they were together he held her hand and gazed deep into her eyes, deep into her soul, and instead of calling her Gwendolyn, or Gwen, or the hateful Gwennie, he called her Beauty.

"I think I'm falling in love with you, Beauty."

With that, the long dormant butterflies in her stomach fluttered awake, wildly batting their wings.

"What's got you grinning like that, heh?" Ethel asked, eyeing her suspiciously.

Gwen would quickly wipe the smile from her lips and squeak, "Nothing."

Edgar took Gwen to a friend who owned a four-story limestone house in Crown Heights. The friend, a short, jowly Afro Indian man from Trinidad, rented rooms for ten dollars a week. The room on the very top floor had once functioned as the maids' quarters when the house was owned by a well-to-do white family in 1898.

The present owner had dubbed that room "the Nest," not just because it sat at the very top of the house, but because he rented it to lovebirds for fifteen cents an hour.

The room was threadbare, freezing in the winter and scorching in the summer. The mattress was lumpy, and the bedsprings squealed. But it had a private bathroom and two windows overlooking a back-yard filled with fig trees.

It was in that room that Gwen and Edgar first consummated their relationship.

Irritated by the shrieking bedsprings and the raucous sounds of Edgar and Gwen's lovemaking, the couple who lived in the room beneath them would place Lord Kitchener's "Jump in the Line" on their phonograph and raise the volume up to ten. So, for years, like one of Pavlov's dogs, whenever Gwen heard "Shake, shake, shake, señora, shake your body right . . ." she creamed herself.

Cut pumpkin can't keep is Bajan speak for "once virginity is lost, it is impossible to abstain thereafter." That was the platitude Ethel clucked when she walked in on Gwen in a state of undress and saw the swell of her midsection.

Ethel was a harsh woman, not unlike other women who'd been cut from stone, whether it was Barbadian limestone or American granite. It was hard being a woman in this world, harder still if you happened to be Black. Ethel realized very early on in life that she had to be a *hard* woman to survive in this world and she didn't know why Gwen didn't understand this. Having a baby without a husband, when she already had two children, wasn't going to make Gwen's life easier, it was going to make it more difficult. Talking to Gwen was like talking to a wall, and that infuriated Ethel.

Aubrey gently patted her hand. "Calm down, calm down, Ethel. Why you let that child vex you so? What's done is done; the baby already cooking in da oven. There's nothing we can do."

Well, that's where he was wrong. There was something she could do. The optimum time to rid Gwen of that baby would have been when she first missed her period. Now three months in, it would be uncomfortable for Gwen but not impossible. Ethel was an obeah woman. People came to her for spiritual guidance and her wish bags—potions and tinctures for migraines, menstrual cramps, infidelity, and unexpectant or unwanted pregnancies.

While the peacock flower wasn't native to America, grown primarily in tropical environments, Ethel had some dried seeds and petals, procured from a friend of a friend who had smuggled them in from Barbados. The flower had been used by Caribbean women of African and indigenous descent to thwart unwanted pregnancies for centuries. Ethel's own mother, Elizabeth, as fair-skinned as Edgar, a product of settler colonialism, had passed the wisdom down from her mother, and her mother's mother, threading all the way back to slavery times.

Ethel was so angry with her daughter that she had a mind to secretly slip the solution into Gwen's morning porridge or evening tea. Aubrey saw the notion smoldering in Ethel's eyes like brimstone. He curled his fingers tightly around her hand and uttered a firm no.

EDWARD ST. CLAIR TAYLOR WAS born on February 11, 1946, just seven days before Gwen's twenty-second birthday. At the hospital, Edgar stood staring at his son through the glass of the infant ward. Edward, who would come to be known as Eddie, was as red as his father. (Describing someone as red is Caribbean-speak for "light-skinned.")

"Family can't hide," Edgar chuckled to himself.

After Eddie was born, Gwen ditched the surname McFadden and adopted Taylor, even though she was still married to Harold and Edgar was still married to his wife, Corrine.

"What?" Ethel cawed when Gwen told her. She thought her daughter had gone mad, or daft, or both.

Gwen saw the move as an act of radical manifestation.

Ethel cupped her hands to Gwen's cheeks and sadly moaned, "Cuhdear," which is Bajan-speak for "poor thing."

Edgar never left Corrine, and Corrine never left Edgar, even after Gwendolyn sent her a letter detailing the affair she'd had with her husband, accompanied by a photo of the child who was produced from the affair. She told Corrine that she and Edgar were deeply, madly in love, and the two had plans to marry as soon as she stopped being a bitch and put her John Hancock on the divorce papers that Edgar said she had refused to sign.

There were no divorce papers.

In the wake of that discovery, Corrine cussed and cried and smashed up the remaining pieces of china salvaged from the last tirade she threw when confronted with Edgar's womanizing ways.

"Go to that little whore in Brooklyn, see if I care!" she screamed.

Oh, she cared all right. She didn't have a job, so what would she and her six children do without Edgar? Marriage and motherhood were her prison, and Edgar was the warden. Corrine did not leave Edgar, and Edgar did not abandon Corrine for Gwendolyn, but both women were freed of him in 1959, when a blood vessel in Edgar's brain erupted and he died.

That said, Gwendolyn continued to carry his last name, using it on documents, both government and otherwise, and *Mrs. Taylor* was how her daughters-in-law addressed her, as did everyone else who made her acquaintance after 1947.

WHEN I SAW THAT RED STREAK IN MY UNDERWEAR, I WASN'T ALARMED, because Vivian had prepared me for the day. She too had started menstruating at an early age. What she hadn't prepared me for was the ways in which this monthly inconvenience would bring an end to the happiest part of my life.

"Hmm, she got her cycle? Well, that mean she could breed now.

Sorry, Robert, I don't want to be held responsible if she comes here and can't keep her purse closed," Anita said into the phone from her house in Barbados. The decision was kept from me until a week before school let out.

"So, we're going to send you to sleepaway camp this summer instead of Barbados," Vivian casually mentioned one Saturday morning as she spilled Cocoa Puffs into my cereal bowl.

My jaw dropped. "Camp?"

"Yes, *sleepaway* camp." She stressed *sleepaway* to emphasize that it wasn't just a regular day camp, like the ones my friends went to. It was special.

My bottom lip quivered. "How come I'm not going to Barbados? Did I do something wrong?"

"You didn't do anything wrong, Bernice, it's just that your father thinks you should have a new experience."

"But I don't want a *new* experience," I blubbered. "I want Barbados." I swiped away the trail of tears dripping down my cheeks.

"Oh, Barbados ain't going nowhere. It'll be there next year." She was standing in front of the refrigerator now, her hand resting atop the open door, as she studied the shelves of plastic containers filled with leftovers. Finally, she reached for the carton of milk and brought it to the table.

"Next year?" I asked, brightening a bit. I could get through another year, it would be difficult but not impossible.

"Well, maybe," she breathed uncertainly. "We'll just have to wait and see. Now go on and eat your cereal before it gets soggy." She reached for her pack of Newports. "I went to camp when I was your age, and I loved it." Her face glowed with the happy memory. "Camp Sharp-a-roon," she sang.

"Is that where I'm going?"

"No, you're going to a different camp."

"And Reggie?"

Vivian cocked her head, the happy glow dimmed. "Well, he's going to Barbados."

She'd barely finished her sentence before I was bawling again.

Vivian put one hand on my shoulder and squeezed. "Bernice, camp is going to be so much better than Barbados, you'll see," she said, using her free hand to swipe the tears from my cheeks.

Sleepaway camp was fine, but it was not better than Barbados. Barbados was heaven, and at best, sleepaway camp was purgatory.

Little did Reggie or anyone know, but that summer, 1975, in Barbados would be his last because while roughhousing with friends, Reggie would break a glass panel in the wooden door of Anita's home. That was enough for her to wash her hands of him, and so the following year, we both spent the summer at sleepaway camp.

The next time I would set foot on Barbados was in 1987, when I was twenty-one and pregnant.

PART TWO

SOMETHING
IN THE WATER

Don't drink the water and don't breathe the air!

—TOM LEHRER

10

In January 1977, James Earl Carter Jr., a peanut farmer from Georgia, was sworn into office as the thirty-ninth president of the United States. Robert watched the swearing-in on the black-and-white console television in the living room. He sat on the plastic-covered green sofa, staring at the screen, mumbling to himself between puffs of his filter-free Camels.

I remember my eleven-year-old-self thinking, *Wow, a peanut farmer could become president?* That's all I knew of Jimmy Carter. I didn't know he was an educated man and had been governor of Georgia. All I'd ever heard was that he was a peanut farmer.

Three days later, on January 23, Vivian and I sat on the couch in the living room watching the first episode in the miniseries *Roots*, based on the book of the same name written by Alex Haley. It was my first up-close and personal experience with the institution of slavery. Over a week and a day, I watched with open-mouthed fascination.

The series made Vivian uncomfortable; it hit too close to home for her liking. During the commercial break, Vivian raked her hands through her hair, looked at me, and said, "I know all about slavery. None of this is new to me." She was referencing her time as a little girl in Sandersville, Georgia.

"Was your grandmother a slave?"

She thought for a second, not clear on the timetable of the births and deaths of her foremothers. "I don't think so, Bernice," she said. "But maybe her mother was a slave?"

"Her mother?"

"Grandma Rosie."

In actual fact, Grandma Rosie, born in 1883, missed being enslaved by twenty years. That said, she'd been born into Jim Crow, which was just a repackaged edition of the tried-and-true version of slavery.

THAT SPRING, I BUDDED RIGHT on time with the red maple trees. It literally happened overnight. I went to sleep with my ironing-board-flat chest and woke up with two peanut-sized lumps.

Until that morning, I'd thought that I was doomed. Vivian had given me a Magic 8 Ball, and I turned to it for advice. *Will I ever have breasts?* And then I shook it so hard my arm nearly dislocated from its socket. The pyramid-shaped object inside the Magic 8 Ball twirled and tumbled, and when it came to a stop, the word on its face was: *NO.*

I was devastated, and even though Vivian tried to console me, reminding me that it was just a toy and someday soon I would have tits, I didn't believe her.

At the time, my friend Deborah, two years ahead of me in age, had been wearing a bra for three years, and Annette, who was my age, had already graduated from a triple A to a double A–size bra in just six months and couldn't stop bragging about it.

It's about damn time! I thought as I stood in the bathroom mirror that morning admiring myself.

My interests changed, right along with my body. Sex became

a curiosity, especially since I had started sneaking to read the racy paperback novels that Vivian kept in her bureau drawer, buried beneath her bras and panties. Jackie Collins and Harold Robbins ushered me into a far different world from my children's books.

I'd had a longtime crush on Michael Jackson. In fact, my first erotic dream was about him and his brothers. In the dream, the Jackson 5 were standing naked—save for bejeweled cowboy hats and cowboy boots—in my bedroom, performing "The Love You Save." I knew that Michael was unobtainable, and so my fascination with the opposite sex drifted closer to home.

After I'd practiced on my dolls, my pillow, forearm, and palm, I finally experienced my first real kiss with a boy named Garfield, who was the grandson of the Jamaican couple across the hallway who had sheltered me and Reggie back in the days when Robert wouldn't allow us to have a house key.

It was in the middle of the day, I can't imagine where my parents or Reggie might have been, but I was home alone in the apartment when I let Garfield in. It was a brazen decision for a goody-two-shoes child like me. Had I gotten caught, I may not have survived to tell the tale.

The first kiss was awkward, he was a pro after all, and I was a novice. At first when he stuck his tongue in my mouth, I recoiled, but after a few minutes, I got the hang of it and really started to enjoy it. He pushed me against the wall, and that was fine too. I could feel his hardness against my thigh, feel both of our hearts banging away in our chests. I was dizzy with desire, and then he slipped his hand beneath my shirt, and I came to.

I pushed his hand away. "What are you doing?"

"What?" he shot back, annoyed. "Let's go to your bedroom?"

I looked at him like he was crazy. I had already violated one of Robert's commandments: *Thou shalt not let a soul in this house when your mother or I aren't here.*

"You gotta go," I said, yanking the door open and shoving him out into the hallway.

The postman, who was filing envelopes into the mailboxes on the wall, looked up from his task.

"Hey, man," Garfield tossed at him as he pimp-walked across the hallway.

Not taking his eyes off me, the postman nodded. I hurriedly shut the door. For the next few days, I worried myself sick that the postman would report to Robert what he'd seen.

I have eyes everywhere.

THAT SUMMER, BEFORE I HEADED off to sleepaway camp, Vivian put a permanent relaxer in my hair. I was the last of my friends to do it. It burned like hell, but it was worth the agony to feel my hair feather across the back of my neck.

I'd been at camp for nearly two weeks, when, on July 13, we were in our cabins, tucked under the camp-issued scratchy blankets, whispering and giggling with one another when the lights went out. Big Allis, the largest generator in the city, shut down, plunging all five boroughs into darkness. What ensued was twenty-five hours of looting, violence, arson, and general chaos.

The following month, on August 10, David Berkowitz, a serial killer—dubbed the Son of Sam—who'd terrorized the city for a year, was finally apprehended and the citizens released a collective sigh of relief. But then, six days later, the world found itself grieving the loss of Elvis Presley, who was dead from an overdose at the age of forty-two. Elvis had been a staple of my childhood, forever young and handsome in the movies I watched growing up.

That September, I turned twelve years old.

THAT CHRISTMAS EVE, AS WAS tradition, Robert was out in his green Buick, hopped up on Hennessy, driving around Brooklyn, looking for the tallest evergreen for the cheapest price that he could find. Everyone else I knew had had their tree—both artificial and real, up for at least two weeks. Others put up their trees right after Thanksgiving.

One year, Aunt Anna put up her artificial tree and never took it down. It stood in the corner of her crowded living room, dripping in ornaments, keepsakes, and cobwebs, wearing a white-winged, Black-faced cherub as a crown. Like a mute family member, that Christmas tree bore witness to countless family gatherings, fights, fornications, tears, laughter, tender moments, soap operas, the nightly news, late-night talk shows, and the birth of trash TV and then, later, pay TV. A shrine to Jesus and Saint Nicholas and all the Christmases past, it remained standing in that corner for decades, until Anna's death in 1996.

"Why can't we have a white Christmas tree?"

I'd posed the question every year, and every year Vivian said, "Go ask your father." Of course, I didn't.

But this year, she didn't say a word, she just kept digging through the carboard box of Christmas ornaments. For days she'd been preoccupied; deep in thought, it seemed to me. So deep that I felt that my interruptions and queries hit her ears like the sound of breaking glass or clattering pots.

"Mommy?"

Her head snapped around. "What?" The irritation in her voice was iridescent on her face.

I lowered my eyes. Vivian wasn't generally snappy with us and when she was, it was usually the runoff from Robert having aggravated her.

BUT SHE WAS NOT WITHOUT her coping mechanisms. In addition to playing bingo as a form of escape and enjoyment, Vivian smoked weed. She smoked before she went to her job at Herzfeld & Stern, the brokerage firm where she worked in the new-accounts department, and then again when she returned home in the evening. She'd come in, greet Reggie and me, set down her purse, sling off her coat, and then close herself away in the bathroom for twenty or thirty minutes. When she emerged, there was always a weird odor clinging to her clothes and hair. To me, it smelled like a mixture of air freshener and skunk.

I'd seen the yellow, white, and red Big Bambú wrapping paper with the illustration of a slick-looking man in a yellow fedora. But I didn't know what they were for and never put two and two together when Robert called her a pothead.

But that year, when Thelma and Vivian came to visit me and Reggie at sleepaway camp, Vivian took me for a walk in the woods and explained things to me.

"See this," she said, after slipping the rolled joint from the front pocket of her jeans. "I want you to know that I do this, okay?" She looked warily around before lighting up. I was confused, because to me, it looked like a cigarette, and I already knew she smoked.

Vivian puffed on the end, inhaled deeply, and then exhaled with a cough. Reading my face, she said, "This is not a regular cigarette, this is a reefer cigarette."

"Ohh," I said.

I knew what reefer was because Thelma called it dope, as in, "These fools out here knocking people in the head, robbing them for money to get that reefer-dope!"

According to Thelma, a boy not old enough to piss straight but already a hoodlum had jumped out of the shadow in the stairwell and pounced on Aunt Ruby when she'd gone to the letter box to collect her social security check.

Ruby was up in age but still tough. She put up a fight, until the assailant clobbered her over the head and she finally let go of the thin paper envelope. By then, of course, it was ripped in half and that made the perpetrator angrier. He clubbed her one more time and fled the building, leaving her crumpled on the floor, dazed and panting. She was never the same after that.

Addicts smoked reefer-dope. *Is Vivian an addict?* The thought crossed my mind, but I quickly dismissed it. As far as I understood, addicts were dirty and homeless, thieves and hoodlums, and Vivian wasn't any of those things.

BUT THAT CHRISTMAS, EVEN AFTER she'd visited the bathroom to smoke her reefer-dope, she still seemed agitated.

"Nothing," I mumbled, reaching into the white Seagram's Gin box, and plucking out a red ornament shaped like a bell.

Robert returned home sometime after eleven. He walked into the house, shrugged off his coat, retrieved his toolbox from the bottom of the hall closet, and headed back out into the hallway where he'd left the behemoth tree.

He attacked the base of the trunk with his saw. Carving away at it for nearly thirty minutes until it fell off, landing in a bed of sawdust. Forehead glistening with perspiration, he hauled the tree into the living room and raised it in the center of the floor. "C'mon," he demanded.

Vivian and I helped him hoist the tree into the red-and-green metal tree stand and held it steady as he twisted the four screws into the bark. When it was secure, we all took a step back to admire it.

Reggie, who had been watching from the sidelines, ambled to my mother and rested his head on her arm.

It was the moment of truth.

Robert used a kitchen knife to slice through the white twine, and one by one and then two by two, the limbs sprang free, filling the entire apartment with the scent of fresh pine.

After Reggie and I helped to string the lights and hang the ornaments, we went off to bed.

"PSST, YOU AWAKE?"

Of course I was awake. It was the night before Christmas. Who could sleep? I was lying there envisioning all the toys and clothes

I'd circled in the Sears Christmas catalog sitting under the tree. I'd been staring at the underside of my eyelids for what seemed like forever. "Yeah," I said.

We crept out of our beds and tippy-toed across the floor to the bedroom door. I closed my hand around the glass doorknob and turned. We hadn't even crossed the small alcove that separated the bedrooms from the living room when Robert barked, "Get back to bed!"

We might have bested him, if not for my bangles turning me into a walking siren. I'd had the bracelets for so long, that I no longer registered the sound they made.

We scurried back into our beds, pulled the covers over our heads, and began the waiting game once again. After a while though, our exhaustion overwhelmed our excitement and we collapsed into sleep.

A few hours later, Vivian was shaking us awake. "Come and see what Santa left you."

Groggy with sleep, we stumbled out into the living room and were met with a heap of wrapped gifts topped with colorful glittering bows. Robert and Vivian both loved Christmas, but it was easy to tell that Robert's adoration for the holiday exceeded Vivian's. It was the one day of the year when he looked genuinely happy. Maybe he was trying to re-create his own childhood Christmases, or perhaps he was creating the Christmas he'd always longed for as a child.

"There's another one there." He'd point, saying, "Open that one."

With every unwrapping, the smile on his face grew and the light in his eyes brightened. Sometimes he even chuckled when we squealed with surprise and joy.

I have a handful of fond childhood memories of Robert, and Christmas morning is one of them.

However, by the time our relatives arrived for Christmas dinner, Robert had polished off half a bottle of Hennessy, and the happy version of himself was fading away.

"Clean up this mess," he demanded, waving his hands over the dolls, puzzles, books, and other Christmas gifts scattered across our bedroom floor. Behind him, in the living room, the adults fell mute. For a few seconds the only sound in the apartment was Otis Redding's velvety voice sailing from the speakers of my mother's hi-fi system.

Merry Christmas, baby, you sure did treat me nice . . .

"Robert, aww, come on now, leave them chirren alone. It's Christmas, for God's sakes," Aunt Anna declared from her seat on the couch.

Robert had a knack of turning good times into bad ones. It wasn't if he would ruin a celebration but when.

"Robert," Vivian said, "leave them alone."

But he didn't. He remained in the bedroom, snarling at us until Thelma had had enough.

"That's one ignorant son of a bitch," she spat. "Bernice, get my motherfucking coat so I can take my Black ass home. Come on, Wilfred."

The other guests soon followed suit. I stood at the closet, fishing out coats. *Bye, Grandma. Bye, Granddaddy.* Wilfred's kids were always sad to go. *Bye, Minnie. Bye, Sharon. Bye, J.J. Bye, Elaine.* Aunt Anna, her husband, Earl, and their brood of boys followed. *See you, James. Bye, Wayne. Bye, Moe. Bye, Ben. Good night, Aunt Anna. Good night, Uncle Earl. Bye. Bye. Bye. Bye.*

"YOU BETTER WASH THAT."

The apartment was dark, save for the twinkling lights on the Christmas tree and the overhead light in the kitchen. Robert was standing in the doorway of the kitchen, pointing at the roasting pan Vivian had left to soak on the stove.

"I'm tired, Robert. I'll wash it tomorrow." She yawned.

Robert glared at her. "You'll wash it tonight."

Vivian laughed. I'm sure she wasn't just laughing at him but the absurdity her life had become. She calmly folded the dish towel in half and hung it on the hook in the wall over the sink. "'Scuse me," she said, trying to brush past him. He sidestepped her, planting himself firmly in front of her again.

Vivian sighed. She was so tired, so very, very tired. "Get out of my way so I can go to bed."

He did not move and after some back-and-forth, Vivian tried to shove him out of the way. He shoved back, and they tussled for a few seconds, before he shoved her again, hard this time. So hard she went stumbling across the floor and into the refrigerator.

She wasn't hurt, just fed up. When Robert saw the look of revulsion on her face, he smiled. Arms whirling, Vivian launched herself at him, ramming him so hard he flew into the wall behind him.

Free now, she made a beeline to the bathroom, which was the only room in the house that had a lock on the door. But he caught her before she could get to safety, wrestled her into their bedroom, and slammed the door.

As I listened to them fight, tears gathered in the seams of my clenched eyelids. And then there came a sound that was out of place amid the slapping, punching, and screaming.

Clank.

It rang like metal hitting metal. Like when the super was in the basement working on the pipes.

The silence that followed felt like death.

"Vivian?" Robert whispered.

I felt more than heard the fear in his voice.

I don't remember bolting from my bedroom. What I do recall is standing in my parents' room, the torn collar of my father's undershirt, the rumpled brown satin bedspread, and the bottles of perfume and fingernail polish strewn across the dresser and the floor.

Just beyond that melee was Vivian.

She was splayed on the floor, on her back, near the radiator. One arm was stretched over her stomach, the other limp at her side. The thin, pink nightgown she wore was up around her waist, her legs were parted, exposing her privates.

My eyes traveled up to her face, which was turned toward the wall. Blood was seeping from a wound on the side of her head near the temple and smeared on the metal elbow that connected the radiator to the floor.

My breath caught in my throat.

At the sound, Robert spun around and looked at me. His eyes were so wide that the brown corneas looked like specks. "Sh-she fell," he stammered.

I thought to myself, *My mother is dead.* The day I had feared had finally arrived. And then I screamed, "Mommmmmmmmmmmy!"

My howling startled him. He caught hold of me and slapped his moist hand over my mouth.

"Shut up. Shut up. Shut up."

My emotions got the best of me. I was hyperventilating, desperately trying to catch air, but his hand over my mouth was as tight as a seal and I passed out.

The following morning, I awoke in my bed. The shades were raised, and the room was swimming with dazzling sunlight. The small black-and-white television that sat atop the dresser was on, tuned to some holiday cartoon, and Reggie was lying on the floor, on his side, eyes glued to the screen. I could hear Robert snoring in the bedroom and Vivian laughing in the kitchen. I couldn't believe my ears.

I called to my brother.

"What?" Reggie said, not turning around to look at me.

"Where's Mommy?"

"In the kitchen," he said, and then chuckled at the antics unfolding on the screen.

Had I dreamed the fight? The blood and the terror on Robert's face? I climbed out of bed, rubbed the sleep from my eyes, and went to the kitchen.

Vivian was sitting at the white Formica table, head bowed, one hand holding the phone against her ear, the other cradling her forehead.

"You've got to be kidding me," she chuckled into the receiver. Whoever was on the other end of that telephone line had her in stitches.

"Mommy?"

Her head snapped up. "Hold on a minute, Betty." She covered the receiver with her free hand. "Well, hello, sleepyhead," she sang with a smile.

Maybe before was reality and now this was the dream?

"G-good morning," I stammered.

"You hungry?"

I nodded, still unsure of the plane on which this was unfolding.

"Pancakes?"

I nodded again.

"Okay, then go to the bathroom and brush your teeth and wash your face."

I was so happy to see Vivian alive that I wanted to run to her, throw my hands around her neck, and squeeze. But outward expressions weren't something that was encouraged in my house. Neither one of my parents were physically affectionate people. In fact, the only time I ever saw my parents kiss was on New Year's Eve. Reggie and I were in the back seat of Robert's car, returning to Brooklyn from Thelma's house. The radio was on, and the disc jockey interrupted the song to countdown from ten to the dawn of the New Year. When the clock struck midnight, the DJ hollered, "Happy New Year!" and as "Auld Lang Syne" played, Robert and Vivian leaned toward each other and kissed.

I was six years old. I'd never seen them kiss before that, and I would never see them kiss again.

So I steeled myself and said, "Okay, Mommy."

And with that, she pressed the phone back to her ear and turned away from me. "I'm back Betty, go 'head," Vivian murmured into the receiver.

That's when I saw the Band-Aid on her temple. I hadn't dreamed any of it.

11

The irritable mood that plagued Vivian during the holiday season came to light in January, just after the New Year, when one chilly Friday evening, she called me into her bedroom.

"Yes, Mommy?"

I was already cycling through my memory bank, searching for some rule I had broken that warranted her summoning me to her bedroom. We children weren't allowed in my parents' bedroom unless requested, which usually meant that we had done something wrong and she was going to punish us for the infraction.

She patted the empty space on the bed beside her. "Sit down."

Whatever it was, it must be serious, because we certainly weren't allowed on their bed. I crossed the room and sat down.

"I need to tell you something."

My heart fluttered with hope. Finally, she was leaving Robert and wanted me to know that she had filed for divorce. Divorce, the death of my father, and my return to Barbados were the three things that I prayed for daily. I looked into her eyes with happy anticipation. But when she opened her mouth, what came out wasn't what I'd expected at all.

"I'm going to have a baby."

My eyes immediately fell to her midsection before bouncing back to her face.

All three of us had suffered so much because of him, I just couldn't understand why in the world Vivian would want to bring another innocent into such an unhappy and dreadful environment. Even at that young age, none of it made a lick of sense to me.

"Um," I hummed, not knowing what to say, and then I smiled and blurted, "Well, I hope it's a girl."

A pained smile curled her lips as she reached for her lighter and cigarettes on the nightstand. "This is your father's fault," she said, choking back the anger. "He threw away my birth control pills and my douche bag."

I'd only recently learned that's what the brown rubber bag in the shower was called. I hadn't noticed its disappearance.

"I didn't want any more children," she continued as if pleading her case to an attorney. "Your father did this to me."

I understood sex and I understood conception and contraception, so the question that I wanted to ask was: "He treats you so bad, why do you keep sleeping with him?" I could think it, but I could never ask it, because I was a child, and she was an adult and my mother. She might have called me fresh or grown, and even though she rarely hit us, that overstep might have earned me a slap across my mouth.

For a long time, I believed that rapists were deviant men who followed women into elevators or climbed into the open windows of their apartments. I didn't know that rapists could also be priests, presidents, superior court judges, entertainers, uncles, brothers, boyfriends, husbands, and fathers. I didn't know that there was such a thing as birth control sabotage or reproductive abuse and coercion.

I didn't know a person would willingly try to control the reproductive choices of their partners and that specific type of control was called reproductive abuse. Reproductive abuse is when the abuser sabotages or completely disposes of their sexual partner's contraception or forces their partner to have sex when he or she does not want to.

I was twelve years old, and I didn't know.

The wall separating our bedroom from theirs was not particularly thick. I could hear Vivian's telephone conversations, TV dialogue, and, of course, their arguments, but I could also hear the thing that often happened after they argued.

"No, Robert, please no!"

"You. Are. My. Wife."

You. Are. My. Wife.

You. Are. My. Wife.

YouaremywifeMYWIFE

YouaremywifeMYWIFE

YouaremywifeMYWIFE!

I could hear him, even with the pillow over my face and my hands covering my ears.

She confided in me that she had toyed with the idea of aborting the pregnancy, but she knew that Robert would never agree to it, especially since he'd trapped her into the pregnancy to begin with.

Gradually, however, she got used to the idea of a new baby and even seemed to be happy.

There seemed to be an epidemic of pregnancies that year. The mothers of several of my neighborhood friends were pregnant too.

"Must be something in the water." Vivian laughed, rubbing her swollen belly.

"I think it's a girl," she said, patting her swollen stomach. "A big fat girl!"

Now that Vivian seemed to be glad about the baby, I allowed myself to be happy too.

Perhaps the new baby would be a good thing and not a nail in this coffin that we called life with Robert.

Even though she was showing, even though it was obvious Vivian was with child, Robert still threatened Reggie and me with a whipping if we breathed a word to anyone.

"What goes on in this house, stays in this house."

That rule wasn't just for Vivian's pregnancy; it went for everything and anything that happened in that apartment—the good and the bad.

Abusers use this rule to keep their bad behavior hidden from outsiders.

"If it's a girl, I'm going to name her Kimberly," Vivian said.

She'd bought a book of baby names and had circled several possibilities, but it was clear that Kimberly was her favorite; not only had she circled it, but she'd starred it too.

"Kimberly." I rolled the name around in my mouth. "Kimberly," I said again.

Well, it seemed as good a name as any, certainly better than my own name. I hated my name. Bernice was an old lady's name. Bernice was the name of Detective Phil Fish's old white wife on the sitcom *Barney Miller*. I might have adored my name back then, had I known that it was Greek for "bringer of victory."

THE DAY VIVIAN RECEIVED THE news that she was carrying not one but two babies, she came home, climbed into bed, and bawled like she'd been sentenced to life without parole.

The babies were due on July 20, two days before Robert's thirty-sixth birthday, but Vivian went into labor on the thirteenth of May, and the twins were born premature, via C-section, on Mother's Day 1978. Vivian's doctor administered penicillin to prevent infection even though she is allergic to penicillin, has always been allergic to penicillin, her medical records dating back decades state unequivocally that she is allergic to penicillin, which is why her wrist was fitted with a plastic band noting this very crucial fact.

For days after the birth, Vivian lay in that hospital bed, on a slow death march, racked with pain, the stapled wound in her belly leaking fluids, refusing to heal, and Vivian moaning so loud that when I went to visit, I could hear her as soon as I stepped off the elevator. She was nearly dead by the time some physician caught the error, rushed into her room, and tore the privacy curtain aside.

The doctor didn't give her a sedative or a numbing agent, he just sliced through the stitches with a scalpel and shoved his hands into the incision, like a gardener into soil.

Vivian was so weak that all she could do was toss her head and howl as his gloved fingers probed and pressed and pushed and squeezed until all the infection had oozed out.

I imagine that the pain Vivian endured was akin to that of enslaved women who found themselves under the knife of J. Marion Sims, a white slave owner, celebrated in this country as the father of gynecology. Sims performed intrusive surgeries on enslaved women without the benefit of anesthetics. One woman, named Anarcha, suffered under his scalpel more than thirty times. He invented the speculum still used all over the world.

Today, Black women in America are three to four times more likely than white women to die during childbirth due to implicit bias and racism. It affects Black women of all backgrounds; even wealthier patients are not protected from errors of judgment due to prejudice and ignorance. In an interview with the American Heart Association News, Dr. Ana Langer, director of the Women and Health Initiative at the Harvard T. H. Chan School of Public Health in Boston, said, "Basically, Black women are undervalued. They are not monitored as carefully as white women are. When they do present with symptoms, they are often dismissed."

For days, Vivian's symptoms had been dismissed and we almost lost her.

VIVIAN WAS RELEASED TEN DAYS after the birth, but the twins remained in the hospital for weeks. Vivian visited them every day, and sometimes I skipped school to accompany her. They were so tiny, just small balls of flesh in the incubators. Whispering hello, whispering their names, we stuck our hands into the care gloves affixed to the openings of the incubators and stroked their little limbs. *You'll be home soon.* The girl came home first. The boy, who was barely two pounds when he was born, was brought home a week later.

What a wonder they were. I hadn't experienced so much awe since I was standing on the beach in Barbados and witnessed a school of flying fish breach the surface of the water and sail through the air. I spent hours hovering over the crib, gazing down at them, screeching with excitement when they smiled in their sleep. Vivian taught me how to hold them, how to bottle-feed them, burp them, and change their cloth diapers.

I thought I was just performing big-sister duties, I didn't know I was being trained to be a third parent.

It wasn't long before the apartment began to feel cramped and overcrowded. There was the crib, the massive double carriage, the playpen, and two of everything else. It was like living in a storage unit for infants. A storage unit that smelled of talcum powder, A+D ointment, and baby formula. With their arrival, the apartment buzzed with visitors, who came bearing wrapped gifts, boxes of Pampers, and cards filled with money.

This one looks like Robert, for sure!

They both look like him.

Nah, I see Vivian in there too.

Then, of course, they'd examine the skin around the ears to determine just how dark they'd grow to be.

A little over a month after they were born, school let out for the summer. Reggie went off to sleepaway camp alone, and I stayed behind to help Vivian with the babies. For two months, I sterilized bottles and rinsed shitty diapers in the toilet. I helped with their feedings, even in the middle of the night. I accompanied Vivian to their pediatric appointments and strolls through Prospect Park.

When Reggie was home, he'd help here and there, but certainly not to the degree that I was expected to support them.

Robert didn't do any of those things. He didn't even hold them. And when they cried, he admonished Vivian for attending to them, claiming that crying was good for their lungs. "All they want is attention. Stop picking them up, you're spoiling them!"

12

That fall I entered eighth grade.

It wasn't until the twins were born that I started to think seriously about boarding school. As the months went by, the restraint Robert had shown throughout Vivian's pregnancy and those early weeks after she'd given birth was starting to wane. The arguing returned, his drinking increased, and he shouted and shoved her even when she was holding one or both of the babies. As a result, we spent a lot of weekends in Queens with Thelma and Wilfred, and when I say we, I mean my siblings and me.

By then, I was a fully indentured third parent. Which wasn't uncommon in my family or my community at large, where it was customary for the older children to help take care of their younger siblings. That said, my best girlfriends did not have siblings who were less than three or four years their junior. Which is to say, if they had to drag their little brother or sister along with them, the most they would have to worry about was the kid getting a little mouthy. That was minor compared to my charges, who needed feeding, burping, and changing several times a day.

I had my weekend days to myself, but after six, I had to be home to relieve Vivian so she could go play bingo. I didn't think it was fair that I should have to be as involved with the rearing of the twins as I was, but that was a thought that I had to keep to myself. Thelma didn't like it either, but she came right out and told Vivian how she felt.

"Vivian, Bernice didn't have those babies, you did. You shouldn't be dumping them on her as much as you do!"

Of course Vivian pushed back on the allegation, even as she pretended not to see the resentment pulsing in my eyes.

"WHAT HIGH SCHOOL ARE YOU going to go to?"

That was the question of the hour in that final year of middle school. Some of my classmates were hoping to get into Brooklyn Tech; others had their sights on Stuyvesant High School or Bronx High School of Science. Those schools required exceptional test scores, and I was an average student at best.

"Where you wanna go, Bernice?"

I had no earthly idea, but I knew I'd better choose a few schools or else I'd end up in one of those troubled high schools where students stabbed one another in the stairwells, threw chairs at their teachers, and brawled in the schoolyard.

"Uh, I'm going to go to Cathedral High School." I chose it because it sounded prestigious and was in Manhattan.

I know it's difficult to imagine now, but when I was coming of age in the 1970s, Brooklyn was not the center of the world that it has recently become. It was, in fact, Manhattan's unsophisticated little sister, still trying to shake off the country-bumpkin persona that had plagued her since the 1700s. Back in my youth, one had to travel to Manhattan for culture, concerts, luxury-brand clothing, and fine food. It was a treat when Vivian took us to shop at Macy's Herald Square or our annual visit to Radio City Music Hall to see the Christmas Show and the Rockettes. She bought us salted pretzels to keep our minds off the cold biting through our knit hats, gloves, and winter coats as we stood in a line of people that was so long it wound 'round and 'round the block. After the show, we'd go to Macy's and wait on yet another line, so we could sit on the lap of a white man dressed up like Santa Claus.

I loved going to Manhattan, walking its wide sidewalks, gazing up at the tall buildings, and gawking at the smartly dressed people. Manhattan was a bundle of energy—electrifying and exciting, but there was something pulling me in a completely different direction.

Thelma and Wilfred had sent my charismatic and problematic uncle J.J. off to boarding school to save him from the streets and himself. But they failed because wherever J.J. went, there he was. He'd been expelled from a handful of schools before Thelma made the decision to send him to boarding school. He had spent a semester at one school in Florida before he was booted out and landed at Carson Long Military Academy in Pennsylvania. A year later, he was expelled from that school too.

Back in Queens, he regaled us with fantastical tales about his time in these institutions. I listened, entranced; these schools sounded like sleepaway camp, but with teachers and textbooks.

I understood, even at that young age, that going to school in Manhattan would only serve as a Band-Aid to my chaotic home life; one that would be ripped off every day when I returned home to that hellish apartment.

I needed a long-term cure. I knew if I was going to make anything of myself, I would have to get as far away from my home as possible.

My report card shows when things at home went from bad to *really bad* by the rise and fall of my grades—that and handwritten comments from my teachers:

Bernice is a nice and polite child, but she lacks focus.
Bernice needs to apply herself more and stop being lazy.

I wasn't lazy, I was distracted, terrified, and anxious.

I suspect Thelma was aware of my unhappiness, which is why she gave me her copy of the boarding school directory. It was a soft-cover red book, half the size of a telephone directory, that listed every single boarding school in the country and a few abroad. In the solace of my bedroom, I flipped through the thin pages, closely reading through each description. All girls. All boys. Coed. Military. Nondenominational. Methodist. Episcopal. Baptist. Catholic. Quaker. I zoned in on schools in Pennsylvania, because J.J. had gone there and it was familiar from enjoyable visits to Dutch Country on bus outings with Thelma. I drew a little star alongside the names of four schools in Pennsylvania that I thought would be a good fit for me, dog-eared the pages, and tucked the book away on the shelf in my closet.

For now, I would keep my desire a secret, because just the thought of leaving racked me with guilt. This is the penalty of being parentified. When a parentified child finally puts themself first, it feels like a selfish act, when, in actuality, it's an act of self-care.

I would be well into my fifties before I fully understood the concept.

IT WAS EARLY 1979. CHRISTMAS was a blur in my rearview mirror. The twins were crawling, and when they weren't crawling, they were in their walkers, powering themselves through the apartment like Fred Flintstone in his prehistoric car. They were spending more time outside their playpen, which meant that they were getting into things and pulling down things and whining to be held or screaming bloody murder because they were sleepy, cranky, gassy, teething, or all of the above, and in the midst of all that mayhem, my parents continued to argue and fight.

Whenever Robert and Vivian got into it, I gathered the twins and Reggie into my bedroom, turned on the television, and raised the volume to an earsplitting level. I was living in a madhouse, and I was slowly going mad.

"When I go back to work, you'll have to take care of the twins," Vivian said.

Her job had given her a twelve-month maternity leave. She was due back to work in May. Thelma's sister Anna would watch the twins until I graduated from middle school, after which time, I'd assume responsibility for the remainder of the summer.

"Me?" I blurted.

I was looking forward to a summer filled with trips to Riis Beach and Coney Island, block parties, double feature movie flicks, and sleeping in. Summer was supposed to mean freedom, but this would be my second summer of bondage to a pair of babies I had not birthed.

Vivian, who was sitting in her brown recliner, folding clothes, didn't even look up from her task when she said, "Yes, you, Bernice. Don't worry, I'll pay you fifty dollars a week," she added, as if it would soften the blow.

It did not. That announcement made up my mind for me; I was going to go to boarding school.

I GRADUATED ON A WARM June day. The sky was blue, the sun was shining, and the trees were dense with leaves the color of green bell peppers. The day felt like a promise.

Like hope.

Beneath my powder-blue graduation gown, I wore a slick purple skirt suit, purchased from Abraham & Straus. On my feet, my first pair of pumps: black slingbacks with toes so pointy I could corner a roach. There is a photo of me in that purple suit. I am standing in a classroom with a male classmate. His arm is thrown around my neck, he is grinning widely into the camera. I look older than my thirteen and a half years. My smile is lopsided and small, my bump curls are sagging.

As was tradition, each graduating class was allowed to pick a song that best represented who they were and what they aspired to achieve in life. The class of 1979 chose "Ain't No Stoppin' Us Now," by the American R&B duo McFadden and Whitehead.

Back then, I knew very little about my McFadden lineage, but I was aware that Robert's father, Harold, was a musician, and so I thought maybe it was possible that there was a connection somewhere down the line. The song was so popular that it was declared the *new* Black national anthem, replacing "Lift Every Voice and Sing," which had held the honor for seventy-nine years. Even now, when I hear those upbeat, catchy lyrics with their undeniable message, I feel like the singers are speaking directly to me.

After the commencement ceremony, we graduates marched out of the auditorium, clutching our thin paper diplomas, faces plastered with wide smiles, singing along to *the* song of our generation.

13

Five months before I donned my graduation gown and slipped my feet into my first grown-up pair of shoes, my aunt Minnie gave birth to a son on a bitterly cold January day. She was nineteen years old and unmarried. We'd grown up together. She was just five years old when her father, Wilfred, married Thelma.

A year later after their nuptials, I was born, replacing Minnie as the baby in the family. We were more like siblings than aunt and niece, so when Vivian told me that Minnie was pregnant, I was stunned.

"Close your mouth, Bernice." Vivian laughed when my jaw dropped.

Minnie? Pregnant? How would she raise a child? She made a joke about everything; a master impersonator, Minnie could mimic Wilfred, Thelma, and most anybody to a tee. She loved to laugh and loved to make people laugh. That was her gift. If life had dealt her a different hand of playing cards, she might have been a brilliant and successful stand-up comedian.

Minnie was my first close encounter with teenage pregnancy.

You know how when you see a car that you really like or really dislike and suddenly you see that car every day and everywhere? That summer I saw pregnant teenage girls everywhere. They were dropping out of the sky and sprouting up from between cracks in the sidewalks. I couldn't get away from them.

Often, I witnessed strangers cast disgusted looks their way. Judging and tsk-tsking under the breath. The pregnant girls did their best to conceal their jutting bellies beneath oversized shirts and baggy jeans, but the shame they felt was harder to disguise because it clouded their eyes, warmed their cheeks; the weight of it rounded their shoulders.

Whenever I came upon a girl with a protruding midsection, as fascinated as I was, I always quickly averted my eyes because I knew what it felt like to be gawked at. I was worried for myself too, as if pregnancy was something that I could get by osmosis, breathing, or simply talking about sex.

Tall Ricky (not to be confused for short Ricky) on the block had started to court my friend Deborah, and that summer, Annette wore tube tops, which accentuated her budding breasts, that were attracting all sorts of attention from the opposite sex. We three had all experienced our first kisses, and at least one of us had been felt up beneath our clothes. I was not that one. But when a new superintendent moved into 300 Sullivan Place with his family of four, that would change.

Trevor Wilks was the eldest child of the family. He was a brown-skinned, handsome, charismatic Jamaican boy who all the girls in the building and the neighborhood instantly crushed on. In time, his sister, Pat, would be absorbed into our friend group, unaware that we were all fiending after her brother. Lucky for me, the family had moved into the apartment next door to mine, and within months, Trevor and I began a clandestine affair.

"Take off your shorts," he panted one day when we were locked away in his room.

We'd been French-kissing, heavy petting, and dry-humping for weeks. But this next step, I knew I wasn't ready for.

"No, no, I can't," I said.

He kissed me again, roughly shoving his tongue in my mouth while tugging at the zipper of my shorts.

"Nooooo," I squealed, slapping his hands away.

Irate, Trevor rolled off me and fixed his gaze on the cracked ceiling. "You don't love me," he breathed.

I did. I loved him with all my heart.

"You'd let me do it if you loved me."

I didn't know at the time that he had *done it* with several girls in the neighborhood and at least one in the building, who was a week away from discovering that she was pregnant with his child.

"I do love you but . . . but . . ."

"But what?"

I had to think quick. "But I have my period," I sputtered.

He made a gagging sound and scowled. "Oh," he sounded, and then after a moment he threw his legs over the side of the bed and stood up. I heard the heavy zipper of his jeans peel apart before he stood and wiggled out of them. When he turned to face me, I saw the prominent bulge behind the thin white underpants. My breath caught in my throat, and my eyes went to the ceiling.

Trevor climbed back into the bed and straddled me. He reached inside the slat of his Fruit of the Looms, pulled out his penis, and waggled it at me.

I'd seen penises before. My brothers', of course, and one belonging to an old white man who masturbated while sitting next to me in the waiting area in the Port Authority Bus Terminal. When I saw his pink, veined stump, I was so stunned, I just stared. When Vivian spotted what was happening, she jumped up, yanked me out of the chair, balled her fist, and swung. The man dodged the blow, leaped up, and jogged away.

Now, as I lay there staring at Trevor's knob, I imagined that I'd just fallen into a scene in one of those forbidden paperback novels Vivian kept hidden away in her underwear drawer.

"Kiss it," he said.

I placed my hands on his thighs and turned my head away. "No, ewwwww."

"C'mon," he pleaded, inching a bit closer.

I folded my lips into a tight crease and shook my head.

Trevor sighed in frustration, stretched his body on top of mine, and began rolling and thrusting his hips. We locked lips, and I matched his fervor, until we had worked ourselves into a hot, sweaty mess. A few thrusts later, he convulsed, made a gargling sound, fell limp, rolled off me, and drifted off to sleep.

I lay there beside him until the gray light in the room went dark. My eyes were growing heavy when I heard his mother and siblings bustling into the apartment.

Pat creaked open the bedroom door. "Trevor?"

When she saw me standing in the muddy darkness, her eyes stretched. "Hurry up," she said, raking her hand through the air. "My mother is in her bedroom."

Her parents' bedroom was on the other side of the large apartment. The television was on, and the younger children were making enough ruckus that they wouldn't hear me slip out. Pat shadowed me to the front door and I eased out.

"Bye," I whispered.

"Later," Pat said as she softly closed the door.

"HEY," VIVIAN GREETED ME WHEN I appeared in the doorway of our kitchen.

"Hi," I said.

"Y'all have fun?"

"Yep."

I hurried off to my room before she could intuit that I had been doing something I had no business doing. Closing the bedroom door behind me, I reached to pull off my shorts when I saw a milky blotch on my thigh. It looked like dried snot. Too revulsed to touch it, I stared down at it for a good long while trying to imagine how I got snot on my thigh. Four years later, when I lost my virginity, I'd understand that it wasn't snot at all.

Not too long after that incident, I was pushing the twins in their stroller up Rogers Avenue toward Eastern Parkway, when the mother of a schoolmate spied me from inside a store and nearly ran over a customer to get out the door. On the sidewalk she caught me by the elbow.

"Bernice?"

Startled, I swung around and glared at her. I knew that when the twins were in my charge I was expected to protect them with my life. Had the woman been an assailant, I don't know how much my scrawny self could have done to safeguard them, but that wasn't a thought in the moment.

"It's Mrs. Prince," she said, aiming her index finger at her chest. When the uncertainty in my eyes lingered, she added, "June's mother."

"Oooh," I moaned.

June and I had met in kindergarten and had been friends ever since. We were both students at the same middle school, but over the years we'd been absorbed into different friend groups and rarely saw each other outside of school.

"How is June? I haven't seen her in a minute."

Mrs. Prince's eyes bounced down to the twins and then back to my face. She responded to my inquiry with her own: "Those your babies?"

The hostility in her voice felt like a fang. My hand floated to my throat.

"N-no, they're my brother and sister," I responded defensively.

"Are you sure?"

Children had been told that their birth mothers were their sisters, and their grandmothers were their birth mothers. So many lies told to cover up the shame of having had a child out of wedlock, underage, or both. This was a common practice in many families, including my own.

"Y-Yes, I'm sure," I stammered, still shielding my throat.

She eyed me, inspecting my face for the thing that would expose me as a liar. After a few seconds, finding nothing, her eyes softened, her lips turned up at the corners, and her face warmed with relief.

"Oh, oh," she tittered, stooping over to admire the babies. "They're so cute." She pinched their cheeks and stroked their fat little hands. "Twins, my goodness, what a blessing. How's your mother doing?"

"She's good. H-how's June?"

At the sound of her daughter's name, Mrs. Prince erected herself. The eyes were hard again, the smile gone, and the expression on her face had turned as cold as an Artic tundra.

"June. Is. PREGNANT," she spat. "Make sure you don't end up pregnant too," and with that, Mrs. Prince readjusted the handles of her shoulder purse and walked off.

My mind flew to Trevor, but even though I knew I wasn't ready for that next step, I feared my body would trick me into doing something I didn't want to do. Yes, I resolved once again, boarding school would be the safest place for me.

WHEN I SUMMONED THE COURAGE to tell Vivian about my plan, she did not try to dissuade me.

"Are you sure?"

"Yes."

"Okay."

I took the book out of its hiding place in the closet and brought it to her. We sat down at the kitchen table, and I flipped open the book to the first dog-eared page.

"Here is one of the schools that I really like," I said.

Her eyes ranged over the photograph of the school and the information below it.

"Hmm," she hummed when her eyes locked on the tuition cost.

After about twenty minutes of perusing the catalog of schools, Vivian leaned back into her chair and said, "Well, these schools aren't cheap, that's for sure."

Panic flickered in my chest. I hadn't thought about the cost. What almost-fourteen-year-old would?

"C-can't we afford it?" I timidly ventured.

THAT'S WHEN I LEARNED THAT I had money.

I believe things happen for a reason. Even bad things. The car accident was a very, very bad thing. But had it not happened, there wouldn't have been an insurance settlement. That money was placed in the bank in a trust for me and had been collecting interest since 1968. Banks don't pay that kind of interest anymore.

Had I not had that money, I would have had to attend a day school in New York. The money permitted me a choice I would not have had otherwise. In hindsight, I believed that had I not chosen to go away to school, I would not have survived both Robert and the demands and difficulties that come with coming of age.

Not both of those things at the same time. No way. No how.

PART THREE

OUT OF BROOKLYN

It wasn't about standing still and becoming safe.
If anybody wants to keep creating they have to be about change.

—MILES DAVIS

14

I wanted a going-away party but had to settle for an evening at Coney Island with friends because Vivian knew how Robert enjoyed ruining a good time. Of course our parents wouldn't allow us tweens to go alone, so my friend Michelle's aunt, a gregarious twenty-something visiting from Trinidad, agreed to chaperone.

Coney Island is in south Brooklyn, overlooking the Atlantic Ocean. The theme park was a favorite destination for Robert and his brothers when they were teenagers. They'd spend Saturdays there, trolling the boardwalk, swimming in the ocean, and gorging themselves on Nathan's hot dogs and fried clams.

I have my own happy memories of going to Coney Island with Robert and Vivian. I can see Reggie and me in the back seat of that green Oldsmobile, gazing out the open car windows, waiting in quiet excitement for the moment when the Wonder Wheel materialized against the sky. I believe Robert became as excited as we were, because his eyes misted over with nostalgia when he saw that landmark appear in the distance.

On those visits with us, he'd stand aside with his arms folded across his chest or devouring a Nathan's Famous frank in three bites, watching Vivian hoist us onto carousel horses or maneuver a bumper car with us sitting alongside her, screaming with glee. At the end of those rare, light-filled summer days, Reggie and I would get a balloon and a stick of cotton candy. By the time Robert lowered the music and parallel parked his light green Oldsmobile in front of 300 Sullivan Place, Reggie and I were fast asleep, still clutching the empty sticky cotton candy sticks in one hand and the rubber tie of our balloons in the other.

By 1979, the Coney Island of Robert's youth and mine was as dilapidated as Times Square. The streets were strewn with garbage, and many of the original rides were shuttered or in disrepair, save for the Wonder Wheel, the Cyclone roller coaster, and bumper cars. That said, there were a few new additions, thrill rides outfitted with flashing colorful lights, disco balls, and a hype man on a microphone trawling for customers over the popular music thumping out of speakers as large as steamer trunks.

There were still a few stalls that offered Skee-Ball, Whac-A-Mole, and the water-gun-race games, but me and my friends were more captivated with the boys, who, like us, were roaming the park in packs, eyeballing the opposite sex. We were all just a bunch of teenagers in heat.

Our chaperone was in heat too. She was foul-mouthed and spicy, with a behind that stuck out like a shelf. Loud and pretty, she drew the attention of men, even when she wasn't trying.

"All yuh don't want to go on the coaster?"

It was the third time she'd mentioned the roller coaster. She wanted to go, but not by herself, and we were all too chicken to accompany her.

I didn't know that the Cyclone was the second-steepest wooden roller coaster in the world, but what I did know was that there was nothing about those cars streaking along the winding tracks or the passengers screaming for their mothers, God, and Jesus that made it appealing to me.

So we continued circling the park, stopping to play a few of the stall games, and consumed more than our fair share of french fries and soda.

When we found ourselves once again in the shadow of the roller coaster, the aunt said, "All yuh going to send me up there by myself?" She gazed at us unbelievingly.

"Fine," she huffed. "But I'm not leaving without riding that roller coaster."

She walked over and joined the line of people, many of whom had already ridden several times. A bored-looking teenager with a patch over his eye took her ticket stub and ripped it in half. He gave her one half, and the other half he dropped into a metal box. She turned around and waved at us before climbing into the car alongside a woman so thin, I was sure she would slip out from beneath the safety bar on the first high-speed corner.

The Cyclone lurched forward and began its slow rumble toward its first thrill, which was a rapid right turn at a 180-degree angle. We watched with our hands over our mouths. The train slowly juddered up the eighty-five-foot camelback and then *whoosh.* . . .

Game on.

The world-famous Cyclone streaked through a series of dips, left turns, right turns, and U-turns and then the operator threw a lever, sending the train rolling backward on its wheels.

We could hear the aunty screaming and laughing and cussing in Trinidadian patois: *Yuh mudda cunnnnnnnnnnnnnnnnnttttttttttttttttttttttt!*

BACK HOME, IN THE LOBBY of the building, my friends and I hugged goodbye and drifted off to our separate apartments. When I opened the door, the cigarette smoke hit me first and then the rank mixture of Hennessy and perspiration. Robert was sitting at the kitchen table, a Camel short burning away in the green tin ashtray. He was hunched over in the kitchen chair, forearms on his thighs, staring into his tumbler of cognac. The apartment was dark and quiet, save for the light in the kitchen. Vivian was at bingo, the twins and Reggie in Queens with Thelma and Wilfred.

"Good evening," I muttered, stepping quickly past the kitchen.

"Get back here," he snarled.

I stepped back and stood in the kitchen doorway.

"Yes?" I answered, intentionally dropping the *sir*. I'd followed the rules and made it home just as the streetlights flickered on, and still that wasn't good enough for him. Robert was staring at the tumbler, but at the sass in my voice, he turned his head very, very slowly, until his bloodshot eyes were fixed onto my face.

"You're not too old to get slapped in the mouth," he warned.

I was thirteen years old. In a month I would turn fourteen; in four years, I would be eighteen, a high school graduate, and then I'd go off to college some place so far away from him I'd forget he even existed. I kept silent, not daring to look at him, but instead gluing my eyes to the white refrigerator behind him.

"Don't think you're better than me because you're going away to high school."

Neither Robert nor Vivian had finished high school; they'd both dropped out after tenth grade.

"Don't think you're better than your friends or your cousins, because I'm here to tell you that you're not."

I didn't think that I was better than my friends or my cousins. However, I did think that I was lucky—lucky enough to be leaving this hell of an existence.

The school I'd decided to attend was located in Danville, Pennsylvania.

He said he knew people in Danville, because he was a truck driver and had been to Danville many times, and those people would be reporting back to him.

"I've got eyes everywhere, remember that."

How could I forget?

I was so tired; I was falling asleep on my feet. When he saw my eyes slip closed, he slammed his fist down onto the table, startling me nearly out of my skin. He laughed at my reaction. He always derived so much pleasure in terrorizing us.

ONCE, WHEN I WAS ABOUT six or seven years old, I was standing exactly where I was standing on that hot August night in 1979, and Robert was sitting in the same spot at the table. In front of him was a glass filled with Satan's elixir. He was humming to himself, staring down at his hands, ignoring me as if I wasn't standing there with every cell on alert, waiting for what was to come. He'd reached for the glass, drained it, and then slapped his chest as the liquor burned a trail down his throat. After a moment he stood, walked to the sink, and filled a glass with water. I kept one eye on him and the other on the yellow-and-black clock on the wall above the refrigerator. I had been standing there in silence for an hour.

After he drained the glass, he moved back to the table, tucked a cigarette into his mouth, went to the stove, and turned the black knob.

Click, click, click.

When, finally, the blue and yellow flame sprung from the burner, he lowered his head until it was level with the fire and carefully edged the tip of cigarette into the blaze. I'd watched him do that a hundred times, awed that his hair never, ever caught aflame even as I willed and prayed for it to happen.

Little me watched him tilt his head back on his neck and pump out three smoky circles. I watched them float until they evaporated. Chuckling to himself, Robert shook his head in response to some inner dialogue and then sat down at the table again.

"Come here, Bernice."

I flinched at the sound of his voice. It sounded like a clatter, because he hadn't spoken for so long. The silence in that apartment had been broken only by the open and closing of apartment doors, footsteps, and conversations in the hall outside our apartment and my own racing heart.

"Yes, sir," I said, stepping stiffly from the dark hallway into the brightly lit kitchen.

"Stand here."

He aimed his index finger at an invisible spot on the linoleum floor directly in front of him. I planted myself there.

"Hold out your hand."

Because I thought I was being punished for something, I raised my arm palm down. I gritted my teeth and closed my eyes, awaiting the slap to the back of my hand, but it didn't come.

"Turn your blasted hand over," he sneered.

I did as I was told.

When he reached for the burning cigarette, the gray tail of ash crumbled off, scattering over the old ash and cigarette butts. He dangled the cigarette over my open hand and with one tap, sent a flurry of hot ash onto my soft palm.

I shrieked and frantically clapped my palm against my pajama-clad thigh.

"Okay, okay." He laughed, yanking my hand up to his face to inspect the injury. "Oh, it's nothing, see? It's nothing, you're such a baby."

I looked down at the blotch of red unfurling like a ruffled marigold petal. He stood up, tugged me over to the sink, turned on the faucet, and shoved my hand beneath the surge of icy water.

"Hey, hey," he bellowed when my sobbing intensified. "Stop all that crying before I give you something to cry about."

I clamped my mouth shut, but I couldn't lock off the valve that controlled my sobbing. Through my tears, I saw the expression on his face, grotesque, beaming with pleasure.

Now, after frightening me awake, it was the same expression that graced his face.

―――――――

OF COURSE, THAT NIGHT, HE drank himself into the monster, and when Vivian came home from bingo, he goaded her into an argument that escalated into a screaming and shoving match before finally, satisfied, he stumbled into the bedroom and fell across the bed into sleep.

The next morning, Vivian tried to shake him awake, but he only waved her off, turned onto his side, and continued snoring.

"Robert, Robert, we have to take Bernice to school," she implored, rocking his shoulder with her hands.

He swiped at her, opened his bleary eyes, and gazed at her like she was the most hateful thing he'd ever seen.

It was early, not yet seven, but I was wide awake. The truth was, I hadn't slept much at all. My parents' fighting, combined with the anticipation surrounding this new chapter in my life, had not made for a restful night. And now, like always, Robert sowed chaos and disruption where there should have been joy.

Vivian went into the kitchen, lifted the receiver on the wall phone, and dialed Thelma.

"Mama?"

"Yes?"

"I can't wake Robert and . . ."

"I don't know why you stay with that stupid motherfucker, I really don't."

I could picture Thelma standing in her kitchen, eyes afire, gripping the receiver of her own wall phone. "Well, Wilfred will be home soon. We'll come after he gets here. I'll take Reggie and the twins over to Anna's house."

"Thank you—"

Click.

When the doorbell buzzed, Robert was in the kitchen, dressed in his boxers and white undershirt, layering discs of bologna on a slice of Wonder bread slathered in mustard. Vivian pressed the red button on the white intercom box fixed to the wall outside the kitchen.

"Mama?"

"Come on, let's get this show on the road," Thelma's voice crackled back through the intercom.

Robert smirked and shoved the sandwich into his mouth. He didn't say goodbye or good luck. He didn't even help us take my luggage out to the car. He just went into his room and climbed back into bed.

Outside, Vivian and I settled into the back seat of Thelma's brown Buick Regal. I was glad that Reggie and the twins had been left with Anna, because it was rare that I had Vivian to myself.

Thelma had purchased the car in 1975, not long after she'd passed the road test. That was four years ago. Since then, she and Wilfred had put thousands of miles on that car. I'd been a passenger on a few of those journeys. That's how I fell in love with the open road. I found the sound of the tires rolling over the asphalt spellbinding and soothing, creating the perfect atmosphere for my persistent daydreaming. We ate our meals at the counters of truck stop restaurants, alongside the plaid-shirt-wearing, baseball-cap-sporting, pack-a-day-smoking, hard-liquor-drinking trucker gods who steered steel chariots across the highways, byways, and thruways of North America. Whenever Thelma and Wilfred got tired of driving, they'd pull into a rest stop, crack the windows a bit, and we'd inhale the night air and car exhaust and drift asleep to the sounds of streaming traffic.

Sometimes Wilfred drove, but mostly it was Thelma behind the steering wheel, her four-foot-eleven frame propped up on a pillow so she could see over the hood of the car. She may have had a tiny foot, but it was heavy.

"Hey, baby, you might wanna slow down a bit," Wilfred would timidly suggest whenever he spied the needle of the speedometer ticking up into dangerous territory.

"Aww, hush up, man." She'd laugh before pressing her foot down harder onto the accelerator.

The car was always filled with music, but it was Harold Melvin & the Blue Notes that mostly serenaded us from the 8-track tape deck. Thelma had it something bad for Teddy Pendergrass and remained a solid fan when he broke from the group to pursue his solo career. I know and love all his songs, because she played his music relentlessly.

It was a thrill a minute being in the car with her, zipping along. On a trip to Gary, Indiana, the home of the Jackson 5, Thelma was barreling down the highway, when blue lights flashed in her rearview mirror. Reggie and I didn't react until we heard the siren.

The state trooper looked like every state trooper I'd seen in the movies—white, male, uniformed with shiny black boots that stopped just below the knee, wide-brimmed hat low on his forehead, and black aviators. When he made his approach, Thelma cranked down the window. Sensing danger, my brother and I sank into the warm leather of the back seat.

"Good morning, Officer."

"Ma'am." He briefly touched the brim of his hat. "License and registration, please."

"Well, you gonna tell me why you pulled me over?"

"Now, baby—" Wilfred started.

"Don't baby me," she snapped. "He's supposed to tell me why he pulled me over." She turned back to the state trooper. "So, why did you pull me over?"

I could see her angry face reflected in the dark lenses of his aviators. The trooper calmly and robotically repeated his request.

"I will give it to you when you tell me why you pulled me over." They went back and forth like that, and with each response, Thelma's voice climbed an octave until it teetered on the brink of explosion.

Wilfred heard it too and rested a bracing hand on her thigh.

I was still blissfully ignorant of the frequency with which police officers killed Black people. Or how many of those murders began with a traffic stop. But even without that knowledge, fear still grabbed me by the throat.

Presently, as I sit here writing about the past, I stumbled upon an article in the *Guardian*, whose headline states in big, black, bold letters:

US Police Have Killed Nearly 600 People in Traffic Stops Since 2017, Data Shows

Imagine losing your life over failing to signal, expired tags, or running a red light or stop sign.

Thelma shrugged off Wilfred's halting hand and unleashed her fury: "*Stupidhonkymotherfuckingwhiteredneckbastard.*"

The officer's jaw locked, but he didn't say a word.

Wilfred rested his hands, palms up on his lap, and stared out the windshield at the open road before him. When Thelma was done, she hurled her license and registration out the open window. The documents hit the trooper in the chest and dropped to the ground. I'm sure Wilfred's entire life passed before his eyes.

The trooper bent over, retrieved the documents, calmly walked to his cruiser, and climbed in.

Wilfred didn't like to argue in front of us kids, and I can count on one hand the number of times I'd ever heard him raise his voice at Thelma, but when the trooper was out of earshot, he turned to her, flung his hand into the air, and shouted, "What the hell are you doing?!" I could see beads of perspiration on his forehead and in the short hairs of his mustache.

Thelma just smirked at him before moving her eyes back to the rearview mirror. It seemed we sat there for a long time baking in that summer heat. I watched passing cars slow to get a good look at us. Their prying eyes made me feel ashamed.

When the trooper returned to the car, he handed Thelma her documents and a speeding ticket. I don't remember how fast he claimed she'd been traveling, but it was quite a few miles over the limit, and the fee for the violation was considerable.

"Cracker," Thelma snapped, snatching the items from his hand and tossing them into Wilfred's lap.

To that, the trooper touched his black-gloved fingers to the brim of his hat and said, "Have a nice day, ma'am."

"Fuck you." She turned the key in the ignition, and the car grumbled back to life.

"Now, baby, just pull off slow," Wilfred said.

She peeled off.

Reggie and I turned around and peered out the back window at the pulsing blue lights and the trooper who was standing astride next to his cruiser, back straight, cross-armed, and stoic.

From that day forward, I was always a little bit apprehensive when Thelma was behind the wheel.

NOW AS WE CROSSED THE George Washington Bridge into New Jersey, the majesty of the Empire State Building and all the other skyscraping buildings withered and shrank out of sight. For miles upon miles we sped past strip malls, gas stations, and fast-food restaurants. Pushing on into Pennsylvania, the short hills of New Jersey soared into the Pocono Mountains, thick with pitch, eastern whites, and table mountain pine trees. Outside my car window, swathes of land covered in the greenest grass I ever saw gave way to parcels of turned earth the color of chocolate. We zipped past rambling homes with wraparound porches, weathered farmhouses slanted and gray with age, dairy and wheat farms flecked with ten-foot-high hay bales, and giant silver silos twinkling in the early-afternoon sunlight.

"Danville, twenty miles," Thelma crooned from the front seat. "We made good time," she added, and then turned the volume up on Teddy Pendergrass's "Turn Off the Lights."

15

Located along the Susquehanna River in Montour County, Danville, Pennsylvania, was founded in 1792 by William Montgomery, who was a general, division commander, abolitionist, and congressman who'd voted against the Fugitive Slave Act of 1793. For many years, Danville sat at the center of the iron-producing region where mills and foundries were the major employers. The employees themselves were mostly emigrants from Poland, Romania, Czech Republic, and Slovakia. First Catholic Slovak Girls Academy was founded to educate and preserve the faith and culture of the daughters of those immigrants.

Perched on a hill, the stone Baroque-styled building with its twin wings and lofty tower looked over Danville like Christ the Redeemer over Rio de Janeiro. The building was designed by architect Harry Sternfeld of Philadelphia.

A man.

Of course.

Who else but a man, tasked with designing a building to serve as school and home to girls and women, would incorporate a stone tower akin to an erect penis—shaft, glans, prepuce, and all?

In 1939, Slovak Girls Academy was one of eight American buildings selected for the RIBA exhibition in London.

I bet you there was plenty of head nodding, eye winking, and backslapping laughter in those cigar-smoke-choked British conference rooms.

I see what you did there, Sternfeld, you old dog!

You say it's a school for girls?

Catholic girls . . .

Is that right?

Nuns too.

You don't say.

And a priest?

But of course. A man of God to lead the young ladies into union with God . . .

Union, huh?

WITH GOD.

Yes, of course. God.

Wink. Wink.

I ARRIVED AT ST. CYRIL ACADEMY (by the time I became a student at the school, the name had been changed) within days of the premiere episode of *The Facts of Life*. It was a weekly television show set at a fictional prestigious boarding school called Eastland Academy starring George Clooney, Nancy McKeon, Charlotte Rae, and a host of other white actors. I tuned in mainly to see the Black character, Tootie, who was portrayed by Kim Fields. Tootie was the only Black girl in a boarding school filled with white girls. Up until I arrived at St. Cyril Academy, the only Black person I knew who'd attended boarding school was my uncle J.J. The show was on the air until 1988, and I watched weekly from its inception to its end, always comparing Tootie's boarding school experiences with my own.

The similarities were few, save for the drama that accompanies teenage girls living together under one roof.

On that first day, the nuns checked our belongings for cigarettes, alcohol, drugs, and unsavory literature.

"Hmmm," one nun sounded after scooping up the two Stephen King novels I'd packed. "This is not appropriate reading material for young minds," she'd said, tucking the paperbacks under her arm and walking out of the room.

We underclassmen slept in dormitories of three to four students, furnished with twin beds, bureaus, desks, and chairs. Down the hall were white-tiled showers and toilets. My dorm room looked out over a grassy courtyard, about half the size of a football field. The core curriculum courses were language arts, history, math, and religious studies. In addition, we took classes in stenography, dressmaking, dance, and the visual arts. Our meals were taken in a large cafeteria, located in the basement of the building. It was in that cafeteria that I would have my first taste of rhubarb and strawberry.

All the day students were white girls from Danville and the neighboring towns of Bloomsburg-Berwick, save for Christen, whose parents were of Lebanese and Sicilian descent, and who was just a tad lighter than me, with thick, wavy dark hair. In America, she is legally white because the Supreme Court says that people from Syria/Lebanon are racially white. Which proves yet again that race is a social construct without biological meaning.

"Don't get involved with no cliques, mind your business, keep your head in your books, and get your education." Those were Thelma's parting words to me.

But cliques would be impossible to avoid because it's only natural to gravitate to people with whom you share commonalities. Which is why I immediately bonded with girls—Black and non-Black—who hailed from New York, New Jersey, or were of Caribbean descent. My boarder friends were Estela, a chubby, fair-skinned girl from Santiago, Dominican Republic, and Micky, who was also Dominican but darker complexioned and lived in Manhattan, not far from

Pascale, the baby of the group, who was of Haitian descent. My day school besties were Laura, who was half white and half Filipino, and Amy and Lori, both of whom were all-American white girls.

In those early days, my interactions with many of my white classmates were fraught with questions that I found ridiculous and demeaning. *Do you live in the projects? How can you afford this tuition on welfare? Can I touch your hair? Does your black rub off? Do you know your father?*

Danville reminded me of the fictional town of Mayberry from *The Andy Griffith Show*. Because people of color were virtually non-existent in Danville, when a townie spied a non-white girl roaming through town, they gawked and pointed in guarded amazement like spectators at a zoo.

On Saturdays, we boarders went into town to lunch at the Arthur Treacher's or Randello's hoagie shop. Oftentimes, we'd go to the local Woolworths to buy books, magazines, candy, and millinery supplies for sewing class. Even though I knew my white classmates were secretly slipping nail polish and lip gloss into their pockets and backpacks, it was me and the other Black girls the store employees hawkeyed and shadowed up and down the aisles.

Sunday mornings, we were all required to attend 8:00 a.m. Mass in the chapel. The service was conducted by Father Long, whose sermons perfectly matched his surname.

Arthur J. Long was a tall silver fox with a deep, droning voice and penetrating blue eyes. He smelled of nicotine and cologne, and occasionally I caught a whiff of alcohol on his breath when I stood before him at the altar to receive the host.

"The body of Christ."

"Amen."

I'd believed in God once upon a time, but not as much by then. I couldn't understand why there was war, disease, and famine in the world. Why hadn't God intervened? Better yet, why had God allowed any of it to happen in the first place? I mean, if God knows the beginning, the middle, and the end, wouldn't they have known that we humans weren't going to do right? That we were natural sinners, no matter how minute the infraction? Instead, this God sets us up to fail and then, as punishment, condemns the sinner to hell for eternity? If this is the logic, doesn't that make God out to be a sadist? Truth be told, Christianity never spoke to me on a soul level, and in the ensuing years, as I grew into womanhood, a deep connection is what I would seek out when I began seriously considering a spiritual practice.

The only reason Vivian decided to enroll us in Catholic school was because she believed that the institution would offer a better education for children than public school. I don't know how true that was or is, especially because parochial schools aren't state-funded, so teaching certificates are not required.

Confession was my least favorite thing about being a Catholic. I didn't like being confined in the dark, in a box the size of a utility closet, professing transgressions to any man, but especially a white man.

Why was this required? Weren't we communicating directly with God through prayer?

It was all very creepy, and I never went back again.

In 1955, Arthur J. Long became Father Long when he was ordained as a member of the Catholic religious order: the Maryland Province of the Society of Jesus.

From there, he went on to spread the "gospel" in schools and hospitals in Pittsburgh, Philadelphia, and Harrisburg. He came to St. Cyril Academy in 1975, just four years before I arrived.

In 2018, Father Arthur J. Long was named an abuser in the Pennsylvania Grand Jury Report, and listed in the Archdiocese of Baltimore's Credibly Accused of Sexual Abuse of Minors list. In 2023, his name appeared in a report released by Maryland's attorney general, which listed 156 Catholic clergy who had sexually abused at least six hundred children over six decades.

When confronted, Father Long admitted to having sex with "four or five" girls since arriving at the academy.

Wink. Wink.

In 2004, John Jay College of Criminal Justice for the United States Conference of Catholic Bishops issued a report concluding that between 1950 and 2002, 4,392 Catholic priests, deacons, and active clergy were accused of underage sexual abuse by 10,667 individuals.

A series published in the *Boston Globe* uncovered that sexual abuse of minors by Catholic priests stretches all the way back to the eleventh century. It is entirely plausible that the innocence of thousands, tens of thousands, and possibly even millions of children were taken by the heinous acts of those duly ordained men of God.

SOMETIMES I SPENT WEEKENDS WITH my day student friends; it was always a treat to get away from campus, to sleep in a cozy bed and have a home-cooked meal. They all lived in lovely homes, with recreational rooms and generous backyards. Their parents were all professional people: doctors and lawyers, and Lori's people owned a large dairy farm.

In Brooklyn, our kitchen was tiny, leaving little space for a dining table large enough to accommodate a family of six. So we children had our meals in the kitchen while Robert and Vivian ate in the living room, seated on the couch with their plates of food balanced on their laps. In contrast, my friends enjoyed their meals in a separate dining room at a table large enough to accommodate the entire family, plus guests.

Robert believed that children should be seen and not heard, especially during meals, so we always ate our food in utter silence. The parents of my white friends encouraged and participated in mealtime discussions. It was at one of those family dinners that Laura's father, a tall, slim, kind man with glasses, responded aloud to a question that no one had posed:

Of course, the white race is the superior race.

To this day, I do not know who asked the question or if in fact a question was asked. Perhaps this man, who had always been nothing but kind and welcoming to me, found it necessary to remind me that even though I was in his Victorian-style home, sitting at his dinner table, eating the food that had been lovingly prepared by his Filipino wife, I was inferior to him.

I cannot recall if my friend and her siblings fell silent, or if my friend, her siblings, or her mother looked at me for a reaction or in consolation. I remember that I kept my eyes lowered to my plate, that the grip on my fork tightened, and the leisurely pace of my heart launched into a sprint.

Do I believe his declaration was meant to wound and degrade me?

Yes, I do.

The sound drained out of the room, and my soul was jettisoned from my body into the space above the table. It hovered there for long minutes until finally one of her siblings either said something or sneezed or coughed and the spell was broken. My soul plunged back into my body, and the sound returned to the room with the intensity of a frothy, crashing tide.

I would return to that house and eat at that table again and again without further incident. But I would never forget the shot fired, because the wound it left would not allow me to forget. The memory is lodged in me like the bullet it was intended to be.

IN MY SOPHOMORE YEAR, A pair of sisters arrived at St. Cyril. Sheila and Yvonne hailed from Central Islip, Long Island. They'd claimed, quite proudly, that they'd been expelled from some of the best boarding schools on the East Coast. They were dark beauties, whip-smart and supreme orators with comic timing, who smoothly vacillated between African American Vernacular English (AAVE) and so-called proper English. They reminded me a bit of my friends back in Brooklyn, but they were worldly and more sophisticated.

I was immediately transfixed and was proud and happy when

they absorbed me into their orbit. They had stories upon stories about their Black Jewish grandmother, whose antics and lexicon closely mirrored Thelma's. Their tales were outlandishly tall—no two people could *consistently* find themselves in such precarious and hilarious predicaments—but we girls believed every single word. And they didn't just recount, they performed, assuming voices, expressions, and physical attributes. It was like watching a stage play. Their hilarity was side-splitting, and more than a few times, I wet myself with laughter.

Sheila and Yvonne reminded me of all the good parts of home.

AT THE TIME, THE WORD *nigger* was batted around by the adults in my family, as was *motherfucker*, *bitch*, and *bastard*. Those words were off-limits to us children. Nevertheless, we invoked them in hushed whispers when the adults were out of earshot.

The unspoken rule was that the word *nigger* was never, ever to be used in the company of white folks, so the first time it tumbled out of Yvonne's mouth in the television lounge crammed with white girls, it pealed like fingernails being dragged across a chalkboard.

The white girls' heads jerked around. Either Yvonne didn't see them looking or didn't care that they were looking, because she continued talking without missing a beat. Slowly, the white girls returned their attention to whatever drama was unfolding on the television.

I didn't realize I'd been holding my breath until they looked away and the air whistled out of my lungs.

There was a girl, we will call her Veronica, she was about five five with long, thick black hair that she washed daily, so she always smelled like Prell shampoo. She had emerald-green eyes and a prominent nose that I'd seen only on profiles stamped onto ancient Greek coins.

Veronica wasn't exactly a member of our friend group, which is to say she did not eat with us in the cafeteria, and she did not participate in the dance routines we spent hours choreographing. But outside the cafeteria and the dance room, she was always with us, like a white, green-eyed shadow. She seemed to be taken with us Black and brown girls, maybe even obsessed? Thelma would have called her a flunky.

I don't remember from where Veronica hailed, but I know she wasn't raised in the sticks, because she had some swagger and suave that her rural-raised sistren did not. Also, she wielded our lingo like she'd nursed at a Black woman's tit.

Too much?

What I'm saying is that when Veronica used AAVE, it didn't sound forced or awkward like white people parroting jive talk in 1970s blaxploitation movies. Veronica sounded natural, like she'd grown up listening to music by Donna Summer, Stevie Wonder, and Marvin Gaye. She spoke like she knew her way around a plate of fried chicken, black-eyed peas, and corn bread. Like she might not have been able to jump double Dutch but could turn. The thing I'm trying to tell you is that girl clapped on the two and the four and not the one and the three.

"Veronica, you're the Blackest white girl I've ever met!" Yvonne said.

"Sure is," Sheila chimed.

But that compliment would be the nail in Sheila's and Yvonne's caskets, because history tells us when you gift a white person an inch, they always come back to take a yard.

The inevitable happened on a Saturday afternoon. It was late fall, just four o'clock and daylight was fading fast. I can't tell you what Veronica was responding to, when that problematic word rolled across her tongue and out of her mouth, but I do remember how the statement rang in my ears like a gong before a boxing match.

Nigger, pullleassssseeeee.

This is a common response among Black people when confronted with something that is highly unlikely, completely unbelievable, or extremely irritating. Sheila's head turned slowly on her neck. She brushed hair from her face and asked, "What did you say?"

Sparks flashed in Sheila's eyes. Her voice was deadly.

"Yeah, what did you say?" Yvonne echoed, her face screwed tight, like she smelled rotting eggs.

"What?" Veronica bleated, innocently batting her big green eyes. The disingenuous expression gave her away.

Sheila placed her hands on her hips and rolled her neck. "You cannot say that word. Don't you ever let me hear you say that word again," she threatened.

Veronica should have humbled herself. An apology would have instantly doused the impeding five-alarm fire.

But no. "Why can't I say it? You and Yvonne say it all the time."

Yvonne's eyes rolled dramatically as if to say, *This bitch*. The sisters were well versed on the horrors of slavery, Jim Crow, and the civil rights movement. I think one or both of their parents had been members of the Black Panther Party, so they were all too familiar with the history and weaponization of that ugly word. Sheila took a deep breath and launched into its sordid history and why Black people had claimed it, scrubbed it free of the ugly, and spit-shined it up for our own personal use. I'm paraphrasing here, but you get the idea. Sheila ended her lecture with this threat: "If you say it again, I'm gonna personally whup your ass."

"Oooooooh," we spectators sounded, snapping our fingers and snickering.

Veronica's eyes ranged over our jeering faces. She seemed to be searching for an ally; someone who would stand up and defend her white right to use that word. When no one came to her defense, she huffed and stormed out of the lounge.

Sheila's face broke into a triumphant smile. We Black girls closed in around her, slapping fives and belittling Veronica for her egregious misstep. One by one, the white girls pulled themselves up from the sofa and the side chairs and stiffly walked away. War had been declared, but we were none the wiser.

That night, after dinner, when we Black and brown girls were in the dorms, clumped together in one space and outnumbered, Veronica planted herself at the top of the corridor like a gunslinger at a showdown awaiting his challenger. Her people crowded the doorways, giggling, fidgeting, itching for the clash.

"Sheila!"

We all heard it, even those of us who were behind closed doors. Veronica hadn't just yelled Sheila's name, she'd shrieked it like a madwoman in an asylum. I opened my bedroom door just in time to see Sheila's head pop around the doorway of the bathroom. Her hair was covered in a pink-and-green scarf, she was clutching her toothbrush, her lips were pinched together, cheeks bloated with water. She stretched her eyes and bounced her head, which is Blackspeak for "Yeah, what?"

Veronica smirked, parted her lips, and coolly uttered, "Nigger."

We turned to see Sheila's expression but only glimpsed a dark blur streaking down the corridor.

Sheila hit Veronica like a linebacker, knocking her to the floor. She was on her in an instant, pummeling her, unleashing centuries of rage. And then Sheila grabbed hold of Veronica's beautiful mane and dragged her across the marble floor, literally wiping the floor with her.

"I told you. Didn't I tell you? Don't say I didn't tell you!" Sheila bellowed.

Veronica tried and failed to disentangle Sheila's fingers from her hair. Her pleas for help went unanswered, even those girls who'd assured her that they'd have her back.

Then Sheila mounted her a second time, took Veronica's head in her hands, raised it into the air, and smashed it into the floor.

That's when we all reacted. By the time we peeled Sheila off Veronica, the nuns were running down the corridor with their habits fluttering behind them like sails.

Someone had given Veronica a ball of tissue to catch the blood leaking from her nose. Another person was holding a damp washcloth to the back of her head. Her face looked like the strawberry and whipped cream desserts the kitchen nuns were fond of serving. Yvonne and two other girls had formed a human fence around Sheila, who was still snorting and pacing like a bull. My eyes were glazed with tears, and I was trembling because it all reminded me of the bad parts of home.

THERE MIGHT HAVE BEEN TALK of calling the police, talk of pressing charges, I don't know. What I do know is that the sisters were expelled on the spot and within hours their family came to collect them.

I barely slept that night, and the next morning in the cafeteria, the tension was too palpable to ignore.

From over their bowls of cereal and plates of powdered eggs, link sausage, and toast, our white classmates eyed us like leopards in tall grass. Throughout the school day, as Black passed white in the hallways or sat next to one another in the classrooms, that horrid word that had started all the trouble in the first place was whispered and muttered and hissed and hummed. All the stories I'd heard about lynchings and cross burnings jumped to mind. I felt unsafe, utterly convinced that my life was in danger.

I went to the wood-paneled room that held the student mailboxes and pay phone, raised the receiver, and dialed zero.

"This is the operator; how may I help you?"

I turned my back to the door, cupped my hand over my mouth, and whispered, "I'd like to make a collect call, please."

After a few clicking sounds, the phone rang in apartment A5 twice, before Robert's "Hello?" echoed in my ear.

My heart sank when I heard his voice.

You have a collect call from Bernice. Will you accept the charges?

"Bernice?"

Will you accept?

Robert paused, and for a second I thought he was going to say no, he would not accept the charges. He'd done it in the past.

"Yeah."

There was a clicking sound, indicating the call had been connected, and then Robert said, "What do you want?"

"Um, hi, Daddy, can I speak to Mommy, please?"

"Whatever you want to tell her you can tell me."

I heard the steel in his voice, so I knew he'd already had a drink or three. I could have lied and said I was just calling to say hello, but I was desperate.

"They're up here calling us niggers . . ."

The simple truth is that Robert did not like white people. He did not like them, and he did not trust them. My allegation was met with silence. I held my breath and waited.

"Pack your things, I'll be there in the morning to get you," he said.

He was coming to rescue me. Finally, *finally* the protector I had always needed him to be had emerged.

"HEY." MY DOMINICAN FRIEND ESTELA threw the greeting at me as she strolled by the open dorm room door. She doubled back quickly when she realized there was an open suitcase on my bed. "Um, are you going somewhere?"

"Yep. I'm going home. My father is coming in the morning to get me."

Estela shoved her hands into the side pockets of her baggy jeans. "Really?"

I pulled open a drawer, scooped out a pile of underwear, and dumped it into the suitcase. "Yep."

She laughed. "You're joking, right?"

"Nope."

"For real, for real?"

I nodded.

Estela blew air out of her mouth, walked into the room, and folded her arms around my shoulders. "I'm going to miss you, chica."

I WAS SITTING OUTSIDE ON the stone steps between my green Samsonite suitcase and my black trunk when I saw Thelma's Buick Regal turn into the driveway and not Robert's car.

My heart dropped into my stomach.

The passenger door opened, and Vivian climbed out. Her hair was pulled back into a ponytail. She looked tired and inconvenienced.

I stood up. "Hi, Mommy."

She nodded and slammed the door shut.

I hoped against hope that Robert had driven Thelma's car. His car was much older and slower, a gas guzzler. Using Thelma's car would make sense, I told myself. But my delusion was dashed when the driver's door opened and Thelma stepped out.

She'd piled her graying hair beneath a black knit hat, with a green-and-white NY JETS patch on the front. Both the gray sweatpants and oversized black jacket she wore definitely came from the men's department of some clothing store. She always dressed like a man when she was going into battle.

I crooked my head a bit, looking expectantly at the right back passenger door.

"Did Daddy come?"

I had directed the question to Vivian, but before she could answer, Thelma huffed, "Didn't I tell your stupid ass not to get involved in any cliques?"

IN THE PRINCIPAL'S OFFICE, SISTER Donna Marie sat straight-backed in the black leather office chair with her fingers laced on her desk.

Her reddish-blond bangs puffed out from beneath her habit like a hairy cloud.

We three generations of firstborn girls sat across from her, with me in the middle—in the hot seat. After a few minutes of small talk, Thelma leaned forward and asked, "So, what seems to be the problem, Sister?"

Sister Donna Marie winced at her straightforwardness.

"Well . . ." Sister Donna Marie quickly laid out the details about the disturbance, emphasizing how *problematic* Sheila and Yvonne had been and how she and the other nuns had tried to refine them, had tried to save them, but failed because they were just too far gone.

She spoke about them the way missionaries spoke about Africans and First Nations people, as if we needed rescuing from ourselves.

My blood boiled as I listened to her furtively disparage my friends.

"I understand"—she dropped her voice an octave—"that they'd been expelled from several schools before they came to St. Cyril. Well, the real problems started with *that* word . . ."

Sister Donna Marie trailed off, her face taking on the pallor of a ripe cherry.

Her eyes twinkling, Thelma leaned in a bit closer.

"What word?"

Sister Donna Marie anxiously raked her hands up and down her arms as if the temperature in the room had dipped.

"You know . . . *that* word."

Thelma's face twisted with befuddlement. She knew the word, but she wanted to hear Sister Donna Marie say it.

"No, I don't. Please tell me," Thelma pressed.

Sister Donna Marie stole a quick glance at the crucifix nailed on the wall behind us. "Oh no, no, I can't."

"Sure you can," Thelma insisted.

Vivian side-eyed Thelma and went so far as to tap her thigh, saying, "Okay, Mama." In that moment, she was probably thinking what a bad idea it was having brought Thelma there in the first place. Thelma ignored the finger and the plea.

By then, the color had drained from Sister Donna Marie's face, and she was as pale as a parsnip.

"Say it." Thelma wouldn't take no for an answer. "Go on, say it."

And finally, Sister Donna Marie broke. She squeezed her eyes shut and squeaked, "Nigger."

"Yes," Thelma echoed. "Nigger."

Thelma fell back into the chair, glowing with the satisfaction of having consumed a sumptuous meal.

LATER, MY DORM MATES QUIETLY watched as Vivian and I hauled my belongings back up to my dorm room. I was embarrassed, of course. Robert had made me out to be a liar in front of the very same white people he had vowed to deliver me from.

Outside, the shifting afternoon light dragged long shadows across the dead grass. Thelma stood before me, with her hands hidden away in the pockets of her jacket.

"I know you're upset, but you can't let these white people run you away over some stupid word. Honkies gonna be honkies," she said. "They can call you what they want—ignore them." She paused, gave me a hard look before continuing. "Now name-calling is one thing," she said, pulling her balled fists from her pockets and raising them to my face. "But if they put their hands on you, you better whup the shit out of them."

That got her a little stifled laugh from me. Her face softened a bit.

"Bernice, there are white people everywhere, which means Black people will always be niggers. Ain't no way 'round it." Her eyes ranged over the vista and then settled on me again. "It's just a word. There are worse things."

SHE WAS CERTAIN OF IT because, day in and day out, the world reminded her.

In December of the previous year, Arthur McDuffie, a thirty-
three-year-old insurance salesman and former marine and father of
two daughters, was riding his motorcycle in Miami when he allegedly flew through a red light. He was pulled over by Miami Dade
police, dragged off his bike, and a dozen officers savagely beat him
into a coma.

He died from his injuries.

The family pressed charges against the officers, who had attempted to cover up their crime. The case went to court, and on
May 17, 1980, just six months before Veronica hurled that word at
Sheila, a jury of twelve white men acquitted those officers of any
wrongdoing. Following the verdict, Miami exploded, like Harlem
in '35 and Detroit in '43 and Baltimore, Chicago, and Louisville
in '68.

There. Are. Worse. Things.

THELMA GLANCED AT VIVIAN, WHO stood a few feet away from us
with her head cocked, hand cupped around a white Bic lighter,
shielding the flame from the autumn breeze. She stepped closer to
me and lowered her voice. "You wanna go back home to do what?
Be a built-in babysitter?" She waved her hand, as if the gesture
alone would sweep the ridiculousness out of my head.

Of course she was right, and I knew she was right. My eyes
welled with tears.

"Now, now, stop all that," she grumbled. "See, this is exactly
what I'm talking about." She aimed a finger at my leaking eyes. She
hated tears. I folded my lips, tried and failed to blink back the water.

Thelma cleared her throat and pulled a roll of money from her
pocket. She only carried a purse for weddings, funerals, and special

occasions. She peeled off a twenty and shoved it at me. "Here, take this and stop all of that crying." Patting my arm, she said, "Remember what I told you, okay?" And with that she turned and walked toward the car.

Vivian dropped the cigarette butt to the ground and crushed it under the sole of her shoe. She came to me and wiped my wet face with her bare hands. Wrapping her arms around my shoulders, she pressed a kiss on my check and mumbled into my neck, "I'll see you in a few weeks." Thanksgiving was right around the corner.

I watched the car until I couldn't see it anymore and then returned to my room, shame-faced and heartbroken.

In the moment, I didn't feel like there were things more grave than being left behind with people who likely wanted to harm me or worse. But I had a whole life ahead of me that would prove Thelma's words true.

16

Yes, Thelma knew there were worse things than some little nobody white girl calling me a nigger, because she had seen and experienced worse in New York, Detroit, Chicago, and certainly as a child in Sandersville.

And now, as I lay in bed in my dormitory room at St. Cyril Academy, my tears replaced with combustible anger, I wished I had a knob I could turn to extinguish the flames flickering in my chest. Thelma knew there were worse things for sure, worse than what I was crying over, even worse than having her mother die when she was so very young that she could barely remember her touch or the sound of her voice. Thelma would have even forgotten what Lillian looked like if she hadn't been born with her face.

She knew there were worse things a girl my age could experience, because she had experienced those things and they had sent her clear out of her mind.

NOT LONG AFTER THE TWINS were born, Vivian received a call from her cousin Jay Findley May, the son of Vivian's granduncle Buddy, who was Lillian's brother.

He was christened Jay Findley, but down south they called him Spoon because that was his preferred utensil. But his family up in Detroit, those offshoots from Sandersville, they all called him Jay Bird, because he sang pretty like a Blue Jay.

Vivian and Spoon had grown up together in Sandersville, in the house where Spoon's father, Charlie Herman May Sr., called Buddy, was the head of household, having inherited the title after his father died and his brothers fled north during the great migration.

Buddy had married a woman from Ohio named Alberta King and moved her into the house where he had been born and raised and still lived with his mother, Rosie May. There, Alberta gave birth to five children, including Spoon. And although those children were Vivian's cousins, they'd all been reared like siblings, which was appropriate because in the summer of 1978, Spoon called and told her that *his* father was also *her* father, so that made them brother and sister.

The one thing everyone knew about Vivian was her desire to know the name of her father. Whenever she'd asked, Thelma would either ignore the question or throw out some random name before refusing to discuss it any further.

Vivian laughed into the receiver. "Spoon, you been drinking?"

"You know I don't drink, Vivian."

She'd forgotten about that. "Well, I haven't seen you for some time now, maybe you picked up the habit?" She was still laughing even as her mind reached back to a memory that lent credence to his claim.

Because there were so many of them, no one had the luxury of sleeping alone in that crowded house in Sandersville. So they doubled up and tripled up in the bedrooms and in the beds. When they were little kids, before Thelma brought Vivian to Detroit, Vivian and Spoon shared a bed with Helen. Because they were children, they made a game out of most everything—picking cotton, bath time, and that terrible thing that happened at night after they'd said their prayers, climbed into bed, and restlessly waited slumber to claim them.

If they were still awake when Helen creaked the door open, they'd go stiff, clench their eyes shut, and feign sleep. She'd climb in beside them and try to fall asleep, but sleep is nearly impossible when you live under constant threat of violence, even if you're bone-tired from picking cotton for ten hours. Even then, when your body is screaming for sleep, your mind can't risk shutting down or shutting off because it's better to be alert and see it coming.

Vivian remembered that some nights, not every night, Buddy would come tiptoeing into that dark room. He'd throw back the covers and strike a match to make sure he wasn't about to mount his own son or grandniece. Vivian and Spoon watched through squinted eyelids as Buddy defiled his own sister's daughter.

When he was done, he'd use the hem of his bed shirt to wipe his penis clean. If he did that to Helen, then he did it to Anna, and if he did that to Anna, then he did it to Thelma.

Thelma never confessed to it or spoke about it, not to anyone, except maybe God. She tried to rid herself of the memory, but it lurked in the shadows of her mind like a phantom.

And then came the day when I screamed for her from the upstairs bedroom of her home in Queens, and the phantom came flapping out of the shadows.

I WAS SIX YEARS OLD, in the bedroom that I shared with my aunts when I came to visit. I was in the bed, seated atop the blanket with my legs folded beneath me, my hands busy with a tail of lanyard. My aunts were out at the movies, and Wilfred was at work. Thelma was downstairs in the kitchen, washing the dinner dishes. There was music playing on the stereo in the living room, but the volume was low enough so that I could hear the music and Thelma could hear me if I needed her.

J.J., Wilfred's son, was home too, closed away in the tiny room that had been Vivian's bedroom before she got married. The room where I had been conceived. I adored J.J. Family lore says that his name was the first word to sail out of my young mouth. At the time of the incident, he was twelve or thirteen years old.

At some point that evening, he slipped from his bedroom, ventured upstairs, and I looked up from my lanyard to see him standing in the open doorway of the bedroom.

"What you doing, bighead?"

"You a bighead." I giggled in response.

He sauntered into the room, sat down on the corner of the bed, and reached for my bare feet.

"Stoooopppppp," I squealed when he began tickling my soles. I yanked my feet from his reach and wiped the tears from my eyes.

"Lemme see that," he said, pointing to the lanyard.

I handed it to him, and as he scrutinized my work, I studied his hairline and inhaled the Afro Sheen wafting up from his freshly cut crown.

He handed the lanyard back to me. "Nice," he said, and then just as casually asked if he could see my pussy.

I blinked at him, sure that I'd heard wrong. "What?"

"Lemme see your pussy," he repeated, reaching for the hem of my nightgown.

I did not know I was screaming until I saw Thelma in the doorway, her eyes wide with alarm.

"What the hell is going on?"

I aimed my finger at J.J.

When Thelma saw the terror on my face, she didn't ask another question; she pounced on J.J. like a wild cat. He was a full foot taller than her and stronger. He could have shrugged Thelma off or knocked her against the wall, but he didn't. Instead, he cowered under her assault, folding his arms protectively around his head. After he went wailing out of the room and down the stairs, Thelma did not take me in her arms in a comforting embrace, she just took the lanyard from my hand, placed it on the nightstand, told me it was time to go to sleep, and hit the light switch on the way out of the room.

"Good night, Bernice."

Downstairs, she fussed some more with J.J., telling him that she was going to tell Wilfred about what he'd done. Then the music went off, replaced by the flat voice of the white male newscaster.

I wish someone in that house in Sandersville had done for Thelma, Anna, and Helen what she'd done for me.

The following morning, Wilfred guided me in the art of flipping pancakes.

"There you go, Bernice, you got it!"

The family had breakfast as if nothing at all had happened the night before. Which is to say, we didn't talk about it, and I never told Vivian, because I knew she'd probably kill J.J., or at the very least ban me from ever visiting that house again. And my grandparents' house was my safe and happy place until I started going to Barbados.

But I'm talking about it now because I'm tired of keeping it to myself, and I've learned that things that live in the dark, die in the light.

AS AN ADULT, WHEN I embarked on my self-healing journey, I learned about the aftereffects of childhood trauma. I used that information as a lens through which to view Thelma, Vivian, and, eventually, Robert and now myself in a different light.

But in the seventies, I am years away from that awareness, so when my family members refer to Thelma as Sybil behind her back, Vivian and I giggle in agreement. *Sybil* is the title of the book about a woman who claimed she had sixteen separate personalities. It was published in 1973 and sold six million copies. I've never read the book, but I did watch the 1976 made-for-television movie adaptation. I was only eleven years old, and didn't quite grasp the storyline. What I do recall is at the end of the movie, when credits were rolling, Vivian made a comment about how much Sybil's behavior mirrored Thelma's.

The condition is no longer referred to as split personality; now it's described as dissociative identity disorder. It's thought to be a complex psychological condition caused by repetitive physical, sexual, and emotional abuse.

A few years after Thelma purchased the Buick, she was rear-ended. The damage was minimal, but she saw dollar signs. In addition to the whiplash suffered, Thelma claimed that she had lost the feeling in her left leg. She had a physician friend who corroborated the claim, no doubt after she'd promised him a share of the pot.

This was not the insurance company's first dealings with a scam artist, and so they sent Thelma to see one of their own doctors. Vivian accompanied her to the appointment, because Wilfred put his foot down where insurance fraud was concerned. With Vivian's assistance, Thelma hobbled into the examining room on a pair of crutches and plopped down into the chair.

"Mrs. Nettles, are you sure that you don't feel anything in this leg?" the doctor asked. "Absolutely, positively sure?"

Thelma looked him square in the eyes. "I'm as sure of it as my name is Thelma Nettles."

The doctor rolled up Thelma's pant leg and massaged the flesh around her kneecap and her muscled calf. "Do you feel that?"

"No."

The doctor grinned, rose from his wheeled stool, and walked over to the metal cabinet. He returned with a needle that was an inch long.

Vivian hated needles. The sight of them made her woozy. She

pulled her eyes away from the weapon and looked at Thelma to see if her expression had changed. It had not. It was still as placid and serene as if she were asleep.

He sat down again and held the needle ominously a few inches from Thelma's nose. She accepted the challenge with a smile.

"Okay," he sighed, "this is going to pinch a little." He looked deep into her eyes; Thelma held his gaze, and Vivian held her breath.

When he pricked the outer left side of her calf, Thelma didn't flinch.

He then pricked the right side of her calf, and still, she didn't move. "Okay," he murmured. "I'm going to apply a little more pressure, okay?"

"Okay," Thelma responded blandly.

He administered three quick jabs around the perimeter of her knee and one in her thigh, and even though the punctures let blood, Thelma hadn't winced or blinked.

The doctor was aghast. He looked at Vivian, whose expression held as much astonishment as his own. "You didn't feel that?"

"No, I didn't," Thelma said.

It is my belief, that as soon as she saw the needle, Thelma had done what she had in that dark bedroom in Sandersville, and any other time she found herself in harm's way—she willed herself away.

Thelma bought a brand-new Buick LeSabre with the settlement money. That and a Nokia Mobira Senator mobile phone that weighed twenty-two pounds and came complete with a leather carrying case.

EVEN THOUGH BUDDY DIED A year before I was born, that does not stop me from exacting revenge on behalf of Thelma, her sisters, and every child he violated.

Buddy is every bad man I have ever written.

I use my pen as a sword, suffering him on the page until he is dead, and then I resurrect him in the next story and the story after that and agonize him all over again.

I sleep well at night, content in the belief that Buddy is in a hell of my making, one crafted of fire, brimstone, and my words.

THE RACIAL TENSION AT ST. CYRIL held us in a vise grip until we broke for the Christmas holiday. When we reconvened in January 1982, it was as if none of the ugliness had ever happened.

I'd returned to school with a couple hundred dollars, a pair of Calvin Klein jeans, a silver-and-black boom box, and a suitcase loaded with music cassettes by Kool & the Gang, Evelyn "Champagne" King, Prince, and Patrice Rushen. Music had always been the one absolute that we Academy girls could bond over. In the lounge, we'd play one tape after the next, singing our hearts out to Prince's "I Wanna Be Your Lover" and Joan Jett & the Blackhearts' "I Love Rock 'n' Roll."

The semester streaked by without incident, and suddenly it was summer again.

17

That summer, I worked as a file clerk at Herzfeld & Stern, the brokerage house where Vivian had been employed since 1969. By then, Vivian was the supervisor of the new-accounts department. The employees under her direction were all women, most of whom were white.

Eventually, I would learn about the hazards that Black people face when holding positions of power over white people. And I'm sure Vivian was no exception, but if there was any animosity or envy, I was unaware of it because her white coworkers had been in my life since I was a little girl and felt like family. The partners at Herzfeld & Stern adored and respected Vivian because she was a hard worker and congenial. They'd demonstrated their regard in a multitude of ways, but especially with the grand baby shower they threw for the twins at a swanky Manhattan restaurant.

A year or so before that, when she underwent foot surgery, they ferried her to and from work via private car until she was healed enough to safely take the subway again. And she was always well compensated at Christmas.

Before I became a summer employee, my mother would bring Reggie and me to work with her on Saturdays for some double-time-and-a-half money. When we'd exit the subway station at Fulton and Wall Streets, it always felt like we had stepped into a ghost town. This was back before the Financial District was a chic place to live. On Saturdays when we went to work with Vivian, she'd seat us at one of the empty office desks to eat our toasted bagels soaked in butter and jelly, and afterward, we'd stuff envelopes until the first paper cut. Then, we'd spend the rest of the day roaming the office floor, visiting with other Saturday workers, or I'd find an empty desk by a window and read.

When I officially worked there, I spent most of my eight-hour day alphabetizing and filing away hundreds upon hundreds of new-account index cards. I did this in a brightly lit, narrow corridor filled with towering steel-gray file cabinets.

It was boring and tedious work. Work that I could not imagine doing for a lifetime. I felt like I was suffocating, like I was working with a dark blanket over my head. I would experience this cloistered, asphyxiating feeling at every job I held before I became a full-time writer.

The office environment itself was a jovial one. There was lots of conversation and laughter. The guys in the mailroom had a radio that was tuned to a popular R&B station, and so the office was always filled with music, which helped to soften the monotony of our tasks. On my lunch breaks, I usually went outside to get out from under the chilly air-conditioning, grab a slice of pizza, and people watch. Back then, I had no clue that Wall Street was once the site of a very profitable slave market. I didn't know that slavery even existed in the North because we weren't taught that history in school. As far as I was concerned, slavery was a sin of the South and the South alone. I think most people still hold this belief.

～

THE TRUTH, I'D EVENTUALLY COME TO UNDERSTAND, WAS THAT NEW
York was one of the capitals of the American chattel slavery institution, second only to Charleston, South Carolina. This fact was uncovered in 1991 when excavators found the remains of 419 Black
people on a construction site.

When the biological anthropologist Dr. Michael Blakey examined the skeletons, he was quoted as saying, "The bones show the
hardships the Africans faced the moment they stepped off the slave
ships; in some cases, they literally were worked to death."

The construction company went to war against the organization that considered the area hallowed ground and wanted it treated
as such. In the end, the organization won and now a monument
stands in remembrance of those enslaved Africans whom the city
had so casually disremembered.

The incident opened floodgates through which volumes of
hidden history poured. One of the forgotten chapters from that
dark period concerned the luxury clothier Brooks Brothers, a
brand popular among presidents and the 1 percent. Founded in
New York City in 1818, Brooks Brothers made clothing from potato sacks for enslaved people, clothing they called "servant gar-
ments."

Servants get paid, slaves do not.

～

BEFORE I KNEW IT, THE SUMMER WAS OVER AND I WAS BACK AT ST.
Cyril, stepping into the final year of high school.

We girls couldn't stop chattering about the blockbuster movie
E.T. that had reignited the world's interest in extraterrestrial life.
Only the most affluent of us had computers, but that year *Time*

magazine had dubbed the processor Man of the Year. Disco was dead, boogie was on the throne now, and we couldn't get enough of the music by the Gap Band, Gwen Guthrie, and the Bar-Kays.

Times were changing, and we were changing right along with them.

I was a senior now, which meant I had a private bedroom with an en suite bathroom that I shared with Estela. In the three years we'd been at St. Cyril, the two of us had weathered many storms. We'd cried and laughed together, and had our disagreements, but never stayed mad at each other for long. We were bosom buddies. BFFs and day-ones.

And now we were nearly at the end of this chapter of our lives. Sad to be leaving each other but excited for what the future held. Estela and I were already planning my visit to the Dominican Republic.

"Chica," she squawked excitedly as we stretched across her bed, looking at photos from her previous summer at home. "DR is so beautiful; you're going to love it!"

Gazing at the photos, I didn't doubt at all that I would love it, because it looked so much like Barbados to me, with its sandy beaches, palm trees, and crystal-clear waters.

As we inched toward graduation day, I was gripped with excitement and dread. The melancholy rolled in like fog, and planning the trip to the Dominican Republic became the one bright spot in my final year at the Academy. I had accumulated many precious relationships that felt more like kinships than friendships. Apart from the Sheila and Yvonne incident, my time at St. Cyril had been peaceful and joyful. Spending those years surrounded by nature and young girls on the precipice of adulthood had been just what I needed at the time.

St. Cyril had become a haven from the havoc at home. That December, when I went home for the Christmas holidays, events unfolded that would remind me just how bad it was.

IT WAS A FRIDAY NIGHT, ROBERT was at work and Vivian was attending her office holiday party. As usual, I was charged with looking after Reggie and the twins. My cousin James, grandson of Aunt Anna, came over to hang out and help with my sisterly duties. We bought a pizza pie and a liter of Sprite and spent the evening listening to Michael Jackson's *Thriller* album.

It was late when Vivian came home. The twins were tucked into their beds, Reggie was asleep on the futon in the living room, and James and I were in the kitchen, picking at the pepperonis on the last cold slice of pizza. We'd finally retired the *Thriller* album for the night and were listening to *The Quiet Storm* radio show when Vivian came through the door. She was tipsy, we could tell by her stumbling walk and the silly grin plastered across her face.

"I see someone had a good time tonight." James laughed, rising from the table to help her with her coat.

"I'm tired." She giggled, before shuffling off to her bedroom and closing the door. Not long after, we went to bed too.

I didn't know what woke me, but when I opened my eyes, James was standing over me, with my baby brother in his arms. Even in the dark bedroom, I could see the panic on his face.

James whispered, "They're fighting."

THUMP! THUMP!

It sounded like Robert was using her body like a mallet. I could hear the plaster crumbling in the hollow space between our walls.

I jumped out of bed, ran to the door, and swung it open. Reggie was standing in the living room, heaving air like he'd run a fifty-yard dash. He was fourteen years old, tall, and broad-shouldered. He'd had a growth spurt over the past few months, and the hems of his pajama pants now dangled conspicuously high above his ankles. He stood there, one foot ahead of the other, as if some unseen force had stopped him in his tracks.

I turned the knob of their bedroom door and eased it open.

Robert had Vivian in a chokehold. The nozzle of the gun I'd found so many years earlier was pressed against her temple. When I saw that gun, I knew that my long-held fear had finally bore fruit.

"Stop!"

Robert's head reeled around on his neck. His brown eyes were black, blacker than I'd ever seen them.

"Get the fuck out," he snarled, and then lugged my mother's limp body across the room, raised his foot, and kicked the door closed in my face.

I ran into the kitchen and picked up the phone to dial 911. When I pressed the receiver to my ear, I could hear my mother's weeping because the receiver in the bedroom was off the hook. A dial tone was impossible.

Reggie was standing in the doorway, staring at me, waiting for me to make it all stop.

"You have to go to the precinct," I whisper-yelled.

Looking back, I could have gone to a neighbor's apartment to use their phone, but in the moment I wasn't thinking straight.

Reggie went into the bedroom and hurriedly got dressed. Wearing only a dark blue sweat suit and his sneakers, he ran through the bitter December cold to the 71st Precinct on Empire Boulevard.

I went back into my bedroom and found James sitting on my bed, cradling a twin in each arm. They were four years old by then, long and gangly. They no longer liked being held, but on that day, they clung to James like a life raft.

We could hear Vivian's weeping seeping through the wall and Robert chanting:

"I'llblowyourfuckingheadoff.

"I'llblowyourfuckingheadoff.

"I'llblowyourfuckingheadoff.

"I'llblowyourfuckingheadoff."

Each time he uttered the threat I held my breath in anticipation of the gunshot.

And then James cocked his head and asked, "Did you hear that?" I'd heard something, but I thought it had come from outside the window. And then the sound came again, clearer, closer.

It was the crackling of walkie-talkies.

I inched across the room to the doorway and saw five police officers standing in the living room, guns drawn.

My sudden appearance startled them.

"Hands up," they chorused.

My arms rocketed into the air.

"Anybody else in that room?" one of the officers barked, still training the gun on me.

My voice was gone. I nodded.

From behind me came James's quaking voice. "Yes, Officer, I'm here too with a pair of toddlers."

Reggie was standing behind the officers with his fingers laced on top of his head. His eyes darted from me to Robert and Vivian's closed bedroom door.

Had he thought he was too late?

They ordered him into the room with us, and he rushed into my arms, bawling.

An officer kicked in my parents' bedroom door, and suddenly the apartment was filled with barking and shouting voices:

"Drop your weapon!"

"Get down on the ground!"

"Hands behind your back!"

How was this real life? How was this my life?

Suddenly, Vivian was in the room, sniveling and swiping tears from her eyes. We were so grateful to see her alive that we all burst into tears.

"It's okay, it's okay," she said. "I'm okay."

She was already at the closet, ripping clothes from the wire hangers and tossing them onto the bed.

We were leaving . . . again.

As I rose to help, I hoped to God she meant it this time. He had put a gun to her head, for goodness' sake!

The cops didn't arrest Robert because there weren't any bullets in the gun.

"He just had a little too much to drink is all," one officer said when he saw the flabbergasted look on Vivian's face.

"But," he added snidely, "if you feel the *need* to, you can go to the precinct and file a complaint."

They did hang around until we were all packed. As we filed out of the bedroom, I chanced a glance at Robert. He was sitting on the bed in his boxer shorts and T-shirt, head hung, staring down at his clasped hands.

WE WENT TO THELMA'S LIKE we always did.

Mother and daughter sat at the dining room table staring silently at the television in the living room. There really wasn't much to say. In the seventeen years my parents had been married, Thelma had used all the words she possessed to convince Vivian to leave that man who drank and fought her and then promised not to drink and fight her, and then turned around and did it all over again.

Vivian was tired, but Thelma was tired too. We were all tired.

Vivian reached for her Newports and fumbled with the thin plastic wrapping. "I'm done for real this time, Mama, I'm really, really finished with him."

Eyes fixed on the television screen, Thelma leaned back into her chair, curled her hand around her chin, humming, "Mm-hmm."

IN AN EFFORT TO MAKE things feel normal for us kids, Wilfred went out and bought a live tree and ornaments. On Christmas morning, most of the gifts under the tree were toys for the twins. The presents

Reggie and I unwrapped were sweaters and socks and underwear. Our real Christmas gifts came in the form of cold hard cash.

As one day rolled into the next, I noticed that Vivian was coming home later and later from work. When I asked why, she told me that she was putting in overtime.

"You believe that, Bernice?" Thelma sidled up beside me one night when I was standing at the sink washing the last of the dinner dishes. "You really believe your mother is working overtime?"

It was near eight o'clock, and Vivian still wasn't home.

"Humph," she grunted. "Well, if you believe that, I've got a bridge I'd like to sell you."

I knew what Thelma was insinuating, but I wouldn't allow myself to believe it. How could Vivian go back to him after what he'd done to her?

Well, there weren't bullets in the gun. The officers' words floated in my mind. Were they floating in hers too?

"There ain't that much love in the world . . ." Thelma's words trailed off as she climbed the stairs to her bedroom.

A FEW DAYS BEFORE I returned to school, Vivian came to me and said, "Your father wants to see you before you go back."

I just stared at her.

"Bernice, he is *still* your *father*," she added when I didn't respond.

These words have been used for generations to keep children in abusive homes and connected to abusive parents. No matter the offense, we are expected to:

Turn the other cheek.

Kiss and make up.

Let bygones be bygones.

Bury the hatchet.

Absolve.

Forget.

Excuse.

Forgive.

So, I went to see him, not because I agreed with Vivian, but be-cause I believed it. What we believe in and what we agree to don't always align.

I had to take two trains and two buses to travel from Queens to Brooklyn. The Q7 bus was the worst part of the journey because it was notoriously slow and it wasn't uncommon to wait for an hour for it to arrive, which was the case on that frigid December day.

When I let myself into the apartment, I was met with the sound of whistling radiators. I was grateful for the heat, because my toes and fingers were numb with cold. The air reeked of cigarette smoke and fried pork chops. Robert had strung a rope across the width of the living room. It sagged with the weight of his laundered socks and briefs, undershirts, and brown UPS uniforms.

The bedroom door was open, and through the canopy of drying clothes, I could see the sporadic blue-white light beaming off the television screen. Robert was in bed, lying on his side with his back to the open doorway.

"Daddy?"

He didn't move, and so I called again, louder this time.

He jerked awake. "Hello? Bernice?"

"Yes, it's me."

He turned over, sat up, and twisted the bedspread around his waist. "Turn on the light."

I flicked the switch on the wall, and the room flooded with the soft yellow beam.

I didn't want to look at him.

I couldn't look at him.

It'd only occurred to me when I stepped into the apartment that he might have summoned me there to kill me in retaliation for Vivian having left him. I'd heard that men sometimes did things like that. Killed the children and then themselves. Murder suicide.

"How have you been?"

The question surprised me. He'd never asked me about myself, he'd only ever told me how I *should* feel.

"F-fine."

He sighed softly, sadly, and then reached for his pack of Camels on the nightstand.

That's when I allowed myself to look at him. To really look at him. He was in desperate need of a haircut and a shave. I'd never seen him with more than a bit of stubble on his cheeks, but on that day his face was splotchy with whiskers.

He picked up the pack of cigarettes and then, as an after-thought, set them back down. When he looked at me again, I saw that his eyes were puffy and red, as if he'd not slept in days. And his face was drawn, free of the edema that comes with the consumption of copious amounts of alcohol. He looked meek and harmless and pitiful.

"Come over here and give your father a kiss."

A kiss? I don't remember a time when we'd had an affectionate father-daughter exchange like that.

Nevertheless, I took a deep breath, quickly crossed the room, bent over, and brushed my lips against his whiskered cheek. Robert threw his arms around me, and for a weird, wild moment I thought he was going to put me in a chokehold like he'd done to Vivian.

But he didn't, it was just a clumsy, awkward attempt at an embrace, which ended with him patting my back like one pats a dog.

Whatever conversation we had was one-sided, with pockets of hollow silences filled by dialogue and laugh tracks and commercial jingles emitting from the television. Thirty minutes in, the painful visit came to an end.

"Hand me my wallet," he said, pointing at the mahogany wood armoire behind me.

He flipped through the billfold and retrieved two tens and a five.

"Here."

"Thank you," I said as I folded the money and stuffed the bills into the back pocket of my jeans. "Goodbye."

I turned around and practically ran out of the room.

The following week, Reggie was summoned, but when he returned to Queens, he had fifty dollars.

THE WRITING WAS ON THE wall. Vivian was going to go back. The overtime charade came to an end when one night she didn't come home at all.

Tired of waiting up for her, I went to bed. It was nearly dawn when I heard the front door open, and the sound of an idling car swept in with the December chill. I could only imagine that it was Robert's car. I slipped out of bed and stood in the dark space at the top of the stairs, watching as she tiptoed in like a teenager well past her curfew.

She was shrugging off her coat when she spied me glaring down at her. "Who the hell are you looking at like that?"

I withered. "Nobody," I mumbled before heading back into the bedroom.

Days later, I was on a Trailways coach headed back to school. A week after that, when I called Thelma's house hoping to speak with Vivian, Thelma let me know that she, Reggie, and the twins were back in Brooklyn.

I was shattered.

PART FOUR

A MIRROR
TO MY SOUL

*There is always one moment in childhood when
the door opens and lets the future in.*

—GRAHAM GREENE

18

In May 1983, I graduated from St. Cyril and returned home to a transformed neighborhood.

The Chinese restaurant where Vivian, Reggie, and I had enjoyed many egg foo young dinners beneath the colorful paper Chinese lamps, had gotten rid of the cozy red leather booths and now only served takeout from behind bulletproof plexiglass. Henry's greengrocer's was now a bodega run by a family from Puerto Rico. The shoe store, bakery, and clothing boutiques were now beauty salons, barbershops, and Caribbean restaurants. When I'd left for school in 1979, there were still a few white people living on my block, but when I returned, they were all gone. Some had died, and others had simply moved away.

That summer I resumed my job as a file clerk at Herzfeld & Stern. I spent my free time hanging out with Michelle, who was working as a clerk in the billing department of a hospital.

When I was at St. Cyril, I didn't read much, because I didn't have anything to run from. The hours I spent with my head in a book at home had been dedicated to making up dance routines with my friends or hunched over a sewing machine in the home economics classroom stitching together outfits to wear to the dances we had with the boys' boarding schools. The other thing that dampened my interest was that I was growing tired of reading about people who didn't look like me, didn't live in the type of neighborhood I lived in, and didn't listen to the type of music I listened to.

In the language arts classes at St. Cyril, we were assigned books written by Jane Austen, John Steinbeck, Emily Brontë, Nathaniel Hawthorne, Emily Dickinson, Walt Whitman, and Robert Frost. "These books are classics," our teacher told us. "Classics, written by the masters of literature!"

None of the *masters* were Black, and a scant few were women, so what was a young Black girl of American and Caribbean descent, born and raised in Brooklyn, with dreams of becoming a writer, to think?

Well, I'll tell you what I thought. I thought that Black writers did not exist. I knew that they had existed at one time way back during the Harlem renaissance, but that was a long, long time ago, like the prehistoric age. I assumed that they too had gone the way of the dinosaurs and the dodo bird, save for Alex Haley, who was the only living Black writer I was aware of at the time. Joycelyn Elders, a Black American woman who served as surgeon general of the United States under the Clinton administration, said it best: *You can't be what you don't see.*

So, when the time came to apply for college, I ditched the idea of becoming a writer for a career in fashion, only because I liked clothes and I wanted to travel, and from what I'd gathered from flipping through glossy fashion magazines, that industry would satisfy both desires. I applied to the Fashion Institute of Technology, Johnson & Wales University, and Laboratory Institute of Merchandising and was accepted into the latter.

BUT NOW THAT I WAS back home, under Robert's tyrannical rule, I returned to reading with ferocity. All through high school, I'd not written much outside of class assignments, but that summer, I gradually began to revisit the practice that I had started way back when I was nine years old.

The first story I penned at that young age was a racy tale that was largely plagiarized from one of the Jackie Collins's novels Vivian kept hidden away in her underwear drawer. Vivian was in the kitchen preparing dinner when I set the handwritten pages on the table.

"What's this?"

"I wrote a story," I proudly announced.

"Oh?" She lowered the fire under the pot of rice, sat down, and reached for the pages. Beaming, I watched her eyes travel down the length of the written page that was rife with depictions of sexual acts no nine-year-old should have been aware of or privy to. She glanced at me before turning the page over and reading to the end. When she looked at me again, she seemed to be squinting, like one does when they're anticipating imminent discomfort, like the prick of a needle.

"Um, Bernice," she started carefully. "These things you've written about, have you experienced them?"

"What things?"

She shifted uncomfortably in her chair. "The sex things."

I grimaced at the question. Of course I hadn't experienced the sex things; it was just a made-up story, not real life.

"N-no," I stammered.

Vivian nodded and then rested her palm on the paper.

"Are you sure, Bernice?" Her eyes bored into me. "Don't lie to me."

I didn't want to tell her that I had been sneaking to read the paper novels she kept hidden away in her drawer. If I told her that I'd been riffling through her things, I'd get in trouble, and I certainly didn't want that. But I wasn't a liar, because even at that young age, I knew I was horrible at it, and lying usually made things worse.

She extended her hand to me. "Come here." Her voice was so serious, I knew for sure that I was in trouble. I moved closer to her, and she closed her hand around my forearm.

"Bernice, you know you could tell me anything, right?"

"Yes."

"If someone has touched you—"

I snatched my arm away.

"No, no one has touched me," I sputtered angrily.

She'd drilled into me about how men, and sometimes women, touched children inappropriately, and how important it was to tell her when and if that ever happened to me.

"You promise to tell me if that ever happens to you?" she said.

"Yes, Mommy, I promise."

But I hadn't kept that promise. I hadn't told her about the time Henry, of Henry's greengrocer's, had patted me on the behind once when I went in to buy a bag of flour, and I'd certainly not told her about J.J. asking me to show him my pussy.

"Are you sure, Bernice?" she pressed.

"I—I copied it from your books," I finally sputtered.

"My books?" The concern on her face melted into confusion. "What books?"

"In—in your dresser drawer."

The truth shall set you free.

Vivian released the grip on my arm.

"Oh," she sighed, relieved. Then her face hardened. "So you been going through my things?"

She went on to lecture me about respecting her privacy, as well as reading books that were written for children and not adults. She didn't punish me, but she warned me to stay out of her things, or else.

After the lecture, she returned to the stove, raised the lid on the pot, and waved away the cloud of steam that wafted up into her face. When it seemed the moment had passed, I timidly asked if she'd liked the story.

Vivian side-eyed me before nodding. "Yeah, it was really good."

I beamed. "I think that's what I want to be."

"What?"

"A writer. I want to be a writer."

She set the lid back down onto the pot and turned to face me.

"Oh yeah? That's nice," she said, before wagging her finger at me. "I'll tell you one thing: you better stay out of my stuff. You hear me?"

"Yes, Mommy."

Weeks passed before I broke the commandment she'd set. I was helpless, you see, because the books called to me like sirens, and soon enough, I answered. I'm sure Vivian knew, but she never moved the books, and we never spoke about it again. I'd go on to write other stories beyond that filthy first one, stories that closely mirrored my complicated life in apartment A5.

I'D BEEN HOME TWO MONTHS when I discovered *The Color Purple* on the bookshelf wedged between *Carrie* and *The Carpetbaggers*. I plucked the hardcover from the shelf and stared at the cover image of the little country house surrounded by the bold purple letters of the title and the author's name, Alice Walker.

It was a well-read copy with dog-eared pages and annotations in the margins. These notes were not made in Vivian's looping script, which led me to believe that the book had been passed along to her.

I took *The Color Purple* to my bed, lay down, folded one leg over the other, and began.

Dear God,

I am fourteen years old. ~~I am~~ I have always been a good girl. Maybe you can give me a sign letting me know what is happening to me.

The opening lines spoke directly to me, and I felt seen in a way that I had never experienced in my reading life. Here was a girl, a Black girl, just a few years younger than I, who was as tortured as I was.

She was a good girl. I was a good girl. But for her that did not seem to be good enough, because she was Black and ugly and the teenage mother of two children, sired by her father.

When I finished the book, the sun was gone, and the sky was slathered in that soft violet of a summer evening. I closed the book and marveled at the emotions swirling in my chest. Over a span of 245 pages, I had been cracked wide-open. Here, finally, was a story about my people—my messy, beautiful, dangerous, loving, grieving, curious, joyful Black people. Black people like the people who raised me. Black people like the people who raised the people who raised me. I saw my entire family spread across those pages. Every single character in that book was familiar to me. I was so elated, so grateful, that when I closed the book, I wept. I'd never read a book that made me cry.

Then, after the tears, came the giddiness of discovery, the flying falling feeling of tumbling headlong in love.

The obsession was immediate.

I needed more stories written by Black writers about Black people, specifically Black women. And so, with *The Color Purple* as my flare, I trekked off into the literary wetlands in search of more.

By the time I walked into my first class at LIM, I had already lost interest in working in fashion. That first semester, I managed to maintain a decent GPA, but the following semester I flunked out.

19

One of the requirements as a freshman at LIM was to obtain a paid or unpaid internship within the fashion industry. A few of my classmates were able to secure positions as assistant admins, clerks, or gophers with the fashion rags, but most of us found work as sales associates at luxury stores like Saks Fifth Avenue, Barneys, and B. Altman. I was hired as temporary holiday help for the Christmas season rush at Abraham & Straus department store on Fulton Street in downtown Brooklyn. Vivian had shopped there for my entire life. My title was sales associate, but I spent most of my time ringing up purchases and returns on the register and tidying up the sales floor after the store closed.

It was at A&S that I met my first great love.

His name was Ellis, and he worked in the electronics department. He was dark with full lips and an inviting smile. He caught my eye the day I went with Vivian to buy a Commodore computer for Reggie's upcoming birthday.

I stood shyly by, sneaking admiring glances at him as he

explained things to Vivian, using technical language that neither of us understood. At the register, I showed my ID card so Vivian could get my store discount. Ellis looked at the card and then up at me.

"Oh, yeah, I thought you looked familiar," he said, handing the card back to me. "What floor do you work on?"

"Third."

He handed the receipt to me and winked. "See you around."

"He seems nice," Vivian remarked as we made our way to the bank of elevators.

A few days later, I looked up from my register and there he was. "Hi."

"Hi," I chirped, nervously smoothing my hand over my hair. It was near closing time, and I was counting my drawer.

"Did you have a good day?"

"Um, yeah. You?"

"Yeah."

I looked down at the money in my hands. I had no idea how much I'd counted. I would have to start all over again.

"Well"—he smiled—"I'll come by and see you tomorrow," he said before winking and strolling off.

"Okay," I squeaked.

It went on like that for a week or so, him popping up just to say hello. His presence made me feel lightheaded and giddy in a way the man I was involved with at the time didn't.

Melvin was the brother of my good friend Alden, whom I'd met just before I went off to high school, when he started visiting his sister during the summer months. He was from a big Georgia family. There were thirteen or fourteen of them, mostly boys, if I am remembering correctly. The sister lived in my building. She was a single mother of a little boy, and I'd known her for a few years by the time her brothers began coming to visit and then moving to Brooklyn for good.

I'd met Melvin when I was a fifteen-year-old sophomore and he was nineteen. I don't know how long he had his eyes on me, but when I reached the age of consent, he began making his feelings known.

Because he was older than me, already had a child, and drove a van, I knew my parents would balk at me dating him, so we snuck around like thieves.

Our clandestine relationship was almost discovered one night when we were sitting in his parked van in front of the building. It was a steamy night, the windows were down, and it was closing in on midnight when Melvin caught sight of Robert in his sideview mirror.

"Shit," he hissed. "Your father."

It was one of those nights when Robert had doubled back home. My soul left my body as I dribbled out of the seat and down to the floor of the van like hot candle wax.

"Hello, Mr. McFadden," Melvin said, lifting his hand in greeting.

Robert nodded at him, turned, and strolled into the building. When the door had slammed closed behind him, Melvin looked down at me and burst into laughter.

He was always a perfect gentleman, never pressuring me for sex, even though it was clear that's what he wanted. I wanted it too; most of my friends had given their virginity away, and it seemed as though I was the last holdout. Some of them, unbeknownst to their mothers, were on birth control pills.

"When you going to do *it*, Bernice?"

My mind wanted me to do *it*, and my body certainly wanted me to do *it*, but I was still terrified of getting pregnant.

Just make sure he uses a condom. You won't get pregnant if he uses a condom.

Pulling out works too.

Na-aah. My cousin's boyfriend pulled out, and now her mama is planning her baby shower.

A WEEK BEFORE MY EIGHTEENTH birthday, I made up my mind to do *it*.

"Are you sure?"

"Yes."

Melvin shared an apartment on Union Street with an older brother. We planned to meet up there, after his brother went off to his night job. I'd told Vivian that I was going to spend the night with my friend Michelle, who lived a half-hour walk in the opposite direction. I went to Michelle's house at 7:00 p.m. and hung out there until eleven. After which, I told *her* mother that I was going home. I then walked the forty-five minutes to Melvin's.

He was waiting for me with a bottle of Manischewitz wine and a joint. He was tender and patient with me, and I couldn't have asked for a better first experience. But I wasn't in love with him, and I wanted to be in love, and that's what I thought the butterflies were telling me when I was with Ellis.

BUTTERFLIES.

We're told that when we feel butterflies it's a good thing, but the truth is that butterflies are our internal warning system. Melvin was too *nice* and drama-free, being with him never set off my warning system. I would learn far too late in life that people who grew up in dysfunctional and chaotic households often misconstrue emotionally healthy and mature partners as boring. I can't tell you the number of men I kept in the friend zone because of this.

I was smitten with Ellis because he was handsome and charismatic and closer in age. He didn't have any children and was a college student like me. Also, Ellis was of Barbadian descent, so we had that in common.

Ellis had dreams of becoming a pro-basketball player, and I told him I wanted to be a writer.

"A writer? Like romance?"

I shrugged.

Melvin, on the other hand, had graduated high school but

hadn't gone to college and wasn't planning to. He worked as a gas station attendant, and I don't remember what aspirations he had beyond that. And while my maternal people had come from Georgia and he was Georgia born and bred, that wasn't enough to keep me interested. Once Ellis was in my sights, Melvin faded into the distance. It was an amicable parting, because he was moving to Boston where some of his other brothers were already living.

THOSE FIRST FEW WEEKS ELLIS showered me with attention, visiting me on the sales floor several times a day, catching the same train as me, and keeping me on the phone late into the night. During those lengthy conversations we spoke about work, our hopes, dreams, disappointments, and our terrible fathers.

"Yeah, my pops was mad abusive."

His parents had separated when he was a little boy. Ellis's memory of him was fuzzy, save for the violence, which was crystallized in his mind. It wasn't long before I'd developed deep feelings. After we consummated the relationship, I was convinced that I was in love when in fact I was dickmatized.

Dickmatized is a condition of being addicted to a man who's no good for you, and the only explanation is because you have been hypnotized by his penis.

Symptoms include but are not limited to:

1. The inability to see and/or acknowledge red flags.

2. Putting his needs and wants before your own, believing
    what he says and not what you've seen with your own
    two eyes. (See side effect #1.)

ONE DAY, ELLIS AND I were lounging on the couch in the living room of his apartment. His mother was at work, and his younger sister, Diane, was away at boarding school, so we had the place to ourselves. There was a basketball game on the television, which meant that he was paying me no mind, and I was bored to tears. I spotted a book peeking out from the clutter of VHS tapes on the middle shelf of the television stand.

It was *Sula* by Toni Morrison. Diane's name was inscribed on the inside page.

On the television, a player dunked the ball, the crowd cheered. And Ellis pumped his fists in the air, yelling, "That's right, yes!"

I flipped the book over, and read the description: *Two girls who grow up to become women. Two friends who become something worse than enemies . . .*

I waved the book in his face.

"What?" he crowed annoyingly.

"Can I borrow this?"

"Sure, I don't care," he said, leaning closer to the television.

That was my introduction to Toni Morrison. I gobbled *Sula* up as quickly as I had consumed *The Color Purple*. I was mesmerized by the language. I didn't know a novel could read like poetry. I was so obsessed that within weeks I reread the story for a second time, but this time I read slowly and deliberately, pausing to meditate on the imagery, metaphors, and turns of phrase. I wondered if I would ever be able to write like that.

I took my inspiration to the page and penned a few lines about a tall woman with skin as dark as a black hollyhock petal. Eventually I would learn that her name was Sugar.

Alice Walker had planted the seed, and now with the arrival of Toni Morrison, germination was under way. I never returned the book. I still have it. It is a sacred limb on my literary genealogy tree.

20

On an incredibly sunny, bitterly cold February day, Ellis and I were hurrying down Utica Avenue toward his place. As we walked, tiny plastic crack vials scattered like bread crumbs crunched beneath our sneaker-clad feet.

It was 1984, Ronald Reagan was president, and his wife, Nancy, was pleading for Americans to just say no to drugs, this even as the CIA flooded Black and brown communities with crack cocaine that was so highly addictive it made it extremely difficult, if not virtually impossible, to say no.

"Hey, hey," I called to Ellis. "Slow down."

I'd begun to take notice that Ellis made it a habit to walk ahead of me rather than alongside of me.

"Oh."

He slowed his gait.

For the few months we'd been a couple, I'd come to realize that the thing we did most was have sex, which was a favorite pastime for both of us, of course, but I longed to do other things, like go to the movies or out dancing. Things that my girlfriends did with their boyfriends.

Us just having sex made me feel less like his girlfriend and more like a whore.

I reached for his hand, and he snatched it away.

"Hey, hey," he cawed, shoving his hand into his coat pocket. "It's too cold for all of that."

In the warm apartment, I shrugged off my coat and flopped down on the couch. Ellis turned on the television, settled down next to me, threw his arm around my shoulder, and pulled me to him. He bent to kiss me, and I turned my face away.

"What?"

I didn't want to rock the boat, but I needed to speak my mind. "Am I your girlfriend?"

He rolled his eyes. "Yes, I've told you that several times, why do you keep asking me that?"

"Because we don't do girlfriend and boyfriend things, other than have sex."

"What are you saying? You want to have sex with someone else?"

This type of rebuttal, I would learn when I was a very grown woman, is called deflection.

"What? That's not what I said . . . ," I blurted, already panicked that he was accusing me of cheating or wanting to cheat.

"Do you want to break up with me?"

I didn't want that either, I just didn't want to feel like a call girl. "No, no . . . but I . . ."

And then he said the thing that I had long suspected but could not admit to myself.

"Well," he started carefully, "sometimes I feel embarrassed being seen with you because of your . . . face."

My stomach dropped to the floor.

"I mean it's *not me*. You know I think that you're a beautiful person inside and out. But it makes me uncomfortable when I see people staring at you the way they do. . . ."

I just sat there on the couch, shrinking with every word that tumbled out of his mouth.

He closed his hand over mine. "You know what I mean, right?"

I nodded like a fucking idiot. I nodded like his words weren't slicing my heart and drizzling lime juice into the gashes.

"Remember when we talked about plastic surgery. . . ."

Yes, it was true. I had considered plastic surgery, but it had been only a consideration. After all, I'd been living with my scarred face and hand for sixteen years, they were a part of me, like my nose and ears. I never thought about my scars until someone questioned me about them, and that happened with less frequency as the years went by.

But clearly, Ellis couldn't be seen with me the way I needed him to be seen with me because of my disfiguration. Because I was eighteen and in love and desperate not to lose him, I went to Vivian and told her that I wanted to speak to a doctor about getting my face fixed.

"Where's this coming from all of a sudden?" She scrutinized me through a cloud of cigarette smoke.

I shrugged and looked away.

"You know you're beautiful just as you are, right?"

She had drilled that into me ever since I was a little girl when I was bullied in school for the way I looked.

I nodded, mumbling, "Yeah, I know."

That was a lie.

She sighed. "Okay, Bernice. Okay."

My pediatrician referred me to a doctor at Kings County Hospital, which was the same miraculous place where Anna had had her vocal cords rebuilt.

AS I'VE MENTIONED, FIRE SEEMS to be a theme in my family. On March 19, 1958, three days after Vivian celebrated her fifteenth birthday, Thelma was tackling a dirty toilet at the home of the white people she cleaned for, Vivian and Peggy were at school, and Anna was at her job at the Monarch Underwear Company factory, sniffing the air.

"Y'all smell smoke?"

The woman working next to her looked up from her task and inhaled. "Yeah, I do."

Within seconds, there was black smoke foaming across the ceiling, and mass hysteria followed. The workers scrambled to the only exit on the floor and found that the door was locked. Screaming, crying, and gasping for breath, they huddled together in the smoke-darkened room and waited for the end. Anna closed her hands over her mouth and prayed.

Our father, who art in heaven . . .

Suddenly, there was the sound of breaking glass, and Anna lowered her hands to see the silver blade of a flat-head ax glinting in the sunlight. Anna thought she was looking at an angel, but it was an angel in disguise.

The firefighter chopped away the glass, threw a blanket over the bottom side of the jagged opening, and extended his gloved hand to her. "Come on!" he yelled over the roaring flames.

That day, twenty-four people lost their lives in that fire. Eighteen of the dead were women. It's a miracle that Anna wasn't one of them.

The smoke and heat had severely damaged Anna's vocal cords. The doctors at Columbus Hospital told her that she would never talk again and sent her home with her smoke-soaked clothes in a paper bag. In the weeks that followed, Anna went to several doctors, all of whom issued the same grave diagnosis.

"Sorry, Ms. Griffin, there's nothing that can be done."

But Anna was a praying woman and God's good servant and was convinced that the Lord would not desert her in her time of need.

The year was coming to an end when someone referred her to a physician at Kings County Hospital. She walked into that hospital dressed in her go-to Sunday meeting dress, with her Bible in her purse and a rosary clutched in her fist.

After the examination, the hazel-eyed doctor closed his hand over hers and smiled.

"It's not as bad as you've been told. I can rebuild your vocal cords."

"I knew Jesus would fix it. I knew it," she'd say whenever she recounted the story.

On the operating table, just before the anesthesia took hold, she stared up into the bright lights and made a silent vow to God. *Dear Lord, if you give me my voice back, I promise to use my voice to praise your name for the rest of my life. Amen.*

Two months after the surgery, Anna uttered the first words she'd spoken in almost a year. That Sunday, she went to service at Plymouth Congregational Church and sat in the third pew, bubbling with her secret. Then the time came when the Reverend Bert Holmes looked out over his congregants and extended the weekly invitation:

"Is there anyone who would like to come to the altar to accept Jesus Christ as his Lord and Savior?"

Anna rose to her feet, raised both arms into the air, and made her way to the altar.

Before the fire, Anna had read her Bible daily but only attended church sporadically. But since then, she'd attended every Sunday service and midweek Bible study class. God had answered her prayers, and she was now ready to honor the promise she made to him.

"Sister Rose." Reverend Holmes opened his arms, and she fell into them, whispering, "Amen, amen, amen . . ."

When he heard her voice, the reverend reared back in surprise. "You can speak?"

Anna nodded.

The reverend looked out over the congregants and shouted, "She can speak!"

The audience erupted, clapping and yelping with joy.

"Praise the Lord!"

"Thank you, Jesus!"

"Miracle upon miracles!"

I WAS HOPING FOR A miracle too.

The surgeon was a tall, thin Sikh man with bushy eyebrows and a warm smile. He explained that he would cut live skin from the side of my head. "Just a track, it'll be virtually unnoticeable," he assured me when he saw the alarm in my eyes.

"I'll stitch here," he said, running his finger along the part of my face where the fire had eaten away my hairline. "Within a month the live skin will meld with the dead skin and hair will grow.

"Now, for the side of your face," he continued, "I'll insert a balloon in your cheek to stretch the skin out. That will take some time."

"How much time?" Vivian asked.

"Maybe six weeks, depending."

We exchanged glances.

"You'll have to come in every week for me to pump it, and then when it's stretched out enough, I'll cut that damaged skin off and replace it with skin from your belly or your buttocks." He chuckled after he said *buttocks*. "And after a few months, the live skin will fuse and heal and voilà, you'll have a new face."

"How long will that take?" I asked.

"About a year to eighteen months."

I DIDN'T HAVE A YEAR to eighteen months to become beautiful, because I'd learned that Ellis was cheating on me. In my young mind, he was unfaithful because I wasn't pretty enough. I didn't know men cheated no matter how pretty their wives or girlfriends were.

I found out about his infidelity one night when I was over at his house. He'd stepped out to get some Chinese food for us, leaving me in the apartment alone. The phone rang and rang and rang. Then it stopped and rang and rang again. The third time it chimed, I picked up.

"Hello?"

"H-hello? Diane?"

"No."

"Oh. May I speak to Ellis?"

My feathers ruffled. Who the hell was this woman calling to speak to my man? I didn't have men calling my house to speak to me.

"He stepped out, can I take a message?"

She must have detected the ice in my voice, because when she responded, there was fire in hers.

"Just tell him his *girlfriend* called."

"Girlfriend? I'm his girlfriend!"

"Oh, really, and who the hell are you?!"

Ellis came through the door during our verbal jousting. He dropped the bag of food on the table, snatched the phone from my hand, and pressed the receiver to his ear.

"Hello . . ."

As he listened to her rant and rave, his eyes shot daggers into my face.

"Okay . . . okay. I'll call you back," he said.

She slammed the phone down so hard, I could hear it from where I was standing.

Ellis set the phone down, balled his fists, and sneered, "What did you do?"

"She said she was your—"

"Why the hell are you answering my fucking phone? You don't fucking live here. When I'm over by you, do I answer your fucking phone?"

We argued for more than an hour, and somehow by the end I was the one at fault and he was the victim. And then we had sex, and it was all better again.

Dickmatized.

IN THE END, I ELECTED to do the hairline reconstruction procedure. "I'll think about the skin balloon thing," I told the surgeon.

Today, the procedure would be an outpatient surgery, but in 1984, I spent a week in the hospital. After seven days, I returned home, with my head wrapped in so many layers of gauze that I looked like I was wearing a turban. I certainly didn't want to be seen like that, and so I hid out in the apartment for weeks until the bandages were removed. By then, I'd become a member of the Book of the Month Club, and so I had plenty of novels to keep me occupied. I was deeply into horror then, plowing through everything by Stephen King and Dean Koontz.

Weeks later, I returned to Kings County Hospital to have my bandages removed. When the surgeon presented me with a hand mirror, I gazed at my reflection with utter disappointment. I'd expected to look like a supermodel, but instead I still looked like me, save for the track of pink flesh stitched over the cavity of previously exposed charred flesh.

"Awww," Vivian cooed. "Would you look at that."

The wonder in her voice was unmistakable, but I couldn't see the marvel of it all. I lowered the mirror.

"It's healing really well, looks even better than I expected," the surgeon said, beaming.

"How long before the hair grows in?" I asked.

"Hmm, you should start seeing some growth in about six to eight weeks."

Six to eight weeks seemed like a lifetime, and I knew Ellis wouldn't wait around that long.

"Hmm," Ellis said once the bandages were removed. "You still kind of look the same."

21

A few months later, I took my same-looking face to the Dominican Republic.

I arrived on a steamy Saturday, thrilled to be reuniting with my school friend Estela. The sun was high and bright in a cloudless sky so pale blue it was almost white. When I stepped off the aircraft, I took a deep breath, filling my lungs with the aromatic scents that are so unique to tropical locations.

In the terminal, when Estela spotted me, she hollered, "¡Amiga!"

We rushed into each other's arms and squeezed. In the car, Estela spoke excitedly to me in a mixture of English and Spanish. At St. Cyril I'd developed a proficient ability to speak and understand Spanish and Haitian Creole. In the years that followed, I would lose that ability, but in 1984, I was still adept. As Estela chattered on, my eyes drifted to the countryside around us. Palm trees, lush vegetation, small wood houses, elegant casitas, and white sand beaches that stretched for miles. The sea was as beautiful and inviting as I remembered from those summers I'd spent in Barbados as a child. The memories filled me with a dizzying sense of nostalgia.

Estela and her parents lived in a sprawling Spanish-style one-level house in Santiago de los Caballeros, the second-largest city in the Dominican Republic. Her father was a well-to-do business owner, and her mother was a stay-at-home wife. They had servants, which both intrigued me and made me uncomfortable at the same time. Maybe it was because I had family members who had made a living, and some who still made a living, as domestics.

Every afternoon from noon until three, Estela's father closed his shop for siesta and came home to enjoy a lavish lunch of fried fish, mangú, tostones, and arroz dominicano. Afterward, we'd down tasty squares of dulce de leche with cups of heavily creamed and sugared coffee.

Most days were spent on the beach, touring the island, and visiting sights of interest. One day, we found ourselves on a lookout point way up in the mountains. Estela pointed across the lush green carpet of trees.

"That's Haiti over there."

I was stunned, because up until that moment I was under the impression that the Dominican Republic and Haiti were separate islands, not two countries sharing one rock. The other thing I was supremely unaware of at that time was the hostile relationship between the two nations.

CHRISTOPHER COLUMBUS LANDED ON HAITI IN 1492, CLAIMED IT FOR Spain, christened it La Isla Española, and then wasted no time enslaving, murdering, raping, and annihilating the three million Taino people who had called the island home for thousands of years. The French came along in the seventeenth century and set up a colony on the west side of the island called Saint Dominique. Over the next few years, the French and Spanish warred over control of the island, until finally they settled their dispute by splitting the island into two colonies in 1697.

When I was growing up, if you spoke Spanish, you were Puerto Rican. So I just assumed all of my Spanish-speaking classmates from kindergarten straight through middle school were Puerto Rican, because I hadn't been taught otherwise. But when I went off to boarding school, I had Spanish-speaking classmates from Mexico, the Dominican Republic, Costa Rica, Ecuador, and Honduras. I'd gone to middle school with a lot of Haitian kids, and it hurt me to see the indifferent, and often outright cruel, treatment those students received from their classmates and teachers. I knew firsthand what it felt like to be on the receiving end of that type of behavior.

For weeks, the nightly news reported on the hundreds upon hundreds of Haitian refugees, or "boat people" as they were called, risking their lives crossing the ocean in fishing boats built to hold four people but thick with five times that amount. Many made it to Florida, but many more did not when the overcrowded boats capsized, and desperate people were swallowed by the pitiless Atlantic. The survivors settled in Miami and in the Crown Heights and Flatbush neighborhoods that were thriving melting pots of immigrants representing every single Caribbean island.

I didn't know a thing about Haiti or Haitians, other than what I'd glimpsed on the news and gleaned from my friends, who'd been warned to steer clear of Haitians because they practiced voodoo and we didn't want to end up a zombie, did we? When the Haitian children immigrants entered school, they were placed two grades behind because they spoke broken English or no English at all. As soon as the HIV/AIDS epidemic erupted in 1981, Haitian people became the scapegoats alongside gay men—because the disease spread through their communities like wildfire. What the news did not tell us was that the virus had been around since the 1800s.

All I had been told about the Haitian people was negative and disparaging. The information that was purposely kept from me was that in 1791 the twelve-year-long bloody rebellion against their

French enslavers won Haitians their freedom, and on January 1, 1804, Haiti became the first Black republic in the western hemisphere. I wouldn't learn this history for many, many more years, and when I did, the part about Haiti having to pay former enslavers and their descendants reparations over several generations, to the tune of twenty billion dollars, would not be included in that lesson.

Haiti's triumph inspired other Caribbean and Latin American nations, and like a row of toppling dominoes, one country after the next seized their freedom. On February 9, 1822, Haiti abolished slavery in the Dominican Republic, which should have garnered them lifelong gratitude from the Dominican people, but that was not the case. In fact, the event was virtually scrubbed from the history books. One hundred years in the future, dictator Rafael Trujillo, fearful of the darkening of his beloved Dominican population, claimed Haitians were a blight on the country. He branded them murderers and cattle thieves and ordered their extermination. In October 1937, over six days, nearly fifty thousand Haitian men, women, and children were murdered in a genocide known as the Parsley Massacre. Trujillo's own maternal grandmother was Haitian, and that's all I have to say about that.

I was eighteen going on nineteen, and I didn't know so very many things, including the fact that that's how America preferred it.

22

After years of hounding, Robert finally agreed to buy a house. With that, Vivian went on a mission to find one before he changed his mind. Robert didn't participate in the hunt, but we children were with her for every open house and appointment.

There was one house that I was completely enamored with: a three-story brownstone in Fort Greene, Brooklyn. I was struck by the parquet wood floors, pier mirrors, and old-world-style architectural details. I had a great love for brownstones, maybe because I'd spent copious amounts of time with my aunts Ruby and Virginia in their brownstone on St. Felix Street in the same neighborhood.

Unlike today, back in the 1980s there was a surplus of brownstones available for sale on the cheap. In fact, there was a huge billboard on top of one of the buildings in the neighborhood that read: *How to Buy a Brownstone for $1*. That was back when Fort Greene and her sister neighborhoods were crime-ridden and many of the brownstones were dilapidated, abandoned, or both. It's difficult to imagine now, as those neighborhoods are at this time the crème de la crème, with brownstones selling for millions of dollars.

Robert declined to buy the house because it was sixty-five thousand dollars, and his limit for a home was fifty. Vivian wanted the brownstone as much as I did, but she wanted out of that overcrowded apartment even more. She found a solid, two-family brick house, complete with a front and back porch, fenced-in backyard, and semifinished studio basement apartment in the East New York section of Brooklyn, for fifty thousand dollars, a number with which Robert felt more comfortable.

When I told my friends where I was moving, their eyes stretched in horror. "Eww, East New York? Girl, they be wildin' over there."

I didn't know a thing about East New York, other than it bordered Queens.

A few months before we moved into the house, a Black man named Christopher Thomas walked into 1080 Liberty Avenue in East New York, on Palm Sunday, pulled his gun, and murdered eight children and two adults, one of whom was pregnant. Enrique Bermudez, who lost his wife and two children in the shooting, claimed that Christopher owed him $7,000 for drugs that he'd sold him and that Christopher believed that Enrique was sleeping with his wife. Christopher had served time in prison for attempted murder and had been recently arrested for beating his wife. After his release, he was arrested again for attempting to rape and sodomize his own mother.

His own mother.

At his trial, Christopher Thomas said: "Well, I was a little high on my alcohol, and you can't blame me for killing everybody because I had one too many!"

East New York was plagued with so many violent homicides that NYC police officers referred to the neighborhood as "the Killing Fields" and "the Town Without Pity."

ON JULY 4, 1984, MY family and I moved from our crowded apartment in Crown Heights to our spacious home in "the Killing Fields."

Reggie was placed on the top floor, in a tiny room that had a connecting door to the tenant's apartment. Robert, Vivian, and the twins lived on the first floor, and I took the studio apartment in the basement. Robert bought me a new bed and gave me the kitchenette set from Sullivan Place. I placed my growing collection of books on the shelves beneath the staircase that led up to the first floor, and in no time at all, that little basement apartment became the place where I would begin to write in earnest.

That July marked a new chapter in our lives. I would turn nineteen in the fall, the twins would enter first grade, and Reggie would celebrate his sixteenth birthday in his junior year of high school.

Now forty-two and forty-one, Robert and Vivian weren't old, but they were weathered. The decades of fussing and fighting, breaking up and getting back together coupled with rearing four children had taken its toll on them. Now, the ferocity with which they used to brawl was diminishing. They mostly shouted and cussed at each other, but when their disagreements *did* get physical, they now fought with the vigor of two jaded prizefighters long past their prime.

THAT SUMMER, THE JACKSON VICTORY TOUR came to Madison Square Garden, and on August 4, me, my friend Michelle, and thousands of fans crowded in for the show of a lifetime. Michelle and I had balcony seats, just feet above the stage. A little bit closer and we would have been able to touch the studded-gloved god. Michelle scream-cried for the entire concert; I was silent, save for singing along to my favorite songs off the album.

Also, I was debating whether to jump off the balcony and onto the stage for a chance to throw my arms around the man whose music had been so important in my life. I'm sure there were many in the audience contemplating the same thing, and that night when three people acted on it, they were manhandled off the stage by security men who were built like meat lockers.

At the end of the night, we floated out of the arena, sweaty and ecstatic, singing, "Can you feel it?!"

And yes, we'd felt every bit of it.

It was the age of crack cocaine, an epidemic equal to, if not worse than, the destruction HIV/AIDS was reaping in Black communities, and I narrowly missed being a causality of both. I was in a relationship with a man who was slinging his penis around like a fishing net. I smoked weed every now and again and had tried cocaine, but I didn't like the way that booger sugar made my heart race. After a while, the reefer began giving me headaches, so I left that alone too. Rum and Coke and vodka and OJ were more than enough to get me high.

This did not curb my curiosity about crack. There were people all around me raving about its euphoric effects, and I wanted to share in the experience. But when I mentioned my interest to a workmate, who was older and wiser than I, he strongly advised against it.

"Bernice, promise me that you will never, ever touch it. It will destroy you; do you hear me?"

The grave expression on his face scared me.

"Promise me," he said.

"I promise."

That was one promise that I'm glad I kept. I'd learn that when he issued that warning he was already in the clutches of the drug and would battle for more than a decade before finally freeing himself from the addiction.

ONE MUGGY AUGUST NIGHT, MY cousin James and I were hanging out in my basement apartment, listening to music, smoking cigarettes, and drinking. In between sips of his beer and puffs on his Newport, I noticed that his eyes kept traveling to his wristwatch. It was closing in on 2:00 a.m.

"Hey, you got someplace to be?"

"Yeah," he mumbled before bringing the bottle of beer to his lips. He took two gulps, belched, and said, "You wanna come?"

I made a face. "Come where?"

"I gotta get something. Just come on."

I shrugged, slipped my feet into my sneakers, and followed him out into the simmering August night. The neighborhood was very quiet because it was a weeknight and people had to get up and go to work in a few hours. We walked for fifteen minutes, scrambling across the conduit expressway until we reached Fulton Street, a long winding thoroughfare that originates in the posh Brooklyn Heights neighborhood, then snakes eastward through the working-class quarter of Cypress Hills and East New York, ending in Queens at Ninety-First Street. James and I started toward the section of Fulton Street that stretched beneath the elevated train track.

In this part of town, the night was alive. Music streamed out open windows, the stoops were crowded with people smoking, playing cards, and throwing dice. Fulton Street itself was choked with people, pacing in the middle of the street, gathered in clusters on the sidewalk, or seated on the ground with their backs propped up against the graffiti-covered metal shutters covering the closed shops. It looked like a scene out of a movie.

James and I stood under an awning of a bodega and watched as an NYPD cruiser, blue lights flashing, rolled slowly up the street.

"Get out of the street! Get onto the sidewalks!" the officer barked over the PA system.

The sea of people parted, moved onto the sidewalks, and then immediately returned to the street once the cruiser rolled out of sight.

"What's everyone waiting for?" I asked.

"The drug man," James stated matter-of-factly.

Before I could utter another word, the man of the hour arrived in a U-Haul truck. At the sight of it, the horde—James included—

took off like greyhounds. The noise of all those sprinting feet sounded like soldiers charging into war, like wild horses streaking across the plains. I pressed myself against a wall to keep from being swept up, trampled, or both.

I waited around for James, but after fifteen minutes, my gut told me to go home. I always try to listen to my gut, because when I ignore it, I find myself in bad situations.

It was nearly four in the morning when James rang my doorbell. I had fallen asleep in my clothes. The television was on and so were the lights.

"Who is it?" I called from the other side of the door.

"It's me, open up."

He barged past me, went straight to the bathroom, and shut the door. I could hear him sniffing and gagging and retching.

"You okay?" I called from the hallway.

"Yeah," he answered in a strangled voice.

I sat down on the bed and lit a cigarette. A few minutes later, he appeared in the doorway, dabbing a crumpled ball of toilet tissue to his leaking nostrils. His eyes were watery and red, and he had a goofy grin plastered on his face.

"You know it's some good shit when it makes you puke," he said.

"Oh?" I shrugged, tapping the ash off my cigarette into the ashtray.

Upstairs, the telephone rang. We cocked our ears toward the ceiling. Calls that early were never a good sign. A few minutes later, the basement door creaked open.

"Bernice?"

"Yes, Mommy?"

"Come upstairs."

She left the door open and went to sit in the kitchen.

"Oh, I didn't know you were here, James," she said when we both walked into the kitchen.

"Yeah, we we're just hanging out. I was getting ready to go—"

"Aunt Ruby passed away," she said, cutting him off.

My breath rushed out of my body. "W-what?"

"Yeah," Vivian muttered sadly.

James was already crying, walking in circles, chanting, "Oh, man, oh, man, not Aunt Ruby, man this is going to kill Mommy."

23

The mommy James was speaking of was actually his grand-mother, Rose Anna, middle sister of Thelma and Helen. The prayer warrior who prayed for my recovery from the car crash; the one who lost her voice for a year after the factory fire. Rose Anna Hawkins, called Anna, was born in Philadelphia on September 28, 1928. When Anna turned sixteen, she left Sandersville and mi-grated to Brooklyn to live with her maternal aunts, Ruby and Vir-ginia. She wasn't in New York long before she met and married Claudie Griffin, a man fifteen years her senior.

We know very little about Claudie, save for that he was born in Free Trade, Mississippi; had a grammar school education; and was a farmhand before enlisting himself in the army in October 1943, where he served two years before he was discharged in December 1945. Maybe he was in New York looking for a better life than the one he'd left behind in Mississippi when he met the voluptuous, naive, and God-fearing Rose Anna Hawkins. What a thirty-one-year-old man would want with a sixteen-year-old girl takes no stretch of the imagination, but Anna refused to give it to him unless he made her his wife. On March 2, 1946, they exchanged vows at city hall with a pair of strangers standing in as witnesses.

Anna kept him a secret until after the nuptials because she knew that Ruby and Virginia wouldn't approve. After all, she'd only just arrived and that man was too old for her, and besides, he was from Mississippi; they didn't have a soul in Mississippi who could vouch for his character.

"Say what now?"

Ruby's eyes roamed from Anna's glowing face to the face of the strange man standing beside her and then down to the pea-green duffel bag on the floor at his feet.

"This is Claudie. Claudie Griffin. He's my husband," she squeaked again, coiling her arm tight around Claudie's arm.

"Husband?" Virginia's eyes rolled from the top of his head down to his scuffed leather shoes and back up again.

Anna nodded her head. Her stomach was in knots, but she was still smiling.

Ruby and Virginia exchanged sickened glances.

"Um, ma'am . . . I mean, um . . . Ms. Virginia and Ms. Ruby, I loves your niece and . . ."

The aunts listened, stone-faced and silent, as he pleaded his weak case.

"And I got a line on a room in a house not too far from here. Should be available in a few days, and then we'll be out your hair."

A few days stretched into weeks and then months. By then, of course, Anna was big with child. Then one day, Claudie left and never came back.

"I knew he was bad news," Ruby grumbled when four days had passed and Claudie still hadn't reappeared.

"Girl, cut out all of that crying," Ruby admonished Anna. "Leaving is probably the best thing he could have done for you and that baby."

Peggy Ann was born on December 13, 1946. It didn't help

matters that it was Friday the thirteenth. Anna was superstitious; she never opened an umbrella in the house, made sure black cats didn't cross her path, and never ever set her purse on the floor, and whenever she was cooking, Anna always made sure to throw a pinch of salt over her left shoulder to ward off bad luck. But what was she to do with a baby born on one of the unluckiest days of the year?

Claudie's abandonment had destroyed her. Until she went into labor, Anna didn't think anything could hurt worse than her broken heart. Labor pain was excruciating; it felt like someone was hammering her uterus. She stayed home with the baby for six weeks. Truth be told, the novelty of motherhood had lost its shine by week two. She wasn't a fan of her factory job, but she was grateful to be someplace eight or ten hours a day where her child wasn't. If only the baby slept when *she slept* and ate when *she ate* and maybe didn't whine and cry so much.

"That's what babies do," Virginia clucked when she caught Anna rolling her eyes at the sound of Peggy's mewling.

Anna was so tired, she'd drop to sleep standing up at work. When the foreman caught her swaying and snoozing, he threatened to fire her.

Well, this was not how she'd imagined her life would turn out in New York. She should have followed her sister to Detroit; she'd heard that Thelma was having the time of her life up there in the Motor City after having left Vivian in Sandersville with Grandma Rosie.

Not only was Anna exhausted, she was drowning in sorrow. It wasn't uncommon for her to burst into tears for no apparent reason. And she'd lost her appetite, which was cause enough for alarm because Anna loved to eat.

"What's wrong with you?" Ruby asked. "You still pining over that man?"

"No, ma'am."

"Then what?"

Anna shrugged; her eyes pooled with water.

"It's just a touch of melancholy, it be gone soon, and you'll be your own jolly self again. You'll see."

Ruby and Virginia had seen that despondency in new mothers before. They themselves had experienced the gloom that followed childbirth. They knew too that sometimes that fog of sadness moved in and stayed. They weren't sure which side of the spectrum Anna was on, but they kept their eyes peeled just in case. That touch of melancholy must have been postpartum psychosis, because why else would Anna have tried to kill her baby?

Peggy was nearly six months old when Anna took her into the bathroom to bathe her. She pulled the door closed behind her, which wasn't odd, but the turning of the lock was. At the sound of the bolt clicking into place, Ruby sat straight up in her chair.

It was June, the windows were open, and the sidewalk was filled with playing children. The television was also on, so the fact that Ruby even heard the turn of the lock was a miracle.

"Why you lock the door? Anna? Anna, why you lock the door?" Ruby called from the sofa. When she didn't get an answer, she pulled her short, stout body up, crossed the floor, and rattled the knob.

Aunt Ruby was short, but she was mighty. Perhaps something naturally acquired when one has spent decades working in the fields.

"Anna?" When Anna didn't answer, Ruby raised her voice and rapped harder on the solid oak door. "Anna!"

When she still did not answer, Ruby took a few backward steps and rushed the door. She hit it so hard it whipped open.

It took her a second to register the horror before her—Anna on her knees, bent over the edge of the tub, holding Peggy under the rippling bathwater.

"Anna, no!!!"

Ruby knocked Anna aside and snatched the baby out of the tub.

Peggy coughed and gagged and coughed as Ruby pounded her back until she cried.

"It's okay, it's okay," Ruby hummed as she rocked the terrified child in her arms.

She glared down at Anna, who was splayed out on the floor between the tub and the toilet, blinking up at her aunt like she'd just been shaken from a dream. "I—I," she stammered. "I didn't mean to . . ." was all she managed before dissolving into tears.

The aunts kept the baby away from her for a few days, taking turns caring for their great-niece, giving Anna time to sleep and eat. It took a few weeks, but eventually Anna seemed to return to the bubbly teenager that had arrived on their doorstep back in the fall of 1945.

After Peggy lost her first milk tooth, Anna put her name on the waiting list for an apartment in the Breukelen housing projects in Canarsie, Brooklyn, and within a year she was called. The aunts pooled some money and bought her a bed.

"That's the best we can do."

"I thank you kindly," Anna said.

She got a line of credit at a secondhand furniture store, where she purchased a twin bed for Peggy and a brown couch and a glass-and-mahogany coffee table that looked like it had come from some wealthy white person's home. Anna was proud of her apartment and finally felt proud of herself. When Anna called Grandma Rosie down in Sandersville and told her that she had a very nice place with room enough for her to come visit whenever she wanted, Grandma Rosie cawed, "Aww, your mama would be so proud."

Back in the fifties, there were still flowers in the courtyard and white tenants, but both the flowers and the white people grew scarcer and scarcer with each new Black tenant, and by the time Thelma left James Forest for good, and she and Vivian moved in with them in '57, there was nary a white person left, and the only thing blooming in those courtyards were dandelions.

AFTER CLAUDIE, ANNA HAD CAGED her heart away in a barbed wire box. The only men she gave access were the Reverend Holmes and Jesus.

"Well, are either of them fucking you?" Thelma asked.

"Oh, sis," Anna grimaced, blushing.

The sisters took to taking day trips up to Saratoga Springs to watch the horse races. It was there that she caught the eye of a jockey named Benny.

When Thelma saw the heat between them, she smirked. "He ain't much taller than me!"

While Thelma was petite (save for her buxom bosom), Anna was taller, with wide hips and thick legs. She had a penchant for small, delicately framed men, or maybe they had a penchant for her. She and her men always looked like the physical manifestation of the number ten. She and Benny became an item, and before long he was spending his off days in Brooklyn with her. For a while, it was heaven, and then one night, after one too many drinks, he hit her and unleashed hell.

Vivian and Peggy, who were in the living room at the time, scrambled to the kitchen for safety. From there they watched Anna transform into a welterweight wrestler. After he hit her, Anna grabbed Benny by the throat, lifted him off the couch, and shook him like a rag doll. His limbs were still flapping when she slammed him facedown on the floor. Dazed, he twisted his head around on his neck and gazed up at her in disbelief.

He opened his mouth to speak, but she was on him again. After a few cuffs to his head, Anna took hold of his collar with one hand, the other she hooked into the waistband of his trousers, hauled him up from the floor, and heaved him onto that expensive-looking glass-and-mahogany coffee table. The impact sent shards of glass everywhere.

That's the first time Peggy and Vivian ever saw a man cry.

"Did he call the cops?" I asked after hearing the story for the first time.

"Did you?" Vivian laughed.

Which is Black-speak for "Hell no!"

Afterward, Anna patched his lacerations, and they crawled into bed together. The next day he left and never came back.

When I first heard this story, I found it unbelievable, because Anna was the gentlest, kindest, most generous and loving person I knew. I'd seen her frustrated, peeved even, but never enraged. While her temper was a mystery to me, it was legendary with other family members and people who lived in the Breukelen housing projects.

Her daughter, Peggy, was just sixteen when she gave birth to her first son, Wayne. Earl, a.k.a. Moe, came the following year, and James in 1966, when she was nineteen years old. There was a fourth boy, named Benjamin, whom Anna took in and raised as her own, when his mother couldn't. This quartet of boys were affectionately dubbed Miss Rose's Boys, and woe to the person who ever brought harm to any one of them.

The man who owned the corner store learned that the hard way. One afternoon, Anna decided to make one of her famous six-layered coconut cakes. She had all the ingredients but was low on flour and so sent James across the street to get a fresh pack. The store owner knew James, in fact he was well acquainted with the entire family, so why he got it in him to slap James simply because he'd made direct eye contact with him remains unanswered.

Eyes tearing, James ran back home, holding his stinging cheek.

"What happened to you and where's my flour?" Anna asked over the large mixing bowl.

"He . . . he slapped me," James said, sniveling.

Anna's brown eyes turned black. "He who?" she growled.

"The man at the store."

Anna pulled herself up from the table, throwing her tweed coat on over her housedress. She didn't bother to put shoes on, just beelined out of the apartment in her slippers. It was late October, chilly but not freezing. Anna tramped across the fallen leaves, crossing the street against the light, throwing death stares at the motorists angrily honking their car horns.

At the store, the man looked up to see Anna marching through the doorway with all four of her boys in tow. She set her clenched fists on her hips and fixed her eyes on his.

"Did you hit my boy?"

The man didn't miss a beat. "Yes, I did."

"Why?"

"'Cause he was looking at me."

Anna's fists balled tighter.

"You see these boys," she said, sweeping her arm over their heads. "These here are my boys, and I'm the only one who hits them. You better not ever lay a finger on 'nan one of them ever again, you hear me?"

The man's lips curled into a simpering smile.

"And," she added, leaning in so close that he could smell the Pepsi-Cola on her breath, "if you do, I'll kill you."

The man rolled his eyes and chuckled. "Get out of my store."

Anna gave him one last, long fuming look and turned around. "Come on, boys," she commanded. The family filed out of the store.

Maybe the proprietor had made a habit of slapping children without consequence. Maybe he had never had a woman threaten to kill him. Whatever the case, he was, shall we say, perturbed, and before Anna could cross the street, he launched a forty-ounce bottle of Colt 45 at her back.

It missed and shattered on the ground, wetting her legs.

Stunned, she spun around and stared down at the broken glass and puddle of beer foaming at her feet. Her lips parted and then closed. She took a deep breath, glanced up at the sky and then down at her terrified boys.

"Go home. Get home now," she demanded in a calm and even voice. "Go on, it's okay."

The children scampered across the street but did not go into the apartment building as ordered. Instead, they huddled together in the courtyard to watch what happened next.

Anna shoved her hands into the coat pockets and rocked back on her heels. Her eyes ranged across the front of the store. From the owner's vantage point, Anna seemed to be sizing it up. Just as he opened his mouth to holler at her, Anna's right hand rocketed from her pocket. In her hand was a snub-nosed .45. She aimed and fired.

The man hit the floor, throwing his arms protectively around his head.

After she emptied the magazine, she strolled across the street as if nothing at all had happened. Seeing the boys gaping at her, Anna said, "Didn't I tell y'all to take your Black asses in the house?"

The boys ran into the building and up the stairs.

The man lay there for a long while, whimpering into the linoleum and squirming in his urine-soaked pants. When he finally summoned the courage to pull himself up off the floor, he saw that the windows were riddled with bullet pits.

When I heard this story, I posed the same question I had after hearing the first story about my sweet aunt Anna: "Did someone call the cops?"

"Did you?"

THE LAST TIME I'D SEEN Aunt Ruby was at her eightieth birthday party. She was ailing then, but you wouldn't have known it from the glow on her face and the smile plastered to her lips. The family had piled into her tiny one-bedroom apartment in Bushwick, and flung open the windows to let in the crisp fall air to abate the sweltering heat of the apartment. We dined on food and confection that Anna had spent three days and nights preparing, laughing and reminiscing over a life inching toward an end.

For Anna, the death of Ruby was like losing a mother, because when Lillian died, it was Ruby and Virginia, along with Grandma

Rosie, who stepped in and cared for Anna and her sisters like they were their own daughters. Because Anna was so young, she hardly remembered Lillian at all, and that saved her little heart from a heap of grief. But now, with Ruby's death, the sorrow she'd dodged when Lillian passed circled back around and smothered her.

24

I'd asked Ellis to come to the funeral with me. He was, after all, my boyfriend, and boyfriends and girlfriends were supposed to support each other in good times and bad, right?

"Nah, I can't; I got a game. But call me when you get back home, and I'll come over."

Click.

We were drifting apart. The sex haze was wearing off, and I was growing weary of the gaslighting, lying, and cheating. My surgery hadn't really altered my appearance, and so we still had that problem.

I kept asking myself if this was how love was supposed to feel. My gut was telling me no, but when it came to matters of the heart, I was still second-guessing.

I wish I could say that the last straw for me was the day Ellis and I were on the train together and a girl he knew from school stepped into the car.

When she spotted him, she waved, singing, "Heyyyyyy, Ellis!"

"Hey, you!" he called back, quickly rising and crossing the narrow aisle to embrace her. They sat down on the long seat across from me and fell into conversation. I waited and waited for him to introduce me, but he didn't. To keep from staring at them, I took a book out of my backpack, opened it in my lap, and gazed down at the words. This went on for five or six stops, while I sat there fighting back tears.

She never made eye contact with me, which led me to believe that she thought I was just another passenger on the train.

When the train pulled into their station, they got up and walked to the door with his hand resting on the small of her back. As they stepped onto the platform, he threw a quick glance over his shoulder and mouthed, "I'll call you later."

Before the doors slid shut, the girl laughed riotously at something he'd said. Were they laughing at me?

I wish I could say that the humiliation I felt drove me to never see or speak to him again, but I've been transparent and honest with you up to this point, so I won't start lying now.

That said, the incident did motivate me to seriously consider a man who had recently started expressing a romantic interest in me.

Linford was from Guyana, and he was the best friend of my Bajan cousin Lionel. When I first met him in 1977 or so, I was still just a little girl and he was a teenager doing what teenagers do. After a few years in the armed services and a failed relationship with a woman who had his child, he moved back home to Brooklyn. The next time I saw him was late 1984, when I was nineteen years old, and he was twenty-five.

"Hey, Bernice," Lionel's sister, Cherrol, cawed when I walked into the bedroom.

One or two Sundays out of the month I spent the afternoon with my Bajan cousins in their small one-bedroom apartment located in a building on Empire Boulevard and Utica Avenue. That Sunday when I came to visit, Linford was there, seated on the carpeted bedroom floor with his long legs stretched out before him.

"Hey," I called back, waving.

Linford looked up at me, squinting. I sat down on the bed next to my cousin Cherrol.

"Is that—" he started, unable to remember my name. He snapped his fingers as he tried to extract it from his memory.

Cherrol pointed at Linford. "Do you remember him?"

I looked at him. "No."

"That's Linford," she said.

"Okay," I muttered, still not remembering. "Hi, Linford."

"Bernice!" Linford shouted with one last snap of his fingers.

"Wow, you were just a little girl last time I saw you," he said. "Now, you're all grown up."

Famous last words.

Over the next few months, we became reacquainted, friendly even. But then the weather broke, and spring stepped in, sprinkling pearl dust in the air.

"You headed home?" he asked one day as I gathered myself to leave. "Or are you going to your man's house?"

Ellis didn't live too far from there, and they all knew him because on occasion he'd come by to collect me.

"No," I said. "I'm headed home."

"You want a lift?"

"Sure."

He drove a black five-speed sports car. I had never been in anything so slick and fast. We sped up Linden Boulevard with the windows lowered and the music blasting.

In front of the house, he threw the car into park. "Home in one piece," he said, grinning.

"Thanks for the lift," I said, reaching for the door handle.

"Um, listen, maybe we can go out sometime?"

I turned and looked at him. Up until that moment, I hadn't really studied him, certainly not with the eyes of someone contemplating a romantic partnership. Leading up to that point, he was just my cousin's best friend. He was six foot three, dark, with an athletic physique, full lips, high cheekbones, and slanted eyes. Even though he'd been in the country for ten years, his Guyanese accent was still very thick. I liked him well enough; I just didn't think I liked him well enough to date. And besides, Ellis still had my heart in the palms of his hands.

Nonetheless, I said, "Sure."

At the time, I had a job as an accounts receivable clerk at a Japanese apparel company on Madison Avenue called Itokin. I was bored to tears with the work. Why I was even hired for the position is a mystery, because I was a word person and not a numbers person. The following Friday, Linford picked me up after work, and we set off for an evening of film and food.

We parked on Tenth Avenue and walked the few blocks into Times Square. It was early April, winter was a few weeks behind us, but the nights still dipped into chilly territory. That evening, Times Square was flooded with tourists meandering up and down the sidewalks wide-eyed, gaping at the tall buildings and bright lights.

Linford walked ahead of me, parting the sea of pedestrians like Moses dividing the Red Sea. I felt like a queen.

When Ellis walked ahead of me, I didn't feel like that.

I now know that when a man walks ahead of you instead of beside you, that is a demonstration of control.

We had dinner at Mamma Leone's and then went to see *Rambo: First Blood Part II*. In the theater, Linford held my hand for the entirety of the film, and I thought, *Wow, Ellis has rarely done that.*

Back in the car, Linford turned to me and asked, "Are you tired?"

I wasn't tired at all.

"Good. Let's go get ice cream."

I liked ice cream, but it didn't like me, because I was and remain lactose intolerant, just like 80 percent of Black people. But I didn't let that stop me.

"Sure."

We drove to Connecticut for ice cream. The gesture felt so

over-the-top romantic to me that one would have thought he'd flown me out to Paris. It was the longest date of my life. In the nearly ten hours we were together, we talked about his childhood in Guyana, his time in the service, my four years at boarding school, his entrepreneurial dream of owning a string of laundromats, and my desire to become a writer. He spoke with delight about his toddler daughter but had little to say about her mother, except that she was crazy. Isn't that what they always say?

"Do you want more children?"

"Yes, of course." His voice climbed a bit, as if my question was the most ludicrous thing he'd ever heard.

When he dropped me home, it was nearly three in the morning, and I was giddy with adoration. From that night forward, we spoke every day, and then the following week went out again. This was the most time and attention I had received from a man since Melvin, and so when it came time to cut ties with Ellis for good, it was an easy decision.

Of course, Ellis begged and pleaded for me to stay with him. He promised to change, to do better. When I didn't fold, he got nasty. He called me a whore, accused me of having been secretly dating Linford all along. In an attempt to sabotage the relationship, he plastered my door with reams of printer paper that stated: I LOVE YOU FOREVER!!!

When Linford saw them, he bristled with anger, ripping the pages off the door and shoving them into the trash can. "Are you still messing with this dude?"

"No, I'm not."

"Well, call him."

"Call him? For what?"

"So that I can tell him that you're my woman now and he needs to back off."

Cut to me, swooning . . .

I did as he'd ~~asked~~ ordered.

On the phone, Linford repeated his statement about me being his woman now, ending with "Don't call this number again."

And for a few months, Ellis obliged.

WE WERE A COMMITTED COUPLE by the time Mother's Day rolled around. That Sunday, Linford drove Vivian, the twins, and me out to Queens, where he met Thelma and Wilfred for the first time.

He liked them straightaway, and the feeling was mutual.

We sat around the dining room table, eating and laughing at Thelma's outrageous stories. After the meal, he helped clear the table, and then as Vivian and I washed up the dishes, Thelma went out onto the back porch to watch the twins play in the yard. Linford and Wilfred retired to the living room to talk football.

It felt like a jumble of puzzle pieces had all fallen into place, which is to say, in that moment, everything felt right and complete.

The next day, May 13, the twins celebrated their seventh birthday. Vivian brought home paper party hats and a little ice cream cake for them. After dinner, we all stood around the table singing "Happy Birthday." That night, they were bathed and getting ready for bed when, in Philadelphia, the local police department dropped a C-4 bomb on a row house on Osage Avenue, located in the middle-class neighborhood of West Philadelphia, decimating more than sixty homes and killing eleven people, five of whom were children.

This loss of life and destruction of property had stemmed from a longtime conflict between the city of Philadelphia and the activist John Africa Sr. and his family and followers.

In 1972, John Africa Sr. founded the socially and environmentally focused organization called MOVE.

The members championed environmental justice, racial justice, and animal rights and did so loudly and visibly, often walking through neighborhoods blaring their messages through a bullhorn.

After complaints poured in from neighboring residents, the city officials attempted to evict the group, but John, his family, and his cohorts refused to leave.

As a result, the city officials dispatched an anti-tank machine gun as well as five hundred military-grade-artillery-toting SWAT-gear-clad police officers to the row house on Osage Avenue to serve arrest warrants and forcibly remove them from the home.

Gunfire was exchanged, and for more than ninety minutes, the police barraged the residence with ten thousand rounds of ammunition. After that, a helicopter dropped the C-4 bomb that ended the standoff.

It was 1985, I was an impressionable nineteen years old, going on twenty, and I believed as I had been taught, which was that the United States of America was the land of the free and home of the brave and the most compassionate, caring, civil, and just country in the world.

But in 2021, when I was fifty-six years old and well aware of the sins and depravities of these United States of America, it was revealed that the remains of Katricia "Tree" Dotson Africa and Delisha Orr Africa, two of the five children casualties of the MOVE bombing, had never been interred. In fact, their remains were in the possession of the Penn Museum, and the institution had been displaying their remains in exhibitions, private showings, in fund-raising activities, and as props.

IN 1985, I'D NEVER HEARD the phrases "trophies of dominance" or "lynching souvenirs." But in 2021, I was well familiar with both and the practice of the murder of Black people that breathed life into those idioms.

In 2021, I learned too that the most cited case of such barbarity was that of Sam Hose, a Black man who was accused of killing his white landlord and raping his landlord's white wife: "There he was stripped; his ears, fingers, and genitals cut off; his face skinned, and his body burned on a pyre. Souvenir hunters fought over his organs and bones."

At the time of the MOVE bombing in 1985, I wouldn't have considered myself a souvenir hunter, but I was a collector, having amassed souvenirs from my high school senior trip to Disney World and my visit to the Dominican Republic. I also had a scrapbook filled with paper mementos marking special moments in my life, which included a green matchbook cover from Mamma Leone's restaurant, which commemorated the first dinner Linford and I ever enjoyed together.

VIVIAN SAW THE TWINKLING LIGHTS in my eyes and voiced her concern about the age difference. I was a legal adult but still growing mentally, physically, and emotionally. Which is to say that I was still malleable.

She liked him well enough, but her regard for him did not outweigh her concern.

"Six years is a big difference in age," she'd warned. "He has more life experience than you do. I just want you to be careful."

She might as well have been talking to a wall. Her words went in one ear and out the other. Besides, I couldn't hear her over the sounds of wedding bells ringing in my ears.

AFTER TWO MONTHS OF BEING together, Linford and I drove to Detroit to attend my family reunion. It was my first such experience, and I had no idea what to expect.

We stayed with Richard and Lula Mae in their Victorian home on Cadillac Avenue. The same home Thelma and Vivian had fled to that night James Forest tried to run them down in the street. The same home Robert, his brother Bree, and their best friend slept the night they drove up to see about us after the accident; the very home where Vivian and I convalesced after nearly losing our lives in that car wreck.

It was a lovely old house, with a welcoming front porch, tall windows, high ceilings, pocket doors, and a large pantry. Lula Mae showed Linford and me to a sunny bedroom on the top floor that overlooked the street. "This is where you and your mother stayed after the . . ." She trailed off.

I studied the wallpaper, drapes, and moldings. I waited for some recall, but nothing came.

The house was brimming with family. I met so many cousins I couldn't remember all their names. It was overwhelming and thrilling. With each introduction, I searched the family member's face for evidence of our kinship. I didn't have to stare very hard or for very long before I spotted Thelma's nose, Vivian's cheekbones, and Anna's eyes.

At the family gala dinner, we received a pamphlet titled *Lester-Dukes Family History*, detailing our family history over seven generations. On these pages are names of antecedents, some of whom I am familiar with, but many more whom I am not. At the close of the foreword, written by Lolita Davean Brown and Naomi Campbell Reese, are these words:

> *It is our profound hope that present and future generations will use this beginning to delve backwards into time, and again forge our link to our NATIVE LAND—AFRICA!!!*
>
> *The oldest traceable ancestor of the Lester branch, at this writing is a female whose name was Lou Vicey. She was born into slavery somewhere in Georgia about 1835. All knowledge of her surname and parentage is thus far still hidden in the ashes of that period.*
>
> *In her early teens or early twenties she married Will Mills. It is likely that they were owned by the same slave master. About 1854, Lou Vicey gave birth to a daughter who was named Lucy. Lucy spent her early years in slavery and was*

about nine years old when the Emancipation Proclamation was
signed in 1863.

At any rate Lucy grew to young womanhood and around
1868, she met and married Buena Vista Lester, Sr.

That union produced ten children, one of which was my great-
great-grandma Rosie. They called it the family tree, but for me, it
was a lifeline and a crystal ball into the past. Seeing the multitude
of names touched me very deeply and set my imagination on fire. I
read and reread the pamphlet. I did not know a thing about the veneration of ancestors, even as I was actively engaging in the practice.

Decades in my future, I would take an African Ancestry DNA
test and find that my first female maternal ancestor in this country
came from Cameroon, from a tribe of people known as Bamileke.
The Bamileke people had once lived in Egypt but fled when Muslim
Arabs conquered the country and outlawed the practice. When I
read that the Christian Bible explicitly forbids consulting with the
souls of the dead, it got me to wondering what our ancestors had to
tell us that they didn't want us to hear.

OVER THREE DAYS, I HEARD a slew of family stories that had been
passed down through the generations. Some I'd heard before, but
many others were new to me.

My three-times great-grandfather, Buena Vista Lester, was born
into slavery in 1846, in Hancock County, Georgia. His owner was
the prosperous cotton farmer David Dickson. The story was that
David had fathered a daughter with one of his enslaved women.
This was quite common during that time. The thing that made this
story unique was that after Dickson died, it was revealed in his will
that he'd left his entire estate to the child. An estate that was worth
millions.

Millions?

Millions!

It sounded like a tall tale.

Thirty years in the future, in July 2015, I would be attending another family reunion—this time in Macon, Georgia. On a hot July day, my family members and I would board coach buses and travel an hour from Macon to the Dickson Plantation in Sparta, Georgia, where Buena Vista Lester had lived as an enslaved person, from birth to the age of nineteen, when Lincoln signed the Emancipation Proclamation in 1863.

There, we gathered on the porch of the big house to listen to the history of the place, told by the current owner of the property, and learned that the tale, that so many of us assumed was phony, was the God's honest truth. David Dickson had indeed left his fortune to the daughter he'd sired with an enslaved twelve-year-old child named Julia Frances Lewis Dickson. Amanda America Dickson was born on November 20, 1849, and raised by her white grandmother-enslaver, Elizabeth Scholars Dickson. Under her grandmother's tutelage, Amanda learned to read, write, and play the piano. In 1865, she married her paternal first cousin Charles Eubanks, and they had two sons. After two years, she and Eubanks split, and Amanda returned with her children to the Dickson Plantation. In 1885, when David Dickson passed away, he owned seventeen thousand acres of land worth $309,000, the bulk of which he bequeathed to Amanda.

Well, this left his white family members gobsmacked and angry as hornets. They contested the will, of course, but in 1885, the superior court of Hancock County ruled in favor of Amanda. And when the family appealed to the superior court of Georgia in 1887, the decision was upheld. I bet you they saw red.

Amanda's life had one more fascinating story for me. In 1892, she married Nathan Toomer of Chatham County, North Carolina, who had been born into slavery in 1840.

At the age of forty-four, Amanda died in 1893 of neurasthenia— also known as nervous exhaustion. Being Black and female in America is still an exhausting existence. After Amanda died, Nathan Toomer married Nina Pinchback and they had a son, Nathan Pinchback Toomer, who grew up to become a writer. In 1923, at the height of the Harlem Renaissance, he published his novel, *Cane*, under his adopted literary name, Jean Toomer.

How many degrees of separation is that?

After the history lesson, we set off to explore the property. I slipped off my sneakers and walked barefoot across the land where my ancestor was born and raised in captivity. The emotion that swelled in my chest was the same sensation that gripped me when I went into the slave dungeons of the Cape Coast Fort in Ghana.

A cousin walked by, stopped, took a step back, and laid a comforting hand on my shoulder. "You good?"

I dragged my hands across my wet face and nodded. He nodded too and walked on. The slump of his shoulders told me he was feeling what I was feeling.

I couldn't think about Buena Vista without thinking about Amanda. Did they know each other? After all, they were born just three years apart. Had his mother known her mother? Had they been friends, foes, family? I couldn't think about Buena Vista or Amanda without thinking about all the other nameless, faceless humans who'd been enslaved on the Dickson Plantation.

BUT BACK IN DETROIT, THIRTY years in the past, I am at my very first family reunion with my boyfriend Linford.

The present is pleasant, and the future is bright, and I know some things, and I am learning more things. And in time I will understand that the knowledge both known and burgeoning aren't just lessons but seeds that will soon sprout into stories.

25

That September, a few weeks before my twenty-first birthday, I opened my door and found Linford standing on the steps, holding a huge box.

"Surprise!"

"What's that?"

He ambled inside and sat the box on the floor.

"It's a television."

I didn't have a television. I didn't need one, because I spent my free time listening to music, reading, and talking on the phone. But Linford was a sports fanatic, and while he enjoyed music, he did most of his listening in the car. He was spending more and more time at my place. Sometimes, if I had plans after work with friends, he'd go to my house and Robert would let him in. When I arrived home, the clothes I'd left thrown on the bed were neatly folded and dinner was cooked.

"You got a good guy there," Robert commented to me one day. "I hope you don't mess it up."

They were similar, Linford and Robert, but I didn't see it at the time.

The television was remote-controlled. The first one of its kind in our house. Robert and Vivian came down to marvel at it, each taking a turn using the remote to scroll through the channels. The following week, Robert went out and bought one of his own.

After it was set up, Linford pecked me on the cheek. "Happy early birthday!"

A few days later, as Vivian and I were walking the twins to school, she broached a subject we'd covered more than once since Linford and I had started seeing each other.

"You know, I really don't like you taking gifts like that from men," she said as we paused at the corner, awaiting the crossing guard's directions.

He wasn't just any man; he was my boyfriend. Aren't boyfriends allowed to give their girlfriends gifts? I clenched my teeth and tightened the grip on my seven-year-old sister's hand. She tilted her head toward me, wincing.

"When men get mad, they come back for those gifts."

Well, she would know. I can't count the number of times during an argument that Robert demanded back the engagement ring and wedding band he'd given her.

I rolled my eyes in exasperation. "He wouldn't do that," I said.

Cat catch rat, but he thief he massa fish, which is Guyanese-speak for "good and evil often come from the same source."

I didn't have the television for three weeks before we had our first major disagreement and Linford threatened to come and get the television.

I had a new group of friends now, all of whom worked with me at Itokin. They were the people who introduced me to the dance clubs, formerly known as discotheques. On Fridays, we went to after-work parties at the Underground in Union Square. Saturdays found us at the Silver Shadow, Bentley's, and the Garage. I loved dancing my nights away, and I would have loved to have Linford dancing with me, but it just wasn't his thing, and I was fine with that—but he wasn't.

"You dance with men?"

"Um, yes. Who else am I going to dance with?"

"But I'm your man, and I'm the only man you should dance with."

This was bizarre to me. "But I'm just dancing with them."

"Dancing leads to other things."

He was saying that I didn't have a mind of my own. He was saying that even though I was committed to him, some man could persuade me to cheat, effectively dancing me right out of my drawers.

I knew women then and know women now who surrendered their autonomy to please a man, keep a man, or both. But at the time, I didn't count myself among them.

His concern about me cheating by accident quickly escalated to him accusing me of actually cheating. That Friday, my friends and I skipped the after-work party and decided to head home after work to shower, change, and maybe get a disco nap in before heading out. Linford was aware of my plans, and just minutes before I walked out the door, he called.

"I don't want you to go."

This again, I thought. "But why?"

"Because I'm asking you not to go, and that should be enough."

We bickered while my girlfriend Cicely milled around, sucking her teeth, and sighing loud enough for the dead to hear.

"Listen, we gotta go. You coming or not?" Cicely huffed, folding her arms across her chest.

I nodded at her. "Listen, Linford, I'll talk to you in the morning," I said.

Before I could tell him good night, he barked, "Fine, then. I'm coming to get *my* television." And with that, the line fell dead in my ear.

Stunned, I stared at the phone.

Cicely saw the look on my face. "What happened?"

I rested the phone in the cradle. "Give me a minute."

I went upstairs and told Vivian. She gave me that *I told you so* look.

"He ain't taking shit out of here," she said. "Go on out and have a good time. Don't worry about it."

I went out, but I didn't have a good time because my mind was on Linford. I was less worried about losing the television and more concerned about losing him.

In the end, he did not take the television but would continue to complain about my nights out with my friends. In between our spats, he showered me with love and attention. We took road trips to Pennsylvania, Virginia, and Niagara Falls. Near Christmas, as we sat in the darkened movie theater watching the previews, he took my hand, leaned over, and whispered, "I want you to have my baby."

Dumbfounded, I sat blinking at the images on the screen. Suddenly, my head was ringing with the childish rhyme: *First comes love, then comes marriage, then comes Bernice with a baby carriage.* But the marriage part was missing, and motherhood was the furthest thing from my mind. What I wanted was to write and travel, preferably with the man I loved.

But when I suggested to Linford that we should take a trip to one of the Caribbean islands, he balked. "I'll travel when I retire."

I wanted to travel now, while I was young, vibrant, and full of energy. I'd already started saving toward a girls' trip to Ocho Rios, Jamaica.

"Tomorrow is not promised," I quipped in response.

I sat in the darkened movie theater mulling over his request.

I'd spent time with him and his daughter and saw that he was a good father. He played with her and cuddled her and loved on her in a way Robert had never done with his children. I figured if I was going to have a baby, I wanted to have one with a man like that.

I rested my head onto his shoulder. "Okay."

Had I known that some men impregnated women to establish ownership and control, I might have given a different response.

That night, I tossed my birth control pills in the trash, and we got down to the business of making a baby. The months came and the months went, and still I did not conceive.

"Maybe that car accident screwed up your insides?"

The thing that I had kept from him during the dawn of our relationship, when I laid my life on a platter, was the fact that I had had an ectopic pregnancy with Ellis.

I had woken up one morning with a spiky brick in my abdomen, at least that's how it felt. Vivian was heading out the door to work and left Robert to take me to the emergency room. The exam revealed that the embryo had already detached itself and a D&C would not be required. The following day, I experienced a slightly heavy period, which lasted for the normal five days.

I'd never told Linford about that, and now I wondered if my insides were indeed screwed up, but not for the reason he thought.

WE ARGUED AND FUCKED, AND in between, I danced the nights away at the Garage, the Underground, and the Silver Shadow. We argued and fucked, and in between, I traveled to Jamaica with my girl-friends Robyn and Wanda, and my travel fever got worse.

We argued and fucked, broke up and made up, and in between, I read Gloria Naylor, and J. California Cooper, who had written books about the woman I was leaving behind and the woman I was becoming.

And between the arguing, fucking, breaking up, making up, and reading . . . I wrote.

After some time, it was not lost on me that we were fighting more than we were fucking. We seemed to disagree about every-thing and anything. Once, we quarreled over the lyrics of a popular Stephanie Mills song—"You're puttin' a rush on me, but I'd like to know you better . . ."

"Ugh," I groaned, quickly switching the station on the car radio. "I can't stand that song."

"Yeah, why?" Linford asked, shifting down from fourth to third gear.

The lyrics, the instrumentals, all of it grated my nerves. I didn't have the language to explain exactly why, so I simply said, "I just don't like it."

Linford stopped at the red light, turned to me, and said, "You don't like the song because she's talking about being virtuous, and you don't believe in that. You'll give it up after one date."

I certainly hadn't given it up to him after one date, so I didn't know where this accusation was coming from.

His implication hurt me. "What are you saying?"

"You know what I'm saying."

"Take me back home," I sputtered through my tears.

When the light changed, Linford ripped through the intersection, hanging a wild U-turn, and then sped back home in silence. I didn't see or hear from him again for a week.

This behavior became commonplace in our relationship. He'd pick a fight, we'd argue, and for days he'd go silent. This type of conduct is known as ghosting. While it's a hurtful and purposeful act toward the *ghostee*, it also serves to buy time for the *ghoster* to engage with other romantic partners.

I had grown up in a chaotic household, so the chaos in my romantic life did not feel abnormal. That said, the constant turmoil was exhausting. I just wanted peace. I longed for the serenity I'd experienced as a child in Barbados, as a student at St. Cyril Academy, and as a young adult vacationer in the Dominican Republic and Jamaica.

I loved the people I worked with, but I hated my job. Of course Robert was still drinking, which meant that he and Vivian were still fighting. Now, most of their disagreements centered around the twins and Reggie. Robert had taken to terrorizing the twins the way he had Reggie and me when we were their age. Reggie was becoming a man, and that seemed to upset Robert, who constantly reminded Reggie that he was the only man in that house and he'd better not forget it.

All of that combined with what I was going through with Linford made me feel like I was suffocating. I needed oxygen.

I'd been thinking about going back to school. Many of my classmates from high school were now college graduates, some in graduate school, preparing for careers in medicine and education. They were out in the world, renting apartments and buying cars. When I held my life up to theirs, it made me feel like a failure.

All these conditions are what led me to apply to a six-month language-intensive program at an academic institution in Switzerland. Three weeks later, I held an acceptance letter in my hand, complete with a partial scholarship.

Before I shared the news with Linford, I told my parents. Vivian was ecstatic. We waited to break the news to Robert on a Saturday morning, when he'd just come home from work and hadn't had his first drink of the day. He read the letter and then looked up at me.

"So, you want to go to Switzerland to learn French?" The quizzical look on his face was almost comical.

"Yes."

He smirked and looked down at the letter again.

"They've given her a partial scholarship, and so all we'd have to pay for is the other part and her airfare," Vivian said.

Robert nodded, his eyes still dancing over the typed lettering.

I don't remember the out-of-pocket cost, but whatever it was, he agreed to cover it.

That night, when Linford came over with a bag of Chinese food and a liter of Pepsi, I told him my plans.

"Wow," he said as he sank his plastic fork into the container of pork fried rice. "French? Why do you have to go all the way to Switzerland to study French when you could do that right here in America?"

"It's not just about the language; it's about the experience. And I want to have an adventure."

We both shoveled rice into our mouths. "I hope you'll come and visit me," I said, taking a sip of Pepsi.

"Sure." His response did not sound sincere. "But listen, I can't guarantee that I'll be here when you come back."

My heart fell into my stomach. "What? Why?"

I don't know why I thought taking time apart would fix our differences and change his controlling ways. I don't know why I thought this when I saw how miserably it had failed for Vivian.

"Six months is a long time to ask someone to wait," Linford said.

"But I thought you loved me?"

"I do. But it doesn't seem like you love me, because you're willing to leave me to travel to the other side of the world to study a language you can study right here in New York."

How could I explain to this man that it was less about studying another language and more about being happy? Why didn't I just tell him that I wasn't happy?

"Six months, Bernice? C'mon now. All I'm saying is that I'm a man, I have needs. Six months is a long time to ask me to wait."

We sat on my twin bed, staring at the basketball players running up and down the court. I was fighting back tears. I didn't want to cry in front of him. Again.

Linford glanced at me. "Why you so quiet?"

My lip quivered.

"Listen," he said, setting his container of food down on the floor between his feet. "I'll tell you what, if you don't go to Switzerland, I won't become a cop."

His interest in becoming a police officer had been a source of great anxiety for me. When he told me he'd taken the exam, I was very upset, already anticipating the middle-of-the-night call from one of his sisters telling me that he had been shot dead.

It seemed a fair enough bargain. I wouldn't lose him to street violence, and he wouldn't lose me to the Swiss.

When I told Vivian that I had changed my mind about the school, she already knew why, but she wanted to hear me say it.

I told her about the compromise I'd made with Linford.

She rolled her eyes so hard that I thought they'd stick to the back of her head. "Do you think if the shoe was on the other foot, he would do the same for you?" Then she looked me dead in my face and called me a stupid ass.

A few months later, when Linford joined the roster of new police academy cadets, I called *myself* a stupid ass. I should have reapplied to the school or any number of other academic institutions, but on top of having been bamboozled, I felt defeated.

By the time Linford graduated from the academy, we were clinging to a dying root. He had cheated, and I had cheated in retaliation. The trust was gone, and so was our mutual respect. The only thing we had left was sex, and we barely had that.

IN FEBRUARY 1987, MY FRIEND and coworker Wanda and I were in the terminal at JFK airport, waiting to board our flight to Antigua. It was our second island getaway in under a year. We were excited to escape cold, dreary New York for tropical heat and sunny skies.

Hearing his flight being called, the man sitting next to me jumped up from his seat and rushed off to the gate, leaving his *New York Times* behind. I picked it up and flipped through the pages, pausing to scan the headlines:

BROOKLYN BISHOP LIMITS CHURCH
USE BY HOMOSEXUALS

3 LEADING BROKERS SEIZED ON
CHARGES OF INSIDE TRADING

FROM CENTER OF COCAINE TRADE
TO A FLORIDA JAIL

U.S. Jurors Award $7 Million
Damages in Slaying by Klan

I crossed my legs and pulled the paper closer to my face.

*A Federal jury today awarded $7 million in damages against the
United Klans of America and six past and present Klansmen in
the 1981 slaying of a black man whose body was left hanging
in a tree.*

*The verdict by the all-white jury was awarded in a suit
brought by the family of the victim, Michael Donald, 19 years
old, and the Alabama branch of the National Association for the
Advancement of Colored People. Mr. Donald was beaten and
strangled in Mobile on March 21, 1981, and then hanged.*

I read those violent words over and over again.
Beaten. Strangled. Hanged.
Beaten. Strangled. Hanged.
Beaten. Strangled. Hanged.
I wish I could say that I was flabbergasted, but I wasn't. The
previous year in Howard Beach, the neighborhood that bordered
my own, another Michael, Michael Griffith, had lost his life to
white violence, when a gang of racist teens chased him into the
high-speed traffic on the Belt Parkway. He was struck by a car and
died of his injuries. Even though I didn't know Michael Griffith, I
grieved for him like he was family, and now reading this story about
Michael Donald made me feel blue all over again.
Beaten. Strangled. Hanged.
At the news conference, Michael's mother, Beulah Mae Donald,
said, "I'm glad justice was done. Money don't mean a thing to me.
It won't bring my child back. But I'm glad they caught the
guilty and brought them to court because I did everything I could
to help."
Beaten. Strangled. Hanged.

———

AFTER MY TRIP TO ANTIGUA, I wanted to see more of the world more often, but I knew it would be difficult on my salary. So I sought out employment in the travel and tourism industry, where I knew that at the very least I could travel for a fraction of the cost. In the past, I'd applied for positions at hotels, airlines, and tourist boards, but no one ever called me in for an interview except once. I showed up at the Irish Tourist Board in a neatly pressed gray skirt suit and black pumps.

"Good morning," I brightly greeted the red-haired receptionist.

"Good morning." She smiled back at me. "How can I help you today?"

"I have an eleven o'clock interview with Mr. Casey."

The woman blinked stupidly at me. "Interview?"

"Yes."

She stared at me, looked down at Mr. Casey's calendar, and then back up at me. "You're Bernice McFadden?" Her query sounded less like a question and more like a preposterous statement.

"Yes," I said, not quite sure what was happening. Did I have food in my teeth? Was there a strand of hair out of place?

"Um, have a seat, I'll be right back." She rocketed out of her chair and dashed up the hallway and out of sight.

In the reception area, I eased down into one of the cushy chairs and studied the photographs on the wall, depicting images of castles, rolling green hills, and four-leaf clovers. I was already imagining what it would be like to visit the green isle when the receptionist's voice shattered my daydream.

"Mr. Casey will see you now," she said. "Please follow me."

I trailed her down the carpeted hallway to Mr. Casey's office.

"Mr. Casey, this is Bernice McFadden."

I didn't miss the snark in her voice or the smirk on Casey's pale face. The receptionist pulled the door closed behind me.

"Please sit down," Casey said, pointing to the chair before his desk.

He shot me a half smile before lowering his eyes to what I could only assume was my résumé. After a few seconds, he asked me two trivial questions and then thanked me for coming in. It was the shortest interview I'd had in my entire life. When I stood to leave, Casey blurted, "So how did you get the surname McFadden?"

I made a face. "From my father?"

"Oh, okay. Have a good day."

That was the Bernice of yesteryear. The Bernice of today would have given him a history lesson about slave-holding Irish families in America.

Because I was batting a thousand, I enrolled in a travel-and-tourism certificate program being offered at Marymount Manhattan College. Once a week for three months, I traveled to the uptown campus to attend night classes in world geography and hotel and airline operations, all in the hopes that this little piece of paper would gain me entry into the industry.

26

I grew up in a world dominated by whiteness.

Santa Claus was white, the president was white, the queen of England was white, which is why it seemed practical that fairy-tale princesses, fairies, and mermaids were also white. Heroes too were white. Good witches were white women with blond hair adorned in bejeweled white dresses, while wicked witches were white women who wore black clothing or had dark hair to signify their wickedness. In the afternoons on my black-and-white television, I watched Tarzan, a white man in a loin cloth who ruled over the animals and savage Africans on the dark continent. When someone fell sick, the spiritual among us sent white healing light their way. A stint of bad luck was called dark days, and people who did bad things had black hearts. All my life, white represented purity, and black stood for all things sinful.

In school, I'd learned that Black people had contributed little to nothing to America, save for George Washington Carver's work with the peanut and Langston Hughes's famous poem about a raisin that inspired a play written by Lorraine Hansberry. I learned that Rosa Parks was tired, and Martin Luther King Jr. had a dream, and that was the sum of my education regarding the civil rights movement.

But by 1987, I had read dozens of books written by Black writers about Black people and the Black experience here in America and abroad. Since graduation, many of my high school friends had traveled to Europe, the place we'd been taught one should visit if they wanted to immerse themselves in *high culture*. (I know, that was almost me.) But my eyes were opening, and the haze of my Euro-centered education and Euro-centered existence was slowly clearing. While my friends were bouncing around countries that had colonized much of the globe, I was visiting those countries that had been colonized. After I completed the travel-and-tourism program, I treated myself to a trip to Barbados. It was May 1987, thirteen long years since I'd last visited the island.

In the taxi, I gazed out the window, as awestruck as I'd been the first time I came to that enchanted place. It was still as beautiful as I remembered. There had been changes, of course—more paved roads, more cars and transport buses. Outhouses and outdoor showers were fading out of sight, as most homes now had indoor plumbing. There were supermarkets now, though some people still grew their own peas and limes and raised chickens, ducks, and sows in their backyards. Many of the bearded fig trees had been cut down to make way for hotels and vacation homes that sat elbow to elbow along the pristine coastline. And there were many more white tourists than there had been in 1974.

Great Britain loved Barbados so much that they nicknamed her Little England. The Barbadian people are very proud of that distinction and laud it over the heads of those who live on the other Caribbean islands. Of course, England favors Barbados, why wouldn't she? It was in Barbados that England conceived the first British Slave Society, which is the primary link in a succession that would bring England untold wealth and power that she sustains today. In his book *The First Black Slave Society: Britain's "Barbarity Time" in Barbados, 1636–1876*, Dr. Hilary Beckles wrote:

> *Barbados was the birthplace of British slave society and the most ruthlessly colonized by Britain's ruling elites. They made their fortunes from sugar produced by an enslaved, "disposable" workforce, and this great wealth secured Britain's place as an imperial superpower and caused untold suffering.*

It is only in recent years that Barbados has begun to reckon with its past. In 1985, just two years before I returned to the island, Barbados erected a statue of Bussa, an enslaved African man who, in 1816, led the largest slave revolt on the island. Even with the statue as evidence, tour guides have been known to tell tourists that while slavery did not exist in Barbados, indentured servitude did.

The house I had spent three summers in as a child had been moved a half mile up the road and was in the final stages of its transformation from wooden chattel house to walled home. It had a veranda now, and that is the place I spent most of my time when I wasn't on the beach or in the nightclubs. In the early evenings, Dolly, Anita, and I would sit on the gallery to gossip and talk Barbadian politics. Oftentimes, my aunts reminisced about the bygone days, and that was always my favorite part of the conversation. I felt so calm, content, and happy that I thought, *I might be able to make a life for myself on the island.*

It was a revelation. Reconnecting with the island and my family was the very thing I needed during a time when I felt adrift. I started dreaming about moving there for good.

MORE THAN 92 PERCENT OF the population of Barbados is Black. Many white Barbadians can trace their lineage back to Scottish and Irish indentured servants sent by England to work alongside the enslaved Africans. Those descendants are referred to as "Ecky-

Beckys," which is a derogatory term used to describe poor white people.

Frank Baines was one such descendant. He lived across the road from Dolly and Anita in a crumbling chattel house. He was well past seventy and bent over, with wispy gray-blond hair and sun-toasted, deeply lined skin. His eyes were the color of blue sea glass. His children and extended family rarely came to look after him, and so Dolly and Anita, being the kind women that they were, kept an eye out and fed him three meals a day. Even though he was rapidly losing his sight, he still noticed the swell of my breasts. When I handed him a plate of steamed fish and white rice one day, he gazed at my chest, sputtering, "Dem some nice bubbies."

"Eww, you dirty old man!"

Men commented on my legs, and my behind, but my tits were small and usually unworthy of praise. It would be several weeks before I realized what his comment prophesized.

27

When I returned to the States, I immediately made an appointment with my gynecologist, a tiny Asian woman with a bowl-cut hairstyle. When I walked into her office, she peered at me over rimless spectacles and smiled.

"Bernice, I haven't seen you in some time. What brings you in today?"

I got straight to the point. "I want to get back on birth control pills."

Her eyes dropped to my chart. "Hmmm," she sounded. "I've not written you a prescription for quite some time now. It's been more than a year."

I nodded.

"Well, it's protocol to give a patient a pregnancy test before they're placed on birth control. Remember? Just like the first time."

"Okay."

"Take off your jacket. I'm going to draw some blood."

I shrugged off my acid-washed denim jacket, sending the dozens of pin buttons of Boy George, Michael Jackson, and Prince rattling. Similar to Vivian, I did not like needles, so I turned my head away and winced, even before the silver tip pricked my skin.

"It will take about ten or fifteen minutes for the results."

"Okay."

When she returned, she was grinning. "Congratulations!"

"Congratulations?"

"Your test came back positive. You're pregnant!"

I nearly doubled over. It felt like I'd been kicked in the gut. "W-what?"

I should have known. In Barbados, I'd attributed my cravings to PMS and my exhaustion to the fact that I was out partying every night until dawn. And now, Frank Baines's comment about my breasts, which had been swollen and tender for weeks, made sense.

"Pregnant?" I bleated again.

Now that my relationship with Linford was on oxygen; now that I planned to move to Barbados; now I was pregnant? I left the exam room in a daze and walked right past Linford, who was sitting in the waiting area. He caught up to me in the hallway.

"What's happened, what's wrong with you?"

Linford and I had had plans that day immediately following my appointment, which is why he was there. He didn't know that I had decided to get back on birth control pills and so assumed it was just a regular appointment.

"I'm pregnant." I whispered the words because they were still unbelievable to me.

Joy exploded through the concern on his face. He whooped, grabbed me up in his arms, and twirled me around.

That was in May. By July, his elation was a memory, and our relationship was dead.

I WAITED THREE DAYS BEFORE I told Vivian, and even then, I didn't have the courage to tell her to her face. I called her from my work, like a coward.

"I have something to tell you, Mommy."

She was at work too; the chattering of her coworkers and clicking of typewriter keys sounded louder than usual. My mouth was so dry, my tongue felt like sandpaper.

"You're pregnant?" Mothers always know. "Well, I was waiting for you to tell me."

I could tell from her voice that she was smiling. "Are you mad?"

"Why would I be mad?"

"Disappointed?"

"No, I'm not disappointed. Let's talk about this tonight, okay?"

I'd been home for an hour by the time Vivian came downstairs. I was sitting on my bed, nervously twining my fingers when she appeared in the doorway.

"How are you feeling?" she asked, her face glowing with happiness.

"Fine," I squeaked.

After a beat, she came over and sat down next to me.

"My baby is having a baby," Vivian sang, patting my thigh. Her hand paused. "You are keeping it, right?"

Abortion hadn't crossed my mind at all.

"Yes, of course!"

She sighed with relief.

"Good, it'll be nice to have a baby in the house again. By then the twins were nine going on ten. "So, when do you want to tell your father?"

I was scared to death to tell Robert; I had an idea of what his reaction would be, and I wanted to put that off for as long as possible. "Soon," I said.

It was another two weeks before I told Robert. When I finally did, I enlisted Linford to be there with me for emotional support. We confronted him with the news while he was seated at the kitchen table, eating a bowl of his famous beef stew that I hated so much. I'd never developed a taste for it, but he loved it almost as much as he loved Hennessy.

"Daddy?"

When he saw Linford standing beside me, his face darkened. I could tell he *suspected* what was coming.

"Yes?"

"Um, I'm pregnant."

He sucked his teeth, dropped the spoon into the stew, and pushed the bowl away.

"Pregnant?" His eyes bounced to Linford.

"Yes, sir," Linford said.

Robert leaned back into the chair and folded his arms over his chest. "So, you're going to marry her, then?"

"She doesn't want to get married," Linford said, his voice a bit too loud for Robert's liking.

"Are you shouting at me in my own damn house?"

Vivian, who had been standing in the doorway, rushed into the kitchen and planted herself between us and him.

"Okay, okay," she said. "Let's calm down. There's nothing here to argue about. Bernice is pregnant, and they're not getting married, and that's that."

Robert glared at her for a moment before fixing his eyes on Linford again. He reached for the bowl. "Well, for your sake, I hope you plan on taking care of that baby."

"Of course I will," Linford said.

And he did.

NEXT, WE CALLED THELMA TO tell her the news.

"Well, well." She laughed into the phone. "Congratulations, baby. I hope you have a boy; we have too many splits in this family!" She cackled and then called, "Wilfred, Wilfred? Wil-fred!"

Her voice was distant, as though she were holding the phone away from her mouth. "Bernice is having a baby!"

I pressed the phone against my ear, listening hard for his response, but there was none. Early that year, Wilfred had traveled home to Fort Worth, Texas, to visit his sister and her children. He wasn't there three days before Thelma got the worried call.

"Something ain't right with Wilfred. He actin' strange."

His family put him on the next flight headed back to New York. When the plane landed, Thelma was waiting for him at the gate. According to her, Wilfred's trousers were inside out, his shirt was misbuttoned, and he smelled musty, as if he'd not bathed in days. And, she'd said, "He didn't know who the hell I was."

She drove him directly to the hospital, where the doctor confirmed what she'd suspected. Wilfred had suffered a stroke that muddled his speech, slowed his gait, twisted his left hand into a claw, and plastered his face with an expression of perpetual bewilderment.

By the time I discovered I was pregnant, he was still able to walk and talk, but not too long after I gave birth, he had another stroke, which would render him mute and immobile.

"He's smiling," Thelma said into the phone.

I DIDN'T CALL GWEN BECAUSE I already knew she wouldn't be happy for me. I felt this way for two reasons:

1. An out-of-wedlock pregnancy was nothing to celebrate.

2. She was rarely happy about things that did not directly concern her.

When Robert told her that he was looking to buy a house, her response to that exciting news was "Oh, dammit to hell, Robert. A house, really? You're forty-one years old, much too old to buy a house. You won't live long enough to pay off the mortgage!"

When weeks passed and I still hadn't told her, Robert called and told her himself. And what was Gwen's response to that blessed news?

"Make her get an abortion."

"Mother," Robert said, "she's Catholic, it's against her religion."

"Well, if they're not planning to marry and she won't get an abortion, then you should put her out."

When Robert and his brothers were preteens, Gwen had taken in a young girl named Joan, who was the daughter of a friend or family member (it was never clear which), and raised her as her own.

Joan was gone by the time Robert and his brothers met and married their significant others, so none of the daughters-in-law had ever laid eyes on her. Not even a photo. The story of her existence and expulsion was passed from husband to wife and then down to us children like folklore.

"Joan was wild. Mother was at her wits' end. When she came up pregnant, mother had the locks to the apartment changed, packed her bag, and sat it out on the sidewalk alongside the trash cans."

"And then what happened?"

"We never saw or heard from her again."

JUST LIKE WHEN VIVIAN WAS expecting, Robert advised me to keep my mouth shut about my pregnancy. He didn't even want me to tell my siblings.

"It's none of their business," he said.

I didn't push back, because the truth is I was harboring a little bit of shame because out-of-wedlock pregnancies were still stigmatized back then. But it was a hard secret to keep because my body was changing so rapidly.

One summer day, when I was moving into my third month, my siblings and I were walking back from Burger King. It was early evening; the streets were crammed with people out enjoying the hot weather, and even though it was nearly eight o'clock, it was still bright outside.

As we came down the block, carrying our bags of hamburgers and fries, a neighbor-friend of mine named Tonya was sitting out on the stoop of her house. Her little sister was between her legs, and Tonya was braiding her hair.

She waved the comb at us. "Hey, y'all!"

"Hey," we chorused back.

I'd shared my news with her and a few of my other girlfriends, but Tonya was the only one I'd sworn to secrecy because she lived on the block.

As we passed her house, Tonya shouted, "Ooooh, girl, you are carrying that baby all in your ass!"

Her words blasted in my ears like an M-80.

I saw the heads of the other neighbors out on their stoops snap up and around. Soon, all eyes were on me, including those of my siblings.

"Baby?" Reggie exclaimed. "What she talking about?"

My little sister tugged my arm. "You having a baby?"

I shot Tonya a death stare.

"Oh shit, my bad." She laughed. "You ain't tell them yet? I thought they knew!"

Well, the cat was out of the bag, and there was no putting it back in. "Let's talk about it inside," I said, hustling them down to the house.

The twins were thrilled with the news, but Reggie was a little bit ambivalent.

"Are you sure you want to have a baby?"

"Yes, of course I'm sure," I said.

"Does Mommy and Daddy know?"

"Yes."

"Were they mad?"

"Daddy was."

He nodded knowingly. "Wow," he said, reaching for the bag of french fries, "I'm going to be an uncle."

PREGNANCY WAS A WONDER. MY body bloomed and spread like yeasted flour.

Before the wonder, I drank water only if I was forced to, but now I was a desert, parched all the time. Water was the best thing ever, as was white grape juice, olives, and mashed bananas turned with rice, peas, and stewed chicken. I stumbled through my days punch-drunk with sleep. At night when I climbed into bed, I dropped immediately into a deep, deep slumber thick with dreams.

A woman followed me out of one of those dreams and parked herself in my imagination. She was tall and dark, humming with music and a little sadness. I was a little bit sad too. And a little bit angry.

My relationship with Linford was over. He had moved into a new apartment, purchased a new car, and had a new girlfriend. His life was moving forward, and I felt like I was spinning in place.

Looking back, I realize that the woman in my imagination was gestating, just like the baby in my womb. I was carrying two lives; two stories were unfolding within me. My body was host to one and my imagination to the other, and I was acutely listening to both.

That poem is mine, the woman said.

I had penned a few poems over the years. Sad poems and love poems, but I knew the one she was suggesting was unfinished, just a few lines—not even a complete stanza. I fished the unfinished poem out of the folder where I kept my finished works and works in progress. After I inserted the paper into the typewriter, I closed my eyes and listened.

Before my pregnancy, before the lady followed me out of my dreams, I'd been writing from the outside in, but now I placed spirit over ego and began writing from the inside out.

28

It was a Saturday afternoon in early December when a man named John showed up at our house, hoping to talk some sense into Robert.

John and Robert were both drivers for UPS, and John was also the teamsters' union representative. He'd called several times, but Robert had hung up on him, so now he was there in person to try one last time. Vivian wouldn't have opened the door for a stranger, but the man was dressed in the brown UPS uniform, and she thought he was delivering a package. When she opened the door, she saw that his hands were empty.

"Yes?"

"Hello, I'm here to see Mack." Mack is what his coworkers called Robert.

"He's not here right now."

"Oh, dang it," he mumbled, despondent. "Are you his wife?"

"Yes, I am."

"I'm John." The man offered his hand. "I work with your husband."

No one came to visit Robert, except his brothers and a cousin he was close with.

Vivian shook his hand. "Oh, nice to meet you."

In the twenty-two years Robert had been employed with UPS, she'd never met any of his coworkers. Robert, on the other hand, was familiar with the people she worked with because they'd been to Thelma's weekend parties and had attended the huge christening bash my parents threw for the twins.

"Um." John shoved his hands into his jacket pockets. "When do you expect him back?"

"Don't know." She shrugged, and then added with a laugh, "I wish he'd go on back to work because I need a vacation from *his* vacation."

Robert had acquired quite a bit of annual vacation time. So it wasn't unusual for him to take two or three consecutive weeks in a row. Of course, him being in the house 24/7 was a challenge for all of us, because he drank night and day, badgered us kids, and picked fights with Vivian. During one of our recent disagreements, I'd ripped the telephone from the wall and hurled it at his head. Worried that his pestering would send me into early labor, Vivian put me in a cab in the middle of a snowstorm and sent me to cool down in Queens with Thelma and Wilfred.

"For the love of God, when the fuck are you going back to work?!"

He was never going back, but we didn't know that yet.

John nodded thoughtfully. Vivian had confirmed what he suspected. Robert hadn't told her.

"I'll tell him you came by," she continued, "or I can deliver a message. . . ."

From the look on John's face, Vivian sensed that this wasn't a casual visit.

"Mrs. McFadden, I'm probably overstepping, but I think you need to know . . ."

ROBERT WASN'T THE ONLY DRIVER who showed up to work reeking of alcohol. Many tractor trailer drivers drank, smoked marijuana, or engaged in illicit drug use.

The drivers at UPS were members of the powerful union formed in 1903 called the International Brotherhood of Teamsters. In the 1950s the Teamsters Union was thrown into the world spotlight when James "Jimmy" Hoffa was president. During his tenure, he was suspected of being involved in organized crime. In response to this, Robert F. Kennedy, who was the attorney general at the time, formed a task force known as Get Hoffa and set out to bring Hoffa down.

The mission was accomplished in 1964. Hoffa was arrested, tried, and sent to prison. During his incarceration, both John F. Kennedy Jr. and Robert F. Kennedy were assassinated. In 1971, Hoffa was paroled by President Richard M. Nixon. Hoffa disappeared in 1975 and was declared dead in 1982. Maybe he wasn't dead, maybe he fled America for a sunny isle in the Mediterranean to live out his last days in splendor. Who knows. That said, the teamsters had a reputation of fiercely protecting their own, and Robert was one of their own.

"I told him, there's a lot of guys who got drinking problems. I was one of them." John chuckled. "But I went to AA, cleaned myself up, kept my job and my family, and in five years, I'll retire." He paused, took a breath, and looked Vivian square in the eyes. "That's what I want for Mack, but he won't . . ." He trailed off, shaking his head.

They were sitting in the kitchen. Vivian was nervous. She kept looking at the front door. Robert would not react well to walking into his house only to find a man sitting at the table with his wife. Worse yet, when he saw it was John, Lord knows what he might do.

"Mrs. McFadden," John continued, "all Mack has to do is admit he has a problem, and he'll be able to keep his job. Simple as that. They'll send him to AA for as long as it takes. But . . ."

Vivian leaned in. "But what?"

John pushed air out through his nose. "Well, he says he don't have a problem with alcohol. He says the company and the union are trying to railroad him because he's Black."

So, there it was once again. Robert was refusing to take responsibility for his actions. It was always everyone else's fault and never his.

"But that's not true," John said, holding up his hands. "I'm Black too. Many of the drivers are Black." He lowered his hands and shook his head in defeat. "There's just no getting through to him."

Vivian knew this all too well.

We'd been living in the house for only three years and four months, and now Robert didn't have a job, and even with the rental income, Vivian didn't earn enough to pay the mortgage and the bills all while keeping the twins fed, clothed, and in the private Catholic school they were attending.

John sat there looking very sorry for having to deliver such devastating news. "Do you think *you* can talk some sense into him?"

She knew that that would be impossible, but she said she would try. And she would try. And Thelma would try, and Anna would try. Maybe Gwen and his brothers tried as well, but they were all habitual drinkers too, so maybe they also believed that it wasn't about the alcohol, like Robert had said.

WITHOUT ROBERT'S COOPERATION, THE UNION was helpless to protect him, and three days before Christmas, he received his official letter of termination.

"Well, you can get a job driving for some other company," Vivian suggested.

"Why should I? I've taken care of all of you for twenty-two years, and now it's time for all of you to take care of me."

PART FIVE

FROM DAUGHTERHOOD TO MOTHERHOOD

*I'm a Black woman. I come from a Black woman,
who came from a Black woman, who came from a Black woman,
and I'm going to give birth to a Black woman. . . . We are impeccable
and special, and the world is just going to have to deal with that.*

—RIHANNA, SEPTEMBER 13, 2019

29

My due date was January 27, but my contractions didn't start until February 8, just three days before my doctor was going to induce my labor.

It was early in the morning. Linford was at work, and Vivian was at work, so my cousin Lionel drove me to Brooklyn Hospital, where I was examined by the doctor on call.

"You're only one centimeter," he said, snapping off his plastic gloves. "Come back when the contractions are three minutes apart."

Later that evening, when the mucus plug made its appearance, Vivian called a cab, and we piled into the back seat.

"You okay?"

"Yep," I said through gritted teeth.

"Just breathe."

Easy for her to say.

The shocks on the car were shot, so we bounced our way down Atlantic Avenue, which would have been entertaining if I wasn't in pain.

"Hey, hey," Vivian called to the driver. "Slow down, my daughter is in labor."

The driver glared at us in the rearview mirror.

THE CONTRACTIONS FELT LIKE PERIOD cramps, like really bad period cramps, which is to say that they were annoying and uncomfortable, but nothing to wail and scream about like I'd seen women in labor do in the movies and on television shows. Like the woman down the hall was carrying on now.

"Good Lord," I laughed. "You'd think someone was murdering her."

Vivian was sitting next to my hospital bed, smirking and shaking her head. She knew what was coming but kept it to herself, allowing me to wallow in my delusion a bit longer.

I was laboring, but my cervix wasn't opening, and so I was given a shot that would help it along. The medicine halted the contractions and spun me into happy delirium. I was as high as a kite.

"What's so funny?" Vivian asked.

"I don't know," I said, and then giggled myself to sleep.

She took the opportunity to slip out of the room to get a bite to eat and have a smoke, so she wasn't there when the first herculean contraction ripped me out of my sleep. By the time she returned to the room, I was screaming and crying, certain that death was near.

Vivian took my hand in hers and squeezed. "Believe me, Bernice, you are not dying."

Nothing she said could reassure me. I'd never experienced pain like that before or since. I let go of her hand, clamped my fingers around her forearm, and nearly hauled her into the bed with me.

"Bernice!"

At the sound of my mother's frantic voice, a nurse appeared in the doorway. The look on her face was a mixture of amusement and horror. She rushed in and pried us apart.

"Okay, Mama, calm down, calm down," she hummed, stroking my damp forehead. "You're fine, you're fine."

But I wasn't. I looked past the nurse's brown face. "Mommy, I want you to name her Azsá," I panted. "A-Z-S-A. Okay? You got that?"

Vivian nodded.

The name Azsá came to me in a dream I had during my pregnancy. The internet wasn't a thing in 1988, and Google did not exist, so I had no way of checking to see if this was a name of my own creation or one that already existed in the world. In 1988, I defined her name as "gift from the ancestors."

AFTER HOURS AND HOURS OF torturous pain, my doctor gazed between my parted thighs and announced that the baby's head had crowned. She turned to Vivian. "Do you wanna see?"

Vivian rounded the bed and peered beneath the tented sheet. "Oh, wow," she cooed in wonder.

BABY AZSÁ WAS A GIFT for sure and a sign if there ever was one, because she arrived in the world on February 9, 1988, right on Alice Walker's forty-fourth birthday.

The doctor placed the tiny little miracle on my chest, and my heart exploded. Barely seven pounds, and the color of quince fruit, Azsá had a head full of straight black hair, her father's nose, and his eyes. It would be years before I saw any part of me in her features.

"Does she have all of her toes and fingers?"

"Yes, Mommy," the nurse said. "Ten toes and ten fingers."

I smiled, and in a blink, my exhaustion claimed me and I dropped to sleep.

When I opened my eyes again, I was in a dimly lit hospital

room; on the other side of the curtain, a new mother was sobbing. I raised myself up onto my elbows.

"Hello?" I called thickly. "Do you need help?"

She did not answer. I rang the call button, and a second later, a nurse appeared.

"Yes?"

"She's crying," I said, pointing at the curtain. "I think something is wrong."

The nurse marched into the room and snatched the curtain aside.

My roommate was a dark woman, about my age. Her head was covered in thick plaits. She was propped up on two pillows, weeping over the baby in her arms.

"What's the matter, Mommy, huh?" the nurse cooed. "It's a lot, I know. It'll get better, you'll see."

My eyes bounced from the baby to the clear plastic bassinet next to her bed. I looked to the left of my bed. There wasn't anything there but a chair. Where was my bassinet? Where was my baby?

Panic gripped me.

Now, I'm going tell you this thing that I have kept a secret for many years until now: Azsá was born with the umbilical cord wound around her throat.

But that is not the real secret. All through my pregnancy, I was terrified that I would miscarry, because I believed that surviving the car accident had created a cosmic debt and that debt had come due the moment I conceived.

I believed this because the Bible taught me God was a duplicitous being, both loving and vengeful, so I fully expected him to take the life of my child as payment for the one he allowed me to keep in 1967. Job 1:21: "The Lord gave, and the Lord hath taken away; blessed be the name of the Lord."

"Excuse me?"

The nurse turned around. "Mm-hmm?"

"Where's my baby?"

"Oh, we had to put her in the incubator because she was cold."

I threw the covers back and eased myself out of bed.

"Where are you going?"

"I'm going to see my baby."

I shuffled down the hallway, bent over like a century-old woman, holding my empty stomach. When I reached the glass wall of the nursery, I was stunned to see more than a dozen babies wrapped in white cotton blankets striped in pink or blue, depending on the sex. My eyes skipped over the paper labels with surnames scrawled in black marker:

Johnson

Brown

Henry

Francois

Vasques

Finally, I spied baby McFadden.

She was lying on her back, in a diaper and T-shirt, bathed in the yellow light of the warming lamp. My flustered heart settled. I stood there for a long time gazing at this life I had brought into the world.

Later, when I was back in the hospital bed and the nurse rolled her into the room and placed her in my arms, a tide of emotion swept over me and I melted into a sobbing, blubbering mess. It was part joy, part fear, and a general sense of whelm.

I looked over at my roommate, and through my tears I saw her gazing back at me. A silent understanding passed between us.

Linford came in a few hours later. "Hey," he whispered, quickly swiping the knit cap from his head. "How are you doing?"

"I'm okay," I said, tilting the baby up so he could see her.

He bent over and peered into her tiny face. "Are you sure they have the right baby? She looks Chinese."

30

Motherhood is not for the weak.

Leaky breasts, shitty Pampers, the looming threat of SIDS, sleepless nights, teething, and endless trips to the emergency room for fevers that seemed to manifest out of nowhere. New motherhood was hard and arduous love labor, and I don't know how women do it alone. I was so thankful to have Vivian to help me, because without her I might have gone mad.

Azsá advanced quickly. She was just two weeks old when she began holding up her head; a month later, she was rolling over. I did all the things Vivian had done for me when I was baby, including reading to her. Sometimes I read Azsá stories from the cloth books I'd bought her, and other times I made up stories just for her. *Once upon a time in a land far, far away, Princess Azsá . . .*

I'd returned to work in late March, leaving the baby with Ms. Deborah, a neighbor down the street who was a stay-at-home mother of five girls. I wasn't back at work for one month before I was fired.

"You come into work late every day, Bernice," said my supervisor, Sung.

She was telling the truth. I'd been late nearly every day because I'd given birth to a night owl. Azsá slept all day at the sitter's and then stayed up most of the night, crying if I put her down in her crib, so I had to sleep with her on my chest, which meant I didn't sleep much at all.

I was perpetually exhausted.

"Can you please try and keep her awake?" I pleaded to Ms. Deborah.

"Sure, honey, I'll try." I could tell from her tone and the half smile on her face that I had made a ridiculous request.

Losing my job did nothing for my self-esteem. Now, not only was I an unmarried, single mother, but I was an *unemployed*, unmarried, single mother. I cried the whole train ride home. That night, when Vivian came home from work, I went upstairs and delivered the bad news.

"I'm sorry that happened to you, Bernice," she said, pulling leftovers out of the refrigerator. "But you're a smart girl, and you'll get another job in no time at all." She forced a smile, but I could see the worry floating behind it, because my contribution, as small as it was, was necessary to keep the family afloat.

"Get yourself *The Chief*, they've got plenty of city jobs listed there," Robert commented from the living room where he was watching television. *The Chief* newspaper was a publication that listed application periods and examination dates for civil servant jobs.

"Then why don't you go get a job, you lazy bastard?!" Vivian screamed.

Robert laughed until he coughed. He slapped his chest and then went into the bathroom and spit a glob of phlegm into the toilet. He didn't flush it, just left it floating there to further agitate Vivian.

Robert had been home for five months, and his constant presence was fraying all of our nerves but especially Vivian's. Every time she looked at him, she was reminded of his refusal to help support his family. She hated him for putting us in such a precarious situation. She hated him more for this than she'd ever hated him for hitting her. Her eyes turned cold whenever he was in her presence.

As he passed back through the kitchen to the living room, Vivian mumbled something under her breath, angrily snatched the tin foil from the glass baking dish, and crumpled it in her hands.

"Peggy is throwing a boat ride next week, I think," she said, staring down at the pieces of cold chicken. "She's looking for servers, I don't know what she's paying, but you should give her a call."

PEGGY ANN WAS THE PHYSICAL opposite of her mother, Anna. Brown and petite, she had shoulder-length hair that she mostly wore slicked back into a tight ponytail. She loved to laugh, drink, dance, and get high. In nearly every photo I have of her, there is a cigarette dangling from her mouth or pinched between her fingers.

In 1982, when she was thirty-six years old, she married a man named Charles Williams, whom we all called Chuck. He was much older than she was, although I don't know by how much. He was fat and bald with a hearty laugh and always had a camera in his hand or dangling from a cord around his neck.

Chuck took Peggy away from that crowded roach-ridden apartment in the Bruekelen projects; away from her three sons who'd been raised to believe that she was their sister and away from the mother whose love had always been hard and hardhanded. Chuck settled her into his two-bedroom co-op apartment in Flushing, Queens, that had sweeping views of the Manhattan skyline.

In that place, they'd make new memories, happier memories. They'd cook meals together and dance together, and at four o'clock, like clockwork, they'd sit together on the couch and watch that new Black talk show host, named Oprah.

On the evening of October 27, 1986, when the New York Mets beat the Boston Red Sox in the final game of the World Series, Chuck leaped out of his recliner, clapping his jubilation. Indeed, all five boroughs erupted with joy. People threw open their windows and spilled out into the streets, banging pots and pans, lighting firecrackers, and shooting bullets into the sky. With tears of joy streaming down his face, Chuck fell back into his recliner, clutched his chest, and closed his eyes forever.

PEGGY HAD BEEN A WIDOW for nearly two years when she gave the party cruise that none of us would ever forget.

I was still plump from pregnancy, and nursing, so my breasts were full and round with milk. I squeezed my postnatal body into a black miniskirt and button-down white blouse, which I paired with silver pantyhose, black patent leather loafers, and Vivian's black faux fur coat, and headed off to Manhattan.

The boat left the pier at midnight, and for hours we sailed up and down the Hudson, rocking to New Edition, Teddy Pendergrass, and Cherrelle. We docked just as the sky was beginning to pale. It was chilly but not frigid. The plastered guests stumbled down the gangplank into the foggy morning and headed home. I was standing on the deck, smoking a cigarette with James, when the captain, a white man, came bounding down the steps from the top deck. He pulled off his shoes, ripped off his white shirt, and dove headfirst into the dark and dirty river.

"What the fuck?" I murmured in astonishment.

James flicked his cigarette butt over the railing, remarking blithely, "Some jackass done fell overboard."

The captain resurfaced, gulped air, and dove again. When he reappeared the second time, there was a body in the crook of his arm. James and I leaned over the guardrail to get a better look.

It was Peggy.

When we saw her, I threw my hands over my mouth and froze, while James took off running and screaming.

Apparently, Peggy had been standing on the dock, fumbling to light her cigarette. With one hand cupped around the lighter, she whirled 'round and 'round, trying to position her back as a wall against the morning gale, and whirled right off the edge of the pier into the water.

We didn't hear the splash, or maybe we had and thought it was water lapping against the side of the boat. Had the captain not seen her, we wouldn't have known a thing until her body washed up. If her body washed up.

After the crew members stretched her still body across the cold, wooden planks of the pier, the cocaptain straddled her and began pumping her chest and performing mouth-to-mouth resuscitation. James was on the pier by then, still screaming, trying to break through the human barrier surrounding the melee. My scream was locked in my throat. I could not make a sound. As I watched, I thought about what Anna had tried to do to Peggy in Ruby's bathtub all those many years ago.

Just then, Peggy's head jerked, and she began coughing up black water. She'd beat death-by-drowning twice in one lifetime.

But four years later, in February 1992, Peggy rose from her bed in that co-op apartment in Flushing, Queens, and hurried to the bathroom to relieve herself. On the toilet, she rubbed the sleep from her eyes, contemplating the day ahead.

WHEN JIM, THE WHITE MAN she'd been dating, walked into the apartment that evening, he was whistling. He threw the key down on the counter and started toward the bedroom.

"Hey," he called. "Where you at?"

Walking past the bathroom, his eyes fell on Peggy, who was slumped over on the toilet, dead. She was forty-five years old.

31

I wasn't out of work for long before I was hired as a reservation's agent for a luxury hotel brand called RockResorts. It was founded in 1956 by businessman and philanthropist Laurance S. Rockefeller. I'd finally gotten my foot through the door of the travel-and-tourism industry.

That November, I took my daughter to Barbados, for the first of several trips we'd take together over the ensuing years. Anita and Dolly gushed over her. She was carried and kissed and hugged and loved. I took her to visit Grandfather, who was ninety years old by then, and ailing.

"She swimming yet?" he asked, flashing his tobacco-stained teeth at me. His body may have been failing, but his mind was still sharp.

"I'm going to teach her," I said.

"Make sure you do," he said with a wink.

I taught her how to swim in the very same waters where I'd learned—of course, in a less traumatic way. At first, she didn't like the sea. She'd cling to me, screaming holy murder whenever I took her into the water. But I kept at it, and after a few days, she relaxed and began to enjoy it. I suppose the floaty helped; I suppose watching the other children splashing about in the water helped as well. Children learn by example. By the end of the week, Azsá was kicking and doggy-paddling through the water with confidence. When we visited Barbados the following year, she wore the floaty for only the first three days.

I WORKED AT ROCKRESORTS FOR two years, and during that time I experienced their properties in Saint John, Saint Croix, and Virgin Gorda—opulent resorts patronized by Hollywood celebrities, athletes, and the superrich. Whenever I visited the resorts, it always felt like I'd stepped into an episode of the *Lifestyles of the Rich and Famous*. At any moment, I expected Robin Leach to appear.

The call center and corporate offices were located in 30 Rockefeller Plaza, where *The Tonight Show*, *Today*, and *Saturday Night Live* are filmed. Once, when I was in the elevator headed up to work, Arnold Schwarzenegger stepped in. I didn't immediately recognize him; all I saw was a big white man with blond hair. I was quickly debating stepping out of the elevator because I didn't want to be alone in that metal box with a big white man. But then he smiled, and I realized who he was.

"Hello," I said.

He nodded, still smiling. We rode in silence, with my eyes glued to his reflection in the polished chrome doors.

Another time, when I was in the elevator, the doors slid open and in stepped Phylicia Rashad. She was carrying her sleeping daughter, Condola, in her arms.

"Hello," she said sweetly.

"Hi," I piped, trying to keep my excitement under control. I couldn't believe that I was in the elevator with Clair Huxtable! At the time, *The Cosby Show* was the number one show in America.

The series aired on NBC from 1984 until 1992. For his portrayal of Cliff Huxtable, Bill Cosby earned the title of "America's dad." During the first season of the show, I learned Phylicia Rashad's sister was the actress and dancer Debbie Allen. Debbie Allen had starred on yet another popular television series called *Fame*, a musical drama adapted from the 1980 film of the same name. Twelve years after Phylicia Rashad stepped into that elevator holding her baby girl, I would be in California having lunch with Debbie Allen, discussing a movie option for my novel *Sugar*.

Even further in the future, in 2021, Phylicia Rashad would narrate my essay about Zora Neale Hurston, which I contributed to the book *Four Hundred Souls: A Community History of African America, 1619–2019*, edited by Ibram X. Kendi and Keisha N. Blain.

In that moment, my future was staring me square in the face.

But it was only 1989, and *Sugar* was still just a short story.

THE CORPORATE OFFICE WAS SMALL, cozy, and brightly lit. While all the upper management were mostly white men, my immediate supervisor was a Puerto Rican woman. During my time there, I'd become friendly with the office accountant, a white woman named Charlotte, who was tall, string-bean thin, and had curly brown hair. Her spectacles were so thick that her eyes looked as big as globes. She was quick-witted, well-read, and a smoker like myself, which is why I took my smoke breaks at her desk.

She had an assistant named Bianca, an Italian girl with long, wavy black hair and green eyes. Every day, Bianca came to work with face makeup worthy of a fashion shoot. She reminded me of Veronica from St. Cyril. The resemblance was so strong that I imagined they must share the same gene pool. Bianca was ambivalent toward me. Sometimes she was chatty, but most times we shared little more than a hello and goodbye.

Once, when I was sitting alongside Charlotte's desk, smoking a cigarette and reading an article in the latest issue of *Essence*, a magazine written for Black women, Bianca looked up from her *Vogue* magazine and said, "I don't understand why Black people need their own magazines."

I didn't miss the revulsion in her voice. The question coming out of the blue like it did caught me off guard. Charlotte, who was on the phone at the time, peered at me over her spectacles. The expression on her face seemed to say, *Well, tell her.*

I crossed the dark blue carpet to Bianca's desk, reached over the BLT on rye she'd been enjoying, and grabbed the *Vogue* magazine. "Lemme show you something."

Bianca bit into her sandwich and watched as I turned the pages. I can't remember if there was one Black woman or none, but there certainly weren't more than two profiled on those glossy pages. When I reached the last page, I set the magazine back on the desk and said, "This is why we have our own magazine."

Bianca rolled her eyes and slid the magazine out of my reach. "I just asked a question. No need to be nasty."

I hadn't been nasty. I hadn't raised my voice, worked my neck, or rolled my eyes. I simply used the magazine to illustrate my answer.

If damned if you do and damned if you don't were a people, those people would be Black.

FRIDAY, APRIL 21. BIANCA WAS standing at the file cabinet, rummaging through manila folders, when I walked into the cubicle for my midmorning smoke break.

"Hey."

"Hey," I responded. "Where's Charlotte?"

"Bathroom, I think."

I sat down, crossed my legs, and lit my cigarette.

Bianca slammed the drawer closed. "So," she sang, "did you hear about what happened to that woman in Central Park?"

I wasn't one for watching the news. "No. What woman?"

She sauntered over to her desk, plucked up the folded news-paper, and presented it to me. "Here, see for yourself." Her lips were stretched into a grin that was part sarcasm and part glee.

I set my cigarette down in the ashtray and unfolded the paper. There, on the front page in bold, ominous, black letters read:

CENTRAL PARK HORROR

WOLF PACK'S PREY

FEMALE JOGGER NEAR DEATH AFTER
SAVAGE ATTACK BY ROVING GANG.

The unnamed woman, called the Central Park Jogger, had been "bludgeoned with a rock, tied up, raped and left for dead."

BACK AT HOME, MY PARENTS were parked in front of the television together, watching the story unfold. I was surprised to see them sitting hip to hip on the couch, because the only thing they ever did together was fight.

The police had identified and arrested five of the alleged assail-ants. The news outlets had already dubbed them the Central Park Five.

Robert sucked his teeth in disgust. "Those boys didn't do that," he spat at the television.

"They didn't do it," he echoed again before turning to look at Vivian, who was staring at the white newscaster's emotionless face.

"That could have been one of my sons," she sighed sadly. "They're just kids."

In America, Black kids don't get to be kids, especially not in the eyes of white people. Black children have been adultified since slav-ery, perceived as older and less innocent than white children. For hundreds of years, they've used this as an excuse to exact violence on our children.

~

IN SOUTH CAROLINA IN 1944, GEORGE STINNEY, A FOURTEEN-YEAR-OLD Black boy, was accused of murdering two white girls. He was arrested, taken to the police station, and questioned alone in a room without his parents. Who knows what the white police officers said or didn't say, did or didn't do to young George in that room that forced him to sign a confession to the crime.

A tax attorney represented George in the three-hour trial that was void of evidence or witnesses. The jury deliberated for ten minutes, then came back into the courtroom and announced that they'd found George Stinney guilty.

George Stinney was sentenced to death. On June 16, 1944, they strapped Mr. and Mrs. Stinney's fourteen-year-old son, their child, their treasure and gift from God, into an electric chair and fried him to death.

Seventy years later, the court ruled that George Stinney was falsely accused and had not received a fair trial. As a result, his conviction was vacated. George was dead, and George's parents were dead. The new ruling wouldn't bring any of them back.

Penance aids the sinner; it does not erase the crime or the people harmed. Too much, too little, too late.

Perhaps those people who had been alive in 1931, watching the news of the Central Park Five in 1989, were struck with a sense of déjà vu, even though it had been fifty-eight years since two white women in Alabama pointed their ivory fingers at nine Black boys and screeched rape. The papers called those boys the Scottsboro Nine. It took only a week for an all-white jury to convict them of rape and sentence them to death.

But the executioner never did get a hold of those boys, because there were years of stays and retrials and reconvictions. And then the day came when they were released from the nightmare that began when they were boys and finally ended when they were men and had been men, for a good long time by then. I said *released*, instead of *freed*, because Black people in America have never been fully free.

Then, in 1949, four Black males ranging in age from fourteen to twenty-six were accused in the rape of one Norma Padgett, a white woman who claimed that not only had the Black males sexually violated her but they'd savagely beaten her husband too. The Groveland Four: Ernest Thomas, Charles Greenlee, Samuel Shepherd, and Walter Irvin.

It was Florida, for God's sakes, just as bad or worse as Alabama, Mississippi, and Texas, and so Ernest Thomas knew what his fate would be and fled before he could be arrested for a crime he didn't commit. Unfortunately, he was unable to outrun, outsmart, or hide from an angry lynch mob, one thousand people strong.

One bullet would have taken him down, but where was the fun in that? So they riddled him with four hundred.

The remaining accused were found guilty by, you guessed it, an all-white jury. Two of the three were sentenced to death and the other to life in prison without parole. The NAACP got involved, and in 1951, the Supreme Court overturned their convictions, remanding the case to a lower court for a new trial.

White people didn't like that all. Not one bit. But none was as angry as Sheriff Willis McCall. Taking matters into his own hands, McCall took Walter Irvin and Samuel Shepherd into custody and shot them in cold blood. He claimed that they were trying to escape.

Walter Irvin survived the shooting, and he and Charles Greenlee went to trial for a second time. The results of the second trial were the same as the first. Verdict: guilty. Sentence: death. They lingered on death row for years before Charles Greenlee was paroled in 1962 and Walter Irvin in 1968.

In 2019, the state of Florida posthumously pardoned all four men and issued an apology to their remaining family members. Again, too much, too little, too late.

Perhaps those people who had been alive in 1949 watching the news in 1989 balled their fists and grumbled through gritted teeth: "Here we go again."

In 2006, when my daughter is eighteen years old, sitting in the passenger seat of my car, singing along to a popular bop, the disc jockey's voice would cut into the music, reporting the arrest of six Black boys in Louisiana who had been accused of beating a white boy. The DJ referred to them as the Jena Six.

A half hour later, when the update came, it was filled with comparisons to the Central Park Five and the Scottsboro Nine, and it would be my turn to ball my fists, grit my teeth, and grumble, "Here we go again."

THAT APRIL DAY IN 1989, AS THE NEWSREADER FINISHED THEIR REPORT on the Central Park Five, Robert got up from the couch in disgust, grabbed his house keys and wallet, and walked out the front door. Vivian and I exchanged glances. We both knew what the other was thinking: *He's going to get a bottle.* It was one of the few times we couldn't blame him, because living Black in America feels like a phonograph needle caught in the dead black wax of a spinning vinyl record.

PART SIX

CARDINALS

Hold fast to dreams
For if dreams die
Life is a broken-winged bird
That cannot fly.

—LANGSTON HUGHES

32

The 1990s were a darned good decade, and everybody's now coming to realize this, but people also need to know that when the 1990s began, it felt like anything but a decade with a unique tone and texture and attitude. It felt like nothing. It felt blank.

—DOUGLAS COUPLAND

In 1990, a few years after RockResorts was sold to CSX Corp., I found myself, once again, out of work. Within six months, my unemployment benefits ran out, and because I didn't have any savings to speak of, I was left destitute. The country was at war with Iraq, and companies had initiated a hiring freeze. With a child to feed and a family who needed my financial contribution, I had no other choice but to go down to the welfare office and file for assistance. I told Vivian how ashamed I felt about the prospect.

"You better go get your money, you've paid into the system and now you're in need," Vivian said. "There's nothing for you to be ashamed about. That's what it's there for."

It was one of the most humiliating experiences of my life.

I arrived on the appointed day, in an acid-washed denim jacket and a kente cloth pillbox hat hiding my uncombed hair. The waiting room, with its gray walls, gray carpet, and harsh lighting, was one of the most depressing places I'd ever had the displeasure of visiting. Nothing about the space was uplifting or welcoming. It felt, and looked, like a large prison cell. There were a few men there, but most of the people waiting were women, and all were Black and Hispanic. Because of the inadequate number of chairs, some people were seated on the floor. I believe this is purposeful, because it adds to the humiliation of those in need. Floating above the clamor of mothers chastising and comforting crying children, ringing telephones, clients arguing with social workers, was Maury's unmistakable voice blaring from the television housed in a cage attached to the wall: "The DNA test says YOU ARE NOT THE FATHER!"

"Bernice? Bernice McFadden? McFadden, Bernice!"

I leaped out of the uncomfortable metal chair and hurried toward the woman beckoning with her hand. In her cubicle, I sat down across the desk from her. The felt-walled box offered little privacy, so I could see and hear the other social workers in the surrounding cubicles as they carried out personal telephone conversations or interviews with others in need.

My social worker was a Black woman in her late thirties or early forties. She wore rings on six of her fat fingers, the metal was so tight that the flesh oozed over the rims like Pillsbury dough from the can. The lobes of her ears were double pierced. One gold ball sitting atop a gold hoop. And she had a gap the size of a door between her top front teeth.

I'd filled out paperwork, divulging who I was, where and when I was born, where I lived, the name and age of my child, and information about the man who'd fathered her. I was not exactly honest when answering the question about my daughter's father. I knew that for me to receive the maximum benefit, I had to lie.

"Are you getting any support from the father?"

"No."

She eyed me suspiciously. "Why?"

"He left the country. He went back to Guyana," I said, trying my best to hold her gaze.

She grunted. "I don't know why you girls keep having babies with those damn West Indians. They ain't no good."

With her eyes still on me, she hovered her shiny manicured fingernails over the keyboard of her IBM computer.

"Next time you get pregnant, get pregnant by an American man so you can get some child support," she added, before viciously attacking the keys.

I nodded obediently.

I was given a book of emergency food stamps and sent home to wait for word telling me if I'd been granted assistance. A week later, the approval letter arrived.

I took the letter to yet another social service office to get my welfare identification card, which I needed to collect my monthly stipend from my neighborhood check-cashing place. This card required a photo, and once again, I'd worn my kente cloth pillbox hat over my untidy hair.

"Remove the hat, please," said the tired-looking, potbellied photographer.

I froze. My hair looked like a bird's nest beneath that hat.

I'd seen women on the news, women who had dashed out to the local bodega with uncombed hair or braless not thinking that they'd witness some newsworthy event and then hung around to watch only to find themselves staring into a camera with a microphone shoved in their face.

"Look, kids, that's one of them welfare queens Ronald Reagan warned us about."

I removed my hat. The shutter closed and opened.

———

LINDA TAYLOR WAS BORN IN 1926 to a white mother and Black father in a Tennessee town called Golddust and grew up to live a colorful life. In 1974, she was arrested for welfare and social security fraud, having collected tens of thousands of dollars under eighty different aliases. And for that she was dubbed the Welfare Queen.

Ronald Reagan caught whiff of the story during his presidential bid of 1976. He claimed that the welfare system was broken and used Linda Taylor as evidence. Suddenly, and without warning, all Black female recipients of the system were labeled welfare queens, even though white women were and *remain* its biggest beneficiaries.

Linda Taylor loomed over me. The government made me feel embarrassed and ashamed of needing help. As a result, I didn't go to the check-cashing place on the first of the month, when the benefits became available and people lined up out the door. I waited until the second or the third of the month, slipping in well after noon, when the storefront was empty. And I didn't use my food stamps at my neighborhood supermarket, because I was fearful of running into someone I knew.

"Oh, hello, Bernice, I didn't know you were a welfare queeeeeeeeeeeeen!"

I couldn't risk that indignity, so I did my grocery shopping across Conduit Boulevard, in the City Line neighborhood, where I didn't know a soul.

I should have used that time to concentrate on writing my novel. Instead, I'd wasted it groveling in my misery and feeling sorry for myself.

THANKFULLY, I WASN'T ON WELFARE for more than six months before I was hired as a reservation's agent at Leading Hotels of the World. Their call center was much larger than the one I had worked at RockResorts.

Leading Hotels is a luxury brand too, but they have hotels and resorts all around the globe, and I was excited about the travel opportunities that awaited me. I was hired on the one-to-nine shift. I hated the hours, but I was happy to be off welfare and working again.

I also couldn't recognize it for the gift it was. You see, because of my late work schedule, by the time I arrived home, it was 10:00 p.m. Vivian had already fed, bathed, and put Azsá to sleep, so when I came home, I was free to do whatever I wanted, and most nights what I wanted to do was write.

Was it serendipity or the angelcestors at work? Maybe it was a little bit of both.

33

The announcer on the radio told us that a heavy snow was on the way. It was December 18, 1992, and Robert's elder brother, Bree, wasn't feeling his best.

In the car repair shop where he worked, Bree straightened himself and frowned down at the guts under the hood of the Oldsmobile Cutlass Supreme he'd been working on for the past few hours. He'd hoped that he could make it home before the first icy flakes started to fall, because all he wanted to do was climb into bed, pull the covers over his head, and sleep off whatever was trying to pull him under. Now, however, he realized the problem with the Cutlass was going to take more time than expected. He might have been a little further along had he not called out sick the day before, and now everything was backed up.

Earlier that day, when he was getting himself ready to go into work, his wife, Audrey, had shot him a concerned look.

"You going in?"

"Yep."

Her eyebrows rose. "You feeling better?"

"Good enough," Bree said.

Audrey didn't push the issue because Bree wasn't one to fol-low orders or suggestions, not from his wife or his doctor, who'd warned him that his liver and kidneys were so damaged from his excessive drinking that if he took another drink, "You'll be yester-day's news."

Now, Bree looked around the body shop and saw just one co-worker peering beneath a van that was suspended on a lift, six feet in the air above his head. When the man felt him staring, he threw the grease towel in his hand over his shoulder.

"You okay?"

Bree nodded. "Yeah, I'm just going to sit down for a minute."

"Okay," the man said, tilting his head back on his neck, return-ing his attention to the task at hand.

Bree opened the car door. He settled into the driver's seat, closed his eyes, took a deep breath, and willed the awful feeling away.

In his mind, Bree counted slowly down from one hundred, but when he opened his eyes again, he didn't feel any better.

"Fuck it," he grumbled to himself as he pulled the car door closed.

He glanced out the closed window and saw that his coworker had his back turned, busy tinkering with something in the under-carriage of the car. Bree slipped the pint of vodka from the pocket of his jumpsuit, unscrewed the top, raised it to his lips, and took a swig. It took only a few moments for the warm liquor to ooze through his veins. Bree's head went pleasantly light, he took an-other sip and then another. In a blink, the bottle was empty. He shoved it back into the pocket of his jumpsuit and let his head fall back onto the headrest with the euphoria.

More than an hour had passed before the coworker walked over to the car and tapped on the window.

"Bree. Hey, man, wake up." He laughed, yanking the car door open.

When he saw the foam of saliva bubbling from between Bree's parted lips and his wide, glassy eyes staring off into oblivion, the man threw his hand over his mouth and screamed into his palm.

IN 1958, THIRTY-FOUR YEARS BEFORE, to the day, Bree and Robert's father, Harold, had also met his maker. Harold had been dead to them for their entire lives, so when they learned that he was *literally* dead, the emotions that welled up in them left them perplexed. The only thing that Bree and Robert had known about Harold was what Gwen had told them, and she'd told them little to nothing. But the little she had shared was unkind.

"Gwennie, did you know your husband is dead?"

It was a somebody who knew somebody who had dated the man who was the nephew of the mortician who had recognized the name and then the face because the two had come up together as boys in Harlem back in the thirties. By the time Gwen got the news, Harold McFadden had been dead for two decades, having left this life as an inmate at the New Jersey State penitentiary.

After she set the phone down, Gwen thought how much she wanted a cigarette, but she'd quit smoking years earlier by order of her doctor. Her heart was weak and damaged from stress and nicotine and alcohol and had been fitted with a pacemaker to make it work right. She'd given up the cigarettes and had cut back on the alcohol but kept a bottle on hand for days when news arrived out of the blue, setting her hands to trembling.

The rum was in the closet, above the shelf where she stored her trusty typewriter. She retrieved both and settled herself at the dining room table. She poured two fingers of rum, raised the short crystal glass into the air, and said, "To you, Harold, I hope you're rotting in hell."

She emptied the glass in one gulp, cracked her knuckles, and attacked the keys. On that typewriter, Gwen had composed letters to department stores pointing out errors on her bill, she'd typed letters to friends and family, and to TV evangelists (she folded those letters around five-dollar bills), and letters to the wives of men she had taken up with.

That day, the letter she typed was addressed to the United States Social Security Administration, informing the whom it may concern that she, Gwendolyn D. McFadden Taylor, was the widow of the long-deceased Harold Isaac McFadden.

I'm writing to inquire about any death benefits that me and my children may be entitled . . .

She'd sent a similar letter back in 1960, after she learned that the man who'd fathered her youngest son, Eddie, had died. Edgar Milton Taylor had passed away of a brain aneurism on May 28, 1959. That request was denied, of course, because Gwen could not provide proof that they were or had ever been legally betrothed. She thought she'd have better luck when she reached out about Harold's death, because their union was real and not imagined, and she had the marriage certificate as proof.

She took the certificate to the pharmacy across the street from her building, paid a nickel for the copy they made on the Xerox machine behind the counter, and mailed both her typed letter and the copy to the social security company.

She could use the money, no matter how small the amount. Especially since she'd had to return to work because the very same Social Security Administration claimed that she was short two quarters of the forty qualifying calendar work quarters required to receive social security retirement benefits.

It took nearly a month, but finally she opened her mailbox and there was a reply. In the elevator, she clutched the envelope protectively against her bosom. When the doors slid open, she hurried down the hallway and into her apartment. Her heart was racing. She had to be careful about that. So she sat down on the couch, closed her eyes, and took four deep breaths. After a while, her galloping heart slowed to a trot. Using a letter opener, she sliced the envelope clean open and retrieved the letter.

Mrs. McFadden,

The eligible spouse or child must apply for benefits within two years of the date of death.

Sincerely.

Hot tears pooled in her eyes. She could never win. She could never fucking win. Unlucky in love and unlucky in life.

"Dammit to hell," she growled under her breath.

That had been twelve years ago, now it was 1992 and her first child was dead. What must have crossed Gwen's mind when, on December 18, she answered the phone and heard her daughter-in-law's tear-soaked voice sputtering out the bad news? Did the significance of the date leap out at her like a cat from the shadows? Or did it take a few hours or even a few days before the realization settled over her like a web? And when it did, did Gwen think that Harold was sending her a final fuck-you from the other side?

And what about Robert? What did he think when he got the call about his brother's passing? Did he think his time was up too? After all, they'd been born exactly one year apart to the day. Did that mean that on December 18 the following year the reaper would sink his scythe into his heart? Was Robert aware that history rhymed?

When I arrived home from work that evening, Robert was seated in his recliner in the back of the basement, staring at the television.

"I'm sorry about your brother," I offered sadly.

Even though Bree and Robert were exactly one year apart, they were two very different men. Bree was tall and bald, and he liked to laugh and cuss. He was a walker, preferring to stride miles to his destination rather than take the train or the bus. He was an extrovert, a good-time guy, well-known and well-liked.

Robert, on the other hand, was an introvert and still clinging to the hair that had been receding since his twenties. Whereas Bree was always in the streets, Robert was a homebody who didn't really care for company other than his own. The one thing they did have in common was their love of alcohol.

Robert glanced at me, grunted a thank-you, and reached for his mug filled with Hennessy. He wasn't tall like his brother, but he was a respectable five seven or five eight. But as I stood there looking at him, he seemed smaller, half the size of what he'd been when I'd left for work that morning. In fact, he looked like a pitiful little boy with a mustache.

It wasn't until that day that I'd ever considered that Robert could experience an emotion outside of anger or rage. And even though he wasn't crying, I could sense his sorrow. That was the first time I saw him as a human being and not the monster I'd always perceived him as.

"Okay," I mumbled before turning and walking away.

THE DAY OF THE FUNERAL, Gwen was so overcome with grief, she could barely walk, so Robert and Eddie each hooked an arm around her waist and practically dragged her across the sidewalk to the waiting limousine. The scene was pitiful. I had to look away, trying hard to swallow the lump in my throat. Being a mother myself, it was easy for me to imagine her misery.

It was a bright and blustery December day. I remember how the sun rays clung to Gwen's sable coat, and when a gust of wind swept the black pillbox hat off her head and sent it tumbling down Flatbush Avenue, Gwen threw one hand over her shiny gray pin curls and wailed.

Eventually, Gwen's sorrow swallowed her whole and she slipped into a deep depression. For her entire life, she'd been fanatically clean and tidy, but now every time one or both of her sons visited, they found dishes in the sink, Gwen unbathed, and a litter box overflowing with cat stool.

As time went on, things got worse. Her mailbox was crammed tight with social security checks, second and third utility shutoff notices, and, finally, on one visit they found an eviction notice taped to her door.

"Well, you can bring her here to live with us. We'll make room," Vivian offered when Robert told her about Gwen's difficulties.

He brought the offer to Gwen, and she'd said, "Thank you, but no."

She preferred to take her chances in a nursing home with people with whom she didn't have any history. After all, she'd accused Vivian of getting pregnant just to trap her son and had boycotted their wedding. And a few years earlier she'd counseled Robert to force me into marriage and an abortion. Sure, she had become a little forgetful in her old age, but she wasn't so completely demented that she would risk placing life and limb in the care of scorned women. So, Gwen chose to go to the nursing home and hoped that all those crisp five-dollar bills she'd sent to the television evangelists had bought her a place in heaven, because she knew nursing homes were like the sea—neither had back doors.

Her belongings were divided among Robert; his brother, Eddie; and Bree's children. Robert took possession of the china cabinet, which Gwen's mother, Ethel, had brought with her from Barbados in the 1920s, that and the dark brown steamer trunk where Gwen stored her photo albums, documents, and keepsakes.

Before it came to our home, the steamer trunk had sat draped in a mustard-colored throw at the foot of Gwen's bed. For years, I had no idea what treasures that trunk held until my freshman year of high school, when I signed up to take tap dancing class. Gwen was thrilled. She even offered to buy my tap shoes. She never really took much interest in me, at least not when I compared her to

Thelma, the grandmother with whom I spent the most time. I still wasn't quite sure why Gwen had bought tap shoes for me. As far as gift giving went, she wasn't big on it, preferring to stick a five-dollar bill in a birthday or Christmas card. *From your old gray-haired grand-mother.*

When I came home for the Christmas break, I went over to Gwen's apartment to collect the shoes.

"Do you want some tuna fish?" That's what she always offered us grandchildren when we came to visit.

"No, thank you," I declined politely, and sat down on the couch. I didn't want to be there longer than I needed to be. Gwen wasn't the easiest person to talk to.

She walked over to the closet and opened the door. "I have the tap shoes right here," she said, bending over. "Size nine, right?"

"Yes, Grandma."

I looked around the tiny studio. It was as neat as a pin. Not one thing out of place. Gwen was fastidiously neat, something Robert had inherited from her.

Outside her window, the D train rumbled across the elevated tracks, setting the glass windowpanes clattering in their casements. The racket always startled me, but it didn't seem to bother Gwen at all. When the train approached, she'd pause her conversation until it passed, and then casually pick up where she'd left off.

Gwen walked over to me, removed the lid from the box, and plucked out one shiny leather shoe.

"Here," she said, handing it to me. "Try it on."

I took it, turned it over, and ran my finger over the metal plate fixed to the heel of the shoe.

"I was a dancer too," she sighed wistfully as I slipped on the shoes.

I'd heard as much but had never seen any evidence of that past life. I stood up and walked across the carpeted floor.

"How do they feel?"

"They feel good," I said.

"Let's go in the kitchen to try them out," she said.

I hadn't seen her move like that in years. Clearly, she was excited. I stood in the narrow space between the kitchen and the stove. Gwen planted her hands on her wide hips and grinned. "Okay, show me what you got."

I didn't have anything, because my first class wasn't until after the Christmas break. I shrugged, feeling a little embarrassed.

"Um, class doesn't start until next month."

Gwen frowned. "Oh," she spouted, and then, "Well, let me show you how to do it."

She kicked her foot out of her lilac-colored slipper. I couldn't ever recall seeing her naked feet, but I must have seen them in Barbados when we were on the beach. I don't know why I was so struck by that, but I was, and I found myself staring at her neatly cut, highly buffed toenails. She grabbed either side of the doorway, bracing herself against a possible slip and fall.

"This is called a ball heel," she said, demonstrating the move to me. "Bring your foot up like this, and then you bring the ball of your foot down, and then drop your heel." Her bare heel hit the floor with a slap. "Now you try it."

I mimicked her movements with my right foot and then my left.

"Good, good," she exclaimed. "Now, we better stop before the neighbor beneath us complains. She's a son of a bitch."

That was her favorite saying. Anyone who annoyed her was a son of a bitch. The mayor was a son of a bitch, the light company was a son of a bitch, as was the gas company. Sometimes her sons were sons of bitches too.

"I want to show you something."

Gwen went to the bedside table, opened the drawer, and fumbled through the contents until she found a brass skeleton key. She removed the throw from her trunk and wiggled the key into the lock, then gently raised the lid.

I watched quietly from my seat on the sofa, sensing that something momentous was about to take place. I strained my neck to see the contents, but her wide body all but blocked a clear view. When Gwen turned around, she had a photo album and a scrapbook cradled in her arms. She sat down beside me, opened the photo album, and there on the first cellophane-covered page was a sepia-colored photograph of a young, glamorous-looking Gwen dressed in a short flared skirt and sleeveless top. She was bent forward, beaming into the photographer's camera. On her feet were tap shoes.

My mouth flopped open. "That's you?"

"Uh-hmm."

For the next hour or so, we sat there together, hips touching, arms brushing, flipping through photographs and newspaper clippings that chronicled her short life as a dancer.

I was flabbergasted. How had all of this been kept from me until now? I glanced over at the open steamer trunk, wondering what other secrets it held. When Gwen saw me looking, she gathered the album and scrapbook into her arms and abruptly stood up. Her genial demeanor seeped away as quickly as water through wet sand, and just like that, she became the aloof woman she'd been my entire life.

"I'm tired," she huffed. "Time for you to go."

I thought I'd done or said something to upset her.

"Okay," I murmured, reaching for the shoebox on the floor. "Thank you again for the shoes, Grandma," I said, rising from the sofa.

She was already beside the steamer trunk, carefully setting the books back inside.

"You're welcome," she threw over her shoulder.

Up to that point, Gwen hadn't been particularly interesting to me because all I knew about her was that she had a bad heart and was easily agitated. But the tap shoes had opened a gateway through which I'd gained a new appreciation for her.

Now that my curiosity was piqued, I made it my business to visit her more often than I had in the past. And every time I did, she allowed me to look at the album and scrapbook, and sometimes she'd answer one or two of my probing questions. But I had to be careful not to delve too deep, or she'd shut down and send me on my way.

Gwen was a mystery that I wouldn't completely untangle until long after her death.

34

It was 1993, the year of the rooster, according to the Chinese zo-
diac. For the ancestors, the roosters crowing awakened people
and brought light into darkness. It seemed appropriate because
Gwen had been such an enigmatic figure in my life.

Robert placed the trunk and all its treasures down in the basement, just feet away from where I slept. The trunk was locked, of
course, and Robert held the key. Understandably, he was as protective of its contents as Gwen had been and so was hesitant to allow
me access, but I chipped away at him until finally he agreed.

What I found in that trunk was so much more than I could
have ever imagined or hoped for.

In addition to the photographs, playbills, and news clippings
that Gwen had shared with me, there were letters, christening documents, school report cards, naturalization records, and several
communications between Gwen and the NYC Department of Vital
Records. For years, Gwen had been trying to acquire a copy of her
birth certificate, but each and every search came up nil.

In later years, I'd discover that the woman Gwen had known as her sister was actually her mother. Irene was fifteen and unmarried when she became pregnant with Gwen. A scandalous combination in 1922 America.

There were several date planners, which Gwen used as journals, recording every minute detail of every waking day.

> *Thank you, Father God, for waking me up this*
> *morning . . . my knees are achy but thank God I'm alive. It's*
> *raining today. Cat seems to be in a saucy mood. Son number*
> *one called me early this morning, fussing. I hung up on him.*

> *You came by today. The sun was just coming up when I*
> *opened my eyes and saw you sitting in the comfy chair, legs*
> *crossed, gazing out the window, fiddling with your watch. Is*
> *that timepiece still giving you trouble, my love? I'm happy to*
> *send you a new one. Citizen, right?*

> *We were at our place today in Batsheba. Oh, how I love it*
> *here! The sea is like a savage, roaring and pounding the*
> *shoreline. I would be frightened, if you weren't here to make*
> *me feel safe.*

> *I come out of the shower, beaded with water, walked into*
> *the bedroom and there you are, sprawled out on your back,*
> *your sergeant standing at attention once again.*
> *Oh my, Oh my . . .*

I could feel her womanness and girlish giddiness rising off the pages like steam. Playful. Lighthearted. Teasing. Sexual. I had known her my entire life, but I was only just making her acquaintance at the end of hers.

I was puzzled by the entries. Was she in Barbados, or was she here in Brooklyn?

It was baffling, because on any given day, paragraphs placed Gwen and her lover together in their love nest in Barbados and then in the paragraphs that immediately followed, she was complaining about the volume of the television in the apartment next door.

I read and reread the entries. Some days, I thought she was writing crazy, that her dementia had started long before Bree died and we'd all missed the signs. I thought too that she was recounting deep and vivid dreams. I knew that some dreams were so potent that they felt real. I'd had dreams like that. I still have dreams like that.

I HAD SO MANY QUESTIONS, and Robert didn't have any answers and Gwen wasn't talking, and so I took matters into my own hands.

First, I opened an account on Ancestry.com and plugged in all the names and dates I had. That search revealed a bevy of information, including census records, which I had never seen before. When I saw Gwen, Irene, and their parents on the 1930 census record, I squealed like I'd hit the lottery.

The discovery was thrilling and addicting, so much so, that sometimes I'd call in sick to work to spend the day looking through records in the genealogical division of the New York Public Library or at the NYC FamilySearch Center. I spent a good amount of money ordering copies of social security applications and birth and death certificates. Every time I obtained a new document, a new piece to the puzzle of my family, I made a copy for Robert. Eyes shining with amazement, he'd ask, "How did you find this?"

The one piece of documentation that literally knocked the wind out of him was his father's World War II draft card. When I approached him, he was standing in the backyard, puffing on a cigarette, staring up at the squirrels jumping through the tangle of grapevines.

He saw me out of the corner of his eye.

"What?" he asked, without looking at me.

Grinning, I pushed the copy toward him.

Robert tapped the ash off his cigarette and tucked it into the corner of his mouth. Squinting, he carefully studied the paper.

Name	Harold Isaac McFadden
Race	Negro (Black)
Age	23
Birth Date	1 Aug 1917
Birth Place	Louisville, Kentucky
Registration Date	16 Oct 1940
Registration Place	New York City, New York, New York
Employer	Harry Blumfield
Height	5'9½"
Weight	155
Complexion	Dark Brown
Hair Color	Black
Eye Color	Brown
Next of Kin	Chappo Elliot

Robert plucked the cigarette from his mouth and dropped it to the ground. He dragged his hand over his face and took a deep, deep breath. It was clear he was shook.

"Your grandmother's name was Chappo," I said, pointing to her name. "That sounds like an Indian name, don't it?"

Robert folded his lips and nodded. When I turned to leave, he said, "Th-thank you, Bernice."

He'd probably thanked me a handful of times in my life, but I'd never heard the sincerity in his voice like I did that day.

"You're welcome, Daddy," I said.

Gifting my father evidence of his identity and seeing his reaction helped me to understand the importance of knowing from whence we came. I suspect the peek into his family history made him feel less alone in the world, maybe in some strange way it made him feel powerful. Maybe that's why America works so hard at erasing and rewriting the true history of Black people in this country.

SOMETIMES, WHILE I WAS PORING over documents, a story would pop into my head, narrated by a voice that was not my own. There was no small doubt in my mind that my ancestors were gathered around me. I couldn't see them with my naked eye, but I could certainly feel their presence and sometimes, I'd even catch a whiff of cologne, perfume, pipe smoke, or fresh-cut grass.

Science tells us that each human being carries up to twelve generations of ancestral DNA in their body. Had my research activated that DNA? Was there some type of alchemy at play?

Maybe.

Absolutely.

I fully expected to unravel the story of my people; what I did not expect from the process was how it nourished my imagination, which in turn strengthened my storytelling skills.

During that time, *Sugar* was still just a short story. Since the birth of my daughter, I'd submitted it to various literary contests without success. I thought I'd have better luck with a collection of stories rather than just one. So I assembled the stories that I thought held the most promise and slapped on a title: *Oxtails, Pig Tails, and Other Afrocentric Tales*. I don't think I had more than one hundred printed pages, which was far less than what publishers expected for a collection. I didn't know that, and that's why ignorance is bliss.

But then I came across an article in either *Writer's Digest* or *Poets & Writers* that claimed it was virtually impossible for an unknown writer to sell a short story collection without first having published a novel. And with that information, my blissful ignorance was blown to smithereens.

I'd had plans to write a novel but not just yet. The truth was I found the page count intimidating. Short stories were like molehills, and the novel was a mountain I wasn't confident I could scale just yet. But according to the article, as an unpublished writer I was wasting my time, energy, ink, and paper on a pipe dream.

So I had a decision to make.

One night, I spread the stories out on the floor of my apartment, sat down, and waited. I didn't know exactly what I was waiting for, but I knew I'd recognize it when I saw, heard, or felt it. I sat there for some time, floating my hands over the pages like a medium at a séance, humming: *Eeny, meeny, miny, moe, catch a novel by its toe.* . . . It was silly, I know. I get silly sometimes during crucial moments, it's a coping mechanism of mine.

That said, my eyes kept drifting to *Sugar.* I reached for the slim stack of papers. She was the story that had been with me the longest. The one story in my collection to which I felt deeply connected.

"I guess you're the one," I whispered.

35

In 1992, New York had a Black mayor named David Dinkins, but it was Black women who would mark that year for me.

Mae Carol Jemison became the first African American woman to travel into space, and Toni Morrison's *Jazz*, Alice Walker's *Possessing the Secret of Joy*, and Terry McMillan's *Waiting to Exhale* all appeared on the *New York Times* bestseller list at the same time.

It was an exciting time for Black women, especially Black women writers. Not since the Harlem Renaissance had there been a fervor for Black literature. Critics and scholars alike jumped to mark the phenomenon as *the new renaissance* and *the second coming*. At the time, I didn't understand the true significance of the moment, but it did make me feel optimistic about my own literary ambitions. I was a fan of all three women but had only recently discovered Terry McMillan. I'd read her sophomore novel, *Disappearing Acts*, just weeks before her blockbuster *Waiting to Exhale* hit bookstores.

At the time, the corporate offices and the call center for Leading Hotels of the World was located at 757 Third Avenue, directly across the street from a Barnes & Noble bookstore. You can imagine how much time and money I spent in that store. I spent most of my lunch hours browsing through the books. And, of course, every other week when I collected my paycheck, I bought a book for myself and a book for my daughter.

Following the new renaissance, chain bookstores across the country created sections solely dedicated to Black-authored books. I, for one, was in heaven because it made it easy for bibliophiles like me who were exclusively reading Black authors. The downside was that many non-Black readers avoided these segregated sections like colored-only water fountains and waiting rooms of the Jim Crow era.

It was in the "African American Interest" section that I discovered a plethora of brilliant Black writers like Gloria Naylor, Marita Golden, Tina McElroy Ansa, Bebe Moore Campbell, Toni Cade Bambara, Louise Meriwether, Paule Marshall, and J. California Cooper.

J. California Cooper was an author whose books affected me in the same way that Alice Walker's and Toni Morrison's did.

J. California Cooper had begun her writing career as a playwright. It was Alice Walker who'd first published her collection of short stories under her press, Wild Trees. Not only was J. California Cooper writing stories that spoke to me, but she was also writing the type of stories that I longed to write myself.

My friend Robyn had a longtime girlfriend named Cassaundra, and over the years she and I had developed a close relationship. She was a big reader like me, and we were both fans of Cooper's work. It was Cassaundra who took me to my first book event, held at the Black-owned and -operated Nkiru Books, located at 76 St. Marks Avenue in my former childhood neighborhood of Crown Heights.

When we arrived, the small bookstore was packed tight with Cooper devotees, so Cassaundra and I stood at the back, near the door. When Cooper appeared, she was met with squeals and applause. She was tiny, fair-skinned, with a swath of gray-and-black hair. Cooper was witty and soft spoken with a warm smile and eyes that sparkled with wisdom. When she said or read something from her book that struck us, the audience moaned in our throats, amen'd, or raised our hands into the air, shaking invisible tambourines. This book event felt like a Baptist Sunday church service, and Cooper was leading the sermon.

During the Q&A portion of the evening, a sister with a headful of locs dripping in cowrie shells asked, "Where do your stories come from?"

"The trees," Cooper said without hesitation. "I talk to the trees, and they talk back."

Some people nodded with understanding; others looked doubtful.

"And guides," she added. "The guides come sit with me and share their stories. Sometimes they stay for hours, days, or even"—she threw her hands up into the air—"months!

"And sometimes, they disappear mid-story . . ." She paused and cocked her head a bit. "Well, I know they have other people to tend to besides me. I'm not greedy. I don't mind waiting, I'm just glad they thought enough of me to share. So I go on with my life, I work in my garden, I read, and I wait for them to come back 'round."

My God, I thought to myself, *she's describing my experience*. I thought I was imagining the voices in my head. My eyes flooded with tears of gratitude at the relief that I wasn't crazy.

When I returned home that night, I wrote Ms. Cooper a short letter of thanks. I told her that I greatly admired her work and that I was an aspiring writer myself and I hoped that one day, very soon, my novel, *Sugar*, would be published. I told her that I would welcome any advice she was willing to share with me. I included my telephone number and closed the letter with *all my love, Bernice*.

The event had invigorated me. I returned to my manuscript with new eyes and new ideas and settled into yet another rewrite, stopping often to take the time to listen.

Three months later, I came home from work, dog tired. I

plopped down on my bed and pressed the button on my answering machine. There were a few messages from friends, a wrong number, and then came a voice that I did not immediately recognize.

> *Hello? This is J. California Cooper. I'm calling for Bernice.*
> *Bernice McFadden. Bernice? Thank you for your lovely letter, I*
> *certainly appreciated it! You're a writer too, how wonderful! You*
> *asked for my advice and so here it is—keep writing. Never stop*
> *writing. Your time is coming. Okay. You stay blessed, okay?*
> *Have a nice day. Take care of yourself. Goodbye.*
> *   Beep.*

I sat there dumfounded for a moment. I thought to pinch myself, but instead I replayed the message six more times until I was convinced that I wasn't dreaming.

AS I'VE MENTIONED, DREAMS *ARE* powerful.

Back in 1987—back when I was pregnant with Azsá—me, Reggie, and our family friend Spanky, who'd grown up with us on Sullivan Place, went to see the comedian Eddie Murphy at Madison Square Garden. He was so funny that I thought I would laugh myself into an early labor. After the show, sides aching and wet-eyed, we boarded the crowded A train headed back to Brooklyn. We sat huddled together on the seat, recounting and mimicking the jokes and punch lines, before falling all over one another with laughter.

"I'm going to do that," Reggie shouted over the rumbling train.

"Do what?" Spanky asked.

"I'm going to do that. I'm going to be a comedian." The determination in his voice was resolute.

For a short time, he'd talked about becoming a rapper, and then there was a brief period where he fancied himself a hip-hop dancer. This new aspiration was news to me. I didn't think he was particularly funny. In fact, I thought he was corny. But I suspect that had less to do with his talent and more to do with him being my little brother.

When Reggie made that statement, he was just a month shy of his nineteenth birthday. By 1993, Reggie was living in Los Angeles, having made a name for himself as a stand-up comic in New York. As a budding actor, he auditioned for, and was hired as, a cast member on the wildly popular comedy series *In Living Color*. The entire family was bursting with pride for him.

His success inspired me to remain committed to my own aspirations, even in the wake of my mounting frustrations. For nearly a year, I'd labored late into the night during the week and all day on Sundays, metamorphosing *Sugar* from a molehill into a mountain. When I was done, I didn't waste any time composing a query letter and submitting it to various literary agencies and publishing houses.

I thought I had written a marvel of a novel, but the generic *Thank you but no, thank you* rejection letters I received suggested otherwise. I fought to contain my disappointment, reminded myself that not even John-Boy had found overnight success, and he was a white man. Another thing I'd read in one of those writers' magazines was the importance of the opening lines of your story. The writer of the article advised that it was crucial to snag the reader's attention early on, to keep them reading.

One of the ways to do this, the article suggested, was with an inciting incident. I didn't have an inciting incident in the first paragraph of my novel, it was all just exposition, the inciting incident occurred in chapter two. I spent weeks wringing my hands over this problem, until one day the voice in my head whispered, "Just say it."

Jude was dead.

36

One Saturday night in 1993, Robyn, who was another good friend from work and also Azsá's godmother, and I went to see *What's Love Got to Do with It*, the movie version of Tina Turner's life. I had been a fan of Tina's ever since I was a little girl. "Proud Mary" was one of my anthem songs. I could remember how my heart raced as I watched Tina Turner's high-octane performance on the late-night variety show *The Midnight Special*.

Popcorn and sodas in hand, Robyn and I settled down into the leather seats and prepared ourselves to be blown away. The abuse was hard to watch, not only because it was horrific but because it struck too close to home. The movie theater erupted in applause when Tina, played by Angela Bassett, fought back against her violent husband, Ike, and then finally left that fool.

A friend had introduced Tina Turner to Buddhism, of which she became a faithful practitioner. Tina cites that pivotal event in her life as the thing that gave her the strength to leave her abusive relationship for good. Some years after she'd severed ties with Ike, she'd thrill the world with a staggering comeback. Proud Mary indeed!

Inspired, Robyn and I, along with a sizable number of theatergoers, left the cinema chanting:

Nam-myoho-renge-kyo!
Nam-myoho-renge-kyo!
Nam-myoho-renge-kyo!

I THOUGHT THAT MAYBE BUDDHISM could do for me what it had done for Tina, and so I went searching and discovered that, unlike Christianity, Buddhism did not have a supreme being, which appealed to me. Buddhism is a religion of peace and nonviolence, and one of the core beliefs is that life and death are a continuum.

I found comfort in that philosophy because reincarnation seemed plausible to me. It would take a bit longer for me to apply that same understanding to incidents, happenings, and occasions. Even more years would pass before I stumbled upon the theories of *eternal return* and *historic recurrence*, and I've read that Mark Twain asserted that "history never repeats itself, but it does often rhyme."

Evidence of Rhyming History

Rhyming History #1

MARCH 3, 1859: Just outside Savannah, Georgia, 436 enslaved men, women, children, and infants were auctioned off to settle the debt of their owner, Pierce Mease Butler. It was the largest single sale of enslaved human beings in the history of the United States.

MARCH 3, 1910: Five thousand men, women, and children gathered in downtown Dallas, Texas, in broad daylight, to watch sixty-five-year-old Allen Brooks die. Brooks, a Black man, had been charged with the attempted rape of the two-and-a-half-year-old daughter of his white employer. With a rope tied around his neck, Brooks was dragged down the street about half a mile until the crowd reached a telephone pole under the Elks Arch—a gaudy three-story structure at the corner of Main and Akard Streets that welcomed visitors to Dallas with light bulbs, antlers, and a statue of an elk on top.

Photographs were taken of Brooks's limp body, dangling from the light pole like an American flag without a breeze. Some of those photographs were placed on postcards and mailed to friends and family around the country and maybe even abroad too. One read, *Well John—This is a token of a great day in Dallas, March 3, a Negro was hung for an assault of a three-year-old girl. I saw this on my noon hour. I was very much in the bunch. You can see the Negro hanging on the telephone pole.*

MARCH 3, 1931: President Herbert Hoover signed a law officially making "The Star-Spangled Banner" the national anthem of the United States of America. This is the third verse: *No refuge could save the hireling and slave / From the terror of flight or the gloom of graves / And the star-spangled banner doth wave / O'er the land of the free and the home of the brave.*

MARCH 3, 1991: Four white LAPD officers beat Rodney Glen King, a Black man, nearly to death. They claimed that he was resisting arrest, but that allegation would be refuted when the video surfaced showing that the police officers had set upon Rodney King like a pack of wild dogs, taking turns kicking, punching, and clobbering him with their batons. The video, filmed on a Sony camcorder by George Holliday, a white man, would come to be known as the first viral video in history.

RHYMING HISTORY #2

MARCH 16, 1908: Memphis, Tennessee, L. H. Polk, a white man and a collector, severely wounded Nancy Davis, an elderly Black woman, who cleaned his rooms. Polk claimed the shooting was accidental. He was released on a $2,500 bond.

MARCH 16, 1916: Victoria, Texas, a watchman, Anton Chernosky, a white man, shot a Black woman three times, killing her instantly. I do not know the name of the victim because it was inconsequential to the white journalist who reported the incident. She is glibly described as "a Negro woman."

MARCH 16, 1991: South Central LA, California, fifteen-year-old Latasha Harlins, a Black girl, walked into Empire Liquor Market and Deli, grabbed a bottle of orange juice from the shelf, and dropped the bottle of OJ into her backpack. The owner, Soon Ja Du, a middle-aged Korean woman, saw the bottle of juice but not the two dollars clutched in Latasha's hand.

Latasha had every intention to pay for the juice, but Soon didn't give her a chance, instead she called her a bitch and accused her of stealing. Latasha raised the hand holding the money, but it was too late. Soon pounced on her, and the two began to tussle. After a few blows, Soon fell to the floor and Latasha placed the orange juice on the counter, turned, and headed toward the door. Soon Ja Du grabbed her gun, pointed the muzzle at the back of Latasha's head, and pulled the trigger.

Latasha dropped to the floor. Dead.

The orange juice, which Latasha left on the counter, cost $1.79.

On April 21, 1992, Soon Ja Du was convicted of manslaughter. She was sentenced to ten years in the state prison, but her sentence was suspended. Instead, she was given five years' probation, four hundred hours of community service, and a fine.

Seven days later, on April 29, the jury acquitted three of the four officers who'd nearly beaten Rodney King to death.

Mark Twain was certainly onto something. Maybe what Mark Twain said about history rhyming is true, but maybe, too, George Bernard Shaw had a point when he said, "The longer I live, the more convinced I am that this planet is used by other planets as a lunatic asylum."

———

GEORGE BERNARD SHAW'S STATEMENT SCARED me to death. Not only was I worried for myself, but I was worried for my daughter. I hoped that the world would change for the better by the time she was out from under my guidance and protection, but hope is fleeting, and as of today, the planet is as bad or even worse as it has ever been.

37

All this reading, writing, and research exposed a wound I didn't know I had.

A mother wound is generally defined as the trauma created in a person who lacked mothering. Well, I think most African Americans are walking around with mother wounds because of the generation's long disconnection from our ancestral homeland.

I'd always wanted to visit Africa, but since I'd become a mother, that desire to return to the land of my ancestors had started to feel like a hunger. The idea of it became so persistent it was as if the continent itself was calling to me.

That fall, Azsá started kindergarten at the local public school. Kindergarten? The years had passed in a blur. She was nursing, then crawling, then walking, and then talking, and, now, kindergarten?

It didn't seem real.

At age five, she was already a seasoned traveler. I'd taken her to Barbados every year of her life since she was born. In addition to that, I'd taken her to Belize and the Dominican Republic to visit my high school friend Estela. Once I'd made up my mind to go to Africa, I briefly toyed with the idea of taking her along, but in the end, I decided it was too long and laborious a trip for a five-year-old. And besides, I hoped that when I did have the opportunity to take Azsá to the continent, I wanted Vivian and Thelma with us. A first-born girls quartet, traveling back to our ancestral home, together.

AND SO, IN OCTOBER 1993, just a few days after I celebrated my twenty-eighth birthday, I left my daughter in Vivian's care and set off for Kenya with my cousin Lionel. I was so excited; I didn't sleep a wink on the nine-hour flight between London and Nairobi.

As a child, everything I knew about Africa came by way of television programming like *Tarzan* and *Mutual of Omaha's Wild Kingdom*, and movies such as *Call Me Bwana*, starring Bob Hope; and *Road to Zanzibar* and *Road to Morocco*, both starring Bob Hope and Bing Crosby. White men were always the central character in those movies. The Africans themselves were depicted as submissive servants, bumbling idiots, and flesh-eating savages.

As the British Airline 747 made its descent through the night sky, my mood, already jubilant, climbed. By the time we touched down, I was grinning so wide, I looked like a clown.

"Stop skinning your teeth!" Lionel laughed.

Lionel and I had been traveling together for some years because he worked for the airlines and I worked for a hotel company. It was the perfect partnership, one that would take us to most of the Caribbean islands, Central and South America, the South Pacific, and Africa. We would spend the entirety of that decade discovering the world together at little to no cost to us.

At immigration, the agent, a burly Black man with cartoonishly large biceps, closely scrutinized my passport. Just beyond the customs area was a glass wall. Beyond the glass wall were African men and women dressed in jackets, cable-knit sweaters, and knit hats. For one wild moment, I thought I'd landed in the wrong country. My face crumpled in confusion. I'd expected searing heat even at that late hour. It was Africa, after all, I thought it sizzled day and night.

"Ah," the immigration agent sounded. My eyes flew back to his dark face. He was staring at me, but his expression was as unreadable as a blank piece of paper. Was something wrong with my passport? My visa? The elation that gripped me for hours began to unfurl. I took a deep breath and prepared for the worst.

"Is this your first time here in Kenya?"

I nodded. "Yes."

His eyes narrowed. "First time in Africa?"

"Yes."

There was a beat, and then he smiled a huge, toothy smile that illuminated his entire face. Handing me my passport, he said, "Welcome home, sister."

My heart burst, and I didn't even try to fight back the tears.

WE SPENT TWO DAYS WANDERING around Nairobi, which was as cosmopolitan a place as Manhattan, with tall office buildings, crowded sidewalks, and traffic. On the third day, we took a short flight to Mombasa, the historic port city that sits on the Indian Ocean and is the second-largest city in Kenya. Mombasa is a melting pot of cultures, a blend of Africa, Asia, and Arabia, all represented in the architecture, food, and music.

We rented a car and spent every other day driving for hours along dirt roads that cut through residential communities and farmland. We exchanged pleasantries and took photos with majestic Maasai men who were tall and thin and as dark as ebony. They roamed the beach carrying spears, their bodies wrapped in brightly colored red cloth called maasai shuka.

We gorged ourselves on fresh fruit, fruit juices, and dishes that were reminiscent of the soul and Caribbean food we'd grown up eating. And not a day went by when we did not tilt our chin at some man, woman, or child, remarking: *Don't he look like so and so? She look just like so and so, don't she?!*

Between the familiar food and the doppelgängers, the tragedy of centuries-long human trafficking and brutal enslavement of Africans, of my ancestors, crystallized in my psyche.

SIXTY YEARS BEFORE I ARRIVED in Africa, a then twenty-two-year-old Langston Hughes stepped onto the deck of the merchant ship SS *Malone* and gazed out at the magnificent beauty of the West African coast.

Before Langston ever laid eyes on that shoreline, planted his feet in her rich soil, and inhaled her aromatic air, he'd written a stirring poem in her honor. I suspect he was called to do so and helpless to resist because the memory of the place was swimming in his DNA and buried river-deep in his soul.

With *Sugar*, I too had written about a place I had never seen but felt as familiar as any I'd ever been to. It's nothing short of amazing that we have stories running through our veins.

In his autobiography, *The Big Sea*, Hughes wrote this about West Africa: "And farther down the coast it was more like the Africa I had dreamed about—wild and lovely, the people dark and beautiful, the palm trees tall, the sun bright and the rivers deep. The great Africa of my dreams."

IN HIS 1982 STAND-UP SPECIAL, *Richard Pryor: Live on the Sunset Strip*, the comedic legend shared his first experience visiting Africa. In the film, Pryor is dressed in a red suit and a black mock turtleneck.

"You know, it's like I was leavin' and I was sittin' in the hotel and a voice said to me, it said to me, 'Look around, what do you see?' And I said, 'I see all colors of people doin' everything.' You know, and the voice said, 'Do you see any niggers?' I said, 'No.' And it said, 'You know why? 'Cause there aren't any.'" From that day forward, he vowed never to utter the hateful N-word again.

Africa has that type of magic. A visit is life-changing. A visit to Africa will have you changing your mind, changing your habits, and changing the way you see the world.

The promise I made to myself when I returned home from my first trip to Africa was to never put another drop of lye on my hair. I cut most of my hair off and began wearing my hair in protective braided styles. At the time, there were corporations that forbade Black women from wearing braids, locs, or Afros. In the future, legislation called the Crown Act would prohibit race-based hair discrimination. It's mind-blowing to imagine that a law had to be created protecting Black people's right to wear their hair the way it grows out of their scalps.

My commitment to releasing myself from the clutches of that creamy crack was another footfall on my journey. Change was afoot, and I was readying myself for the next chapter. The French fashion designer and businesswoman Coco Chanel reportedly famously said, "A woman who cuts her hair is about to change her life."

And yes, my life was about to change.

THERE WERE FEW OPPORTUNITIES FOR advancement at Leading Hotels, and because finding a home for my novel was taking longer than I imagined it would, I thought it best that I take a second shot at a college education. In the fall of 1994, I enrolled in the undergraduate program at Fordham University in pursuit of a bachelor's degree in liberal arts. I was nervous about returning to school at that big age, but my anxiety eased when I walked into the classroom and saw that most of the students were adults like me. At Fordham, I studied Black women's history under Dr. Irma Watkins-Owens. In that class, Professor Watkins-Owens introduced me to activists like bell hooks, Audre Lorde, Paula Giddings, Sojourner Truth, and Fannie Lou Hamer.

Later, when I was an established writer, I would turn to Irma Watkins-Owens's book *Blood Relations: Caribbean Immigrants and the Harlem Community, 1900–1930* to aid me in conceptualizing Harlem in my novel *Glorious.*

In my African history class, taught by a Black male professor who was born and raised in Kenya, I learned about the Mau Mau rebellion and Jomo Kenyatta, the anticolonial activist and first indigenous president of Kenya.

"You all heard of Adolf Hitler, yes?" said the Kenyan professor.

We nodded.

"What about King Leopold the Second?"

We stared at him in mute silence.

He nodded knowingly. "Open your books to page . . ."

The Belgium-born-and-bred second king of Belgium and sole owner of the African Congo Free State was responsible for the deaths of fifteen million African men, women, and children between 1885 and 1908. The atrocity is often referred to as the hidden holocaust.

It was certainly hidden, from me and generations upon generations of people of all colors, creeds, and backgrounds. I was twenty-nine years old, and as far as I knew, there had only ever been one Holocaust.

Someone asked the professor, "How come we don't talk about King Leopold the way we talk about Hitler?"

He smirked, rocked his head to one side, and stretched his eyes real wide, which is silent Black-speak for "Because the victims of King Leopold's massacre were Black Africans, and Black lives don't matter."

He had many stories about Kenya, but none that affected me more than the one about the children who lived in and around the Kenyan town of Thika, located in south central Kenya. In Thika, there was a massive pineapple plantation owned by Del Monte. It was one of the largest in all of Africa, covering tens of thousands of acres. A tall fence enclosed the plantation and was patrolled by savage mongrel dogs. Children, being children, frequently scaled that fence to steal the luscious fruit. They thought they were quick. Fast on their feet. And some were, but many others were not, and by the time they snatched the fruit from its shrub, turned to double-time it back to the safe side of the fence, one or all those dogs would run them down and make a meal of their flesh.

As a result, there was an excessively high number of amputees in Thika, and people with mangled limbs, missing eyes, and mauled skin. Del Monte never compensated those children or their families because they'd placed *No Trespassing* and *Beware of Dogs* signs everywhere. It wasn't their fault that children did childish things.

WHILE ALL OF MY PROFESSORS had an impact on my development as a writer, reader, and thinker, there was one woman who set me on the track that brought me here to you today. Professor Margaret Lamb was a novelist, playwright, essayist, and my very first creative writing instructor. The first time I walked into her class, I was struck by her appearance because she so closely resembled my first-grade teacher at P.S. 161 who had charged herself as my protector.

Over the next few weeks, we discussed craft and plot and characterization. I learned about point of view, imagery, the difference between metaphors and similes, and the importance of knowing when to use an abstract noun and when to use a concrete one.

Before Professor Lamb, the only people I'd shared my writing with were my teenage sister and two of my boyfriends, none of whom could give me the critical analysis I needed. I shared with her my desire to become a published writer, the steps I'd taken to make that happen, and the rejection letters that arrived weekly, declaring that I did not have what it took.

One night, as I gathered my things to leave, Professor Lamb called to me, "Bernice, do you have a minute?"

Because catastrophizing was a way of life for me, I immediately thought that I was in trouble. I offered a cautious yes.

She rose from her chair and walked toward me. Her face was set. When she reached my desk, she placed her hand on my shoulder and said, "I've really enjoyed reading your stories. I think you're an exceptional writer, and I don't know why you're not published."

"That means so much to me, Professor, thank you."

Buoyed by Professor Lamb's validation, I floated home on a cloud of happiness.

38

When the phone startled her awake, Virginia had been dreaming about Sandersville, Georgia. She and her brother Richard and her sister Ruby were children again, walking through the woods, chattering, giggling, and beating the ground cover with sticks, sending snakes slithering out of their path.

Sunshine dripped down through the canopy of limbs and climbing vines, setting the colorful autumn leaves aflame. It was November, winter was just weeks away, the nights and early mornings were chilly, but the days were warm and bright. They'd heard that snow had already fallen in Philadelphia, where their eldest sister, Lillian, was living.

They'd never seen snow outside of a picture book, magazine, or photograph, and they very much wanted to see the fluffy white stuff in person. They wanted to dig their fingers into it, tilt their heads back, open their mouths, and catch the falling flakes on their pink tongues. They wanted to build snowmen, pound one another with snowballs, or just stand in all that white and listen to the silence. They would never be able to do that in Sandersville, never play in snow, and never look a white person in the eye.

Lillie Bell said, up North, Black people didn't have to step off the sidewalk to let white people pass, and "we can look them direct in their eyeballs when we speaking to them. I'm not saying they like it, but you can do it and go to sleep at night and not worry 'bout being dragged out your bed and lynched or worse."

What's worse than being lynched?

There. Are. Worse. Things.

Virginia wanted to see snow, and she wanted to see the ocean, which she'd heard was bigger than the spring in the woods behind their house, bigger than the Oconee River in Milledgeville, and bigger than the Ocmulgee in Macon.

"Bigger than Ocmulgee?"

"So much bigger than Ocmulgee!"

Yes, all but one of Grandma Rosie's children dreamed about getting up and away from Sandersville and out into the big, wide world.

They'd leave, one by one and then in twos and threes, until one day Rosie May looked around and only her son Buddy was still there.

When it came time for Virginia to leave the nest, she'd wanted to take that yellow-and-white quilt that Lou had stitched together back at the end of slavery times. Lou had called those bright happy colors "freedom colors." When Lou died in 1927, the quilt was passed down to Lucy, and Rosie had inherited the quilt after Lucy passed in 1935.

Rosie May wasn't ready to part with it, because it was the only thing she had that had belonged to her grandmother.

"It'll be here when you come home to visit," she'd said, dabbing the hem of her apron to her tearing eyes. She was heartbroken, of course. Virginia was the last of her children to leave. Rosie thought that by then she'd be used to saying goodbye to her children, but she never did.

———

IN BROOKLYN, VIRGINIA AND HER family moved into a two-bedroom apartment in the Fort Greene housing projects, where her sister Ruby and her family were already living. When they arrived, it was long after Labor Day, the leaves were already changing colors, and there was a noticeable chill in the air. None of that mattered to Virginia, she'd waited all her life to see the ocean, and since she knew tomorrow wasn't promised, she'd rather not wait. They skipped Sunday church service, took the train out to Coney Island, stepped out onto the sun-splashed platform, and inhaled.

"You smell that?" Virginia's husband, Walter, slapped his chest. "That's salt air."

They bought three hot dogs, slathered each with mustard, and followed the smattering of people to the boardwalk. The closer they inched toward the water, the harder the wind whipped. Virginia turned the collar of her coat up around her neck, and her husband and son grabbed hold of the rims of their fedora hats. The beach was empty save for the seagulls and a man walking along the shoreline.

Virginia cast her eyes over the expanse of bucking gray water. "Oh my goodness," she murmured. "It is so much bigger than the Ocmulgee."

"And louder." Walter laughed over the sound of the breaking waves. He and their son, Walter Jr., rolled their trouser pants up to their knees, and the trio started across the sand toward the water.

People only had to see them slogging through the sand in their good shoes, nice suits, and smart dress to glean that they were new in town, immigrants or migrants fresh off the boat, bus, or train. Well, the spectators chuckled to themselves, that had been them once upon a time.

When the family reached the dark wet sand, both husband and son stopped walking, but Virginia kept going, as if in a trance.

"Hey, Ginny," Walter Sr. called out. "Don't get too close now, ya hear."

His voice was shrill, nervous. Neither one of them could swim, so if the sea reached out and snatched her, she would surely be lost. The distress in his voice snapped her back to reality. Virginia looked down just in time to see the foaming water trundling toward her feet. Giggling, she danced out of reach.

"C'mon now," Walter Sr. said. "Let's head back home."

He didn't want to let on, but the fact of the matter was that all that water made him feel small and scared. Walter stared across that big body of water and wondered if he'd have these same diminishing feelings when it came time for him to stand before God.

NOW, LYING THERE IN HER bed, staring into the darkness, Virginia suspected that her moment before God was swiftly approaching.

Her eyes traveled to the open doorway. There in the soft light of the living room were people milling about, waiting, it seemed, on someone or for something. Some faces looked vaguely familiar, others she didn't recognize at all. What she did know was that the horde was growing. There seemed to be twice as many people there that day than the day before.

Virginia had asked Anna, "Why are all of those people here?"

Anna had brought her face very close to hers. "What people you talking about, Aunt Virginia?"

Virginia tilted her chin. "Them people."

Anna turned her head. "I don't see anyone."

Virginia sighed. "My mistake."

Now, Anna was in the living room, whispering about her into the phone. Anna had been staying with Virginia for months, having left her own family behind to care for her aunt in her last days.

Virginia rubbed the sleep out of her eyes, and when her vision cleared, there was Walter Sr., called WC—her first love and ex-husband, dead ten years now. WC grinned at her in that way that always made her knees weak. Her cheeks warmed as she watched him roll a wooden matchstick from one side of his mouth to the other. He pulled his hands from his pockets and waggled his fingers like he was about to perform a magic trick.

Virginia strained to see.

WC balled his right hand into a fist and placed it over his heart. On his wrist was a watch, the last gift she'd given him before their marriage fell apart and they went their separate ways.

Her breath caught in her throat. "You kept it all these years?"

Walter nodded and then raised his left hand and touched the tip of his index finger against the crystal face. He smiled at her, shoved his hands back into his pockets, and walked out of her frame of vision.

Virginia reasoned again that her end must be near; why else would her apartment be filled with ghosts?

Well, she was tired anyhow. Eighty-nine years is a long time to live. Shoot, when she came into the world on June 26, 1907, Harriet Tubman was still alive, as was her maternal grandmother, Lucy, and her great-grandmother Louisa Vicey, both of whom had been enslaved. Virginia was six years old when Harriet Tubman died. By the time Louisa passed away in 1927, at 105 years old, talkies were replacing silent films and Virginia was a grown woman with a husband and a son. She lived through the horrors of Jim Crow; pandemics; epidemics; countless presidents; Bloody Sunday; the March on Washington; the assassinations of Martin, Malcolm, Medgar, John and his brother Robert; World War I and World War II; the Korean War; the Vietnam War; and more race rebellions than she could count.

She was born a Negro, lived as a colored woman, a Black woman, and now in the last days of her life, African American.

She'd battled cancer, and that bitch had taken her breasts, but Virginia had gotten away with her life. Her battle with cancer and the double mastectomy that followed was an open family secret, so I hadn't had any qualms asking her about it. I was twelve years old when I cornered her in the kitchen at an annual family gathering.

"Can I see?"

Virginia lowered the spoon into the bowl of potato salad. "See what, baby?"

I leaned in. "Your chest," I whispered.

She threw her head back and laughed. "Sure."

Virginia took me by the hand, led me to the bedroom, closed and locked the door. There in the silence of the room, she unbuttoned her blouse and rolled the padded mastectomy bra up to her neck.

"See?"

I gazed at the jagged scars where her breasts had been. My curiosity sated, I thanked her.

"You're welcome, baby," she said. "Do you have any other questions about anything?"

I thought for a second. "No."

VIRGINIA HAD OUTLIVED HER PARENTS and every single one of her eleven siblings, as well as her one and only son and one and only grandson. She'd seen a lot of life and a lot of death, and she was tired.

Virginia closed her eyes, and when she opened them again, her sister Ruby was standing over her, grinning like she had a secret. On her head was a colorfully striped child-sized cardboard party hat.

"Chile," Virginia sighed. "It's November first, your birthday was yesterday. Halloween." And then added with a chuckle, "You look silly."

Ruby crossed her eyes, screwed her face up, and stuck out her tongue.

"I sure do miss you," Virginia whispered.

Ruby smiled warmly at her and then aimed her finger toward the foot of the bed.

It took some effort, but Virginia finally raised her head off the pillow. There, folded neatly on the foot of the bed, was the yellow-

and-white quilt she'd begged Grandma Rosie to give her when she left Sandersville for Brooklyn.

"Oooh," Virginia moaned, "I wondered what ever happened to that."

"What's that now, Aunt Virginia?"

Virginia looked over and saw Anna standing in the doorway. Virginia dropped her head back onto the pillow. "Nothing," she croaked.

Anna peered back at her uncertainly. "You ready to eat? You gotta be hungry. You only took three bites of your breakfast."

Virginia's eyes roamed back to Ruby.

"Aunt Virginia? Aunt Virginia!"

Anna's voice sounded like a siren, and Virginia couldn't imagine why she was screeching like someone had just died.

VIRGINIA EVA MAY-CUMMINGS

JUNE 26, 1907–NOVEMBER 1, 1996

Inside the Minton Springs AME church in Sandersville, Georgia, Anna dabbed at her leaking eyes. Virginia had been dead for nine days and nine nights, and Anna had been weeping for just as many days and nights. Virginia had been the family matriarch, the reigning queen mother, and Anna was struggling to imagine life without her. She pressed her handkerchief over her mouth and moaned. Thelma was seated alongside her, hands folded in her lap, stone-faced. If she'd shed a tear, she'd done so in solitude.

Soon the small church filled with family and friends who'd driven in and flown in and bussed in and trained in from New York, Michigan, Indiana, Virginia, North Carolina, Florida, and as far away as California. They filed somberly past the open casket, stopping briefly to peer at Virginia's lifeless face.

"She look good, don't she?"

"I can't believe she's gone."

"I talked to her two nights before she passed. She sounded a little weak, but . . ." The cousin's voice quivered and stalled. A fresh wave of grief washed over her, and she dropped her head into her hands, sobbing.

Two attendants, a set of twin sisters with shiny gray bobs, hurried forward, wrapped their white-gloved hands around the grieving woman's arms, and guided her back to her seat.

AFTER THE SERMON, THE PREACHER offered the podium to the congregation. "Is there anyone who would like to say a few words?"

Anna heaved her four hundred pounds out of the pew and started toward the dais. There she shared her loving memories of Virginia, stopping often to swab at the perspiration clinging to her face and the tears dribbling from her eyes.

Help her, Lord. Help her, Jesus.

It's okay. It's all right. Take your time.

When she was done speaking, Anna turned away from the podium, but then, as an afterthought, turned to face the people one last time.

"One more thing," she breathed, "I wish you all safe travels back home and thank you for coming."

Anna returned to her seat and opened her Bible to the scripture directed by the pastor. Eyes blurry with tears, she followed along as best she could. Her grief was so very, very heavy. And then suddenly that weight was crushing her heart. Anna's breath caught in her throat, the Bible tumbled from her hands down to the floor.

Thelma turned to look at her. "Sis, what's wrong?"

James threw his arm around her shoulder. "What's wrong, Mommy?"

Anna was gasping by then, gasping and tugging at the collar of her dress. "I need some air," she wheezed.

James and a few others helped her out of the pew, down the aisle, and into the room at the back of the church. The pastor bounced his hands in the air. "Everybody calm down. Stay calm."

In the back room, after James unzipped Anna's dress, she reached her hands around to claw at the hook-and-eye panel of her bra. "Take it off, I can't breathe, it's too tight . . ."

The weight grew heavier. James and Thelma fumbled with the tiny fasteners with trembling fingers. Anna's chest heaved and shuddered with every shallow breath.

"Almost there, Mommy," James cried.

Suddenly, Anna's head shot back on her neck, her terror-filled eyes fixed on the ceiling, and her arms began flailing.

"Nooooooo!" she screamed.

The tight throng of people leaped out of striking distance. Their eyes trailed Anna's line of sight to the space above their heads.

"You see anything?"

"What she looking at?"

"No, no . . . noooooooo, get away . . . nooooo!" Anna wheezed, swiping at the invisible assailant. Seconds later, her arms collapsed, and her head slumped to one side.

"Sis?"

ROSE ANNA HAWKINS-TYLER

SEPTEMBER 28, 1928–NOVEMBER 10, 1996

The family had held a funeral service in Brooklyn for Virginia's church family, longtime friends, and those familial who didn't have the means or the time to go down to Sandersville, where she would have a second homegoing service at Minton Springs AME church and then be interred in the church cemetery, where her parents were buried.

My immediate family had attended the first service in Brooklyn.

When we got word that Anna had passed away at Virginia's funeral, we were shocked and saddened. Days later, numb with grief, we boarded a flight to Georgia to say a final farewell to our dear aunt Anna.

It was a pretty day, warm and breezy and full of sunshine. Little white butterflies flitted over the open grave and settled on the tiny ant mounds rising like crumbling clay towers from the knolls of fresh-dug earth. The tree canopy trilled with birds of all sizes and colors, but I thought the prettiest birds were the red ones.

"Cardinals," my cousin said when she saw me staring up at one perched on a low branch.

I'd seen the cardinals here and there around Brooklyn, but they weren't as popular as the infrequently glimpsed blue jay, which symbolized good luck.

"Aaah," I moaned.

"You see them mostly when someone has passed away."

I looked at her. "What?"

"Something about them carrying messages for the spirits." She chuckled.

"Really?" I was intrigued now.

"I don't know, just some old wives' tale." She laughed again. "C'mon, let's get inside."

I hurried to keep up, snatching glances over my shoulder at the crimson-colored spirit transporter.

We walked past a line of parked cars that stretched a mile down the road. Plenty of people had come to say goodbye to Virginia Eva May-Cummings and stayed to say goodbye to Anna.

The women walked ahead, eager to get out of the heat and inside the church, where it was cooler. The men dawdled outside for a bit, puffing on cigarettes, talking cars, football, the rising cost of fertilizer, and the recent reelection of that tenor-sax-playing, smooth-talking, this-is-the-closest-thing-we'll-ever-get-to-a-Black-president Bill Clinton.

At the funeral, I kept my eyes on Thelma, who was seated in the pew, with one arm thrown casually over the back of the wooden bench like she was watching a boring baseball game.

In the church, we firstborn girls sat in a row, me on the outside right, Thelma in the middle, Azsá sat next to her, with her head resting on the swell of her bosom, and Vivian bookended to the left.

I kept my eyes on Thelma, because the story was that after Anna took her last breath, Thelma sprinted out of the church and took off running across the grounds toward the road. They say she was running and wailing like she was being chased down by devil hounds. Three men shot off after her, caught her, and wrapped their strong arms around her until she thrashed and hollered herself limp.

Now, as I vigilantly observed her, it was hard to imagine that she had expelled such dramatic sorrow. Which is not to say that she wasn't grieving, I'm sure she was, but I believe that that part of herself that spirited away in times of distress had done exactly that, which is why the look on her face was flat and emotionless.

Vivian looked as sad as sad looked, but her eyes were bone-dry. She only ever cried when she was fighting with Robert. Azsá, just eight years old by then, may have understood the gravity of the situation, but she was as restless and bored as all the other little children in the church.

"Stop all the squirming," Thelma warned Azsá, and then curled her arm around her shoulders in a tight hug.

As for me, I am the crier in the family, and for the entirety of the service, I held true to my calling.

ANNA HAD BEEN THE THUMPING heart of our family, the one you went to for advice, to be prayed over, a comforting embrace, or a meal. True, she was a fierce combatant, willing to square up with anyone, woman or man, who threatened her safety or the safety of those she loved.

And boy, did she love. She'd loved deeply, wholly, interminably, and sometimes to a fault.

What a blessing she had been to our family. Her passing left a void that started as a pit and continues to expand today.

As the years folded and unfolded, I would never hear Thelma voice just how much she missed her, but I knew she missed her terribly, by the way she'd recall stories about Anna, mimicking the gentle and loving way she'd called her Sis.

IN THE WORDS OF THE famed rapper Biggie Smalls, the final months of 1996 were filled with "a lot of slow singing and flower bringing."

Still ladened with grief, our family staggered into 1997 believing that we had left the misery of death behind. But we should have known better, because the rule of death is that it comes in threes.

On the eleventh day of the New Year, the grim reaper employed his scythe once again, this time on Gwen, and she closed her eyes for good.

GWENDOLYN DOROTHY GILL-MCFADDEN

FEBRUARY 18, 1924–JANUARY 11, 1997

39

After Gwen died, I quit school.

Not only was the tuition steep, and my student loan bill inching into uncomfortable territory, but I was depressed and grieving and found it difficult to focus on my studies.

After five years, I left Leading Hotels of the World for a position as a customer service manager with a small, independently owned Caribbean tour company in Washington Heights, called Sunburst Holidays. The commute from home to work was over an hour long. Each way. Perfect for reading.

The job itself was mostly uncomplicated. I spent most days resolving customer grievances and acting as liaison between travel suppliers and the public.

Before the job, I had never been to Washington Heights. When I arrived there in the fall of 1997, the neighborhood was populated by Latinx people, most of whom were of Dominican descent, which is why it's called Little Dominican Republic. It was once a very affluent neighborhood, populated by wealthy New Yorkers. But those people left when European immigrants, seeking refuge from famine and genocide, began moving into the neighborhood. It was in that neighborhood that Malcom X lost his life to an assassin's bullet on February 21, 1965.

WHEN I ACCEPTED THE POSITION, I'd completed a third draft of my novel. I knew it was the best draft thus far, because the rejection letters were personalized now, and not the prewritten form letters I'd received for drafts one and two.

The parties argued that while I'd written a compelling piece of work, there simply was no audience for the book. The parties in question suggested that I read what was currently trending in African American fiction, rewrite my story to suit, and then resubmit for their consideration. Their contention was baffling, because a blind man could see that my writing style was heavily influenced by Morrison, Walker, and Cooper; and they all had an audience, didn't they?

I was pissed but not defeated. In fact, I was more determined than ever to prove my cynics wrong.

BY NOVEMBER 1997, I HAD been with Sunburst Holidays for a year. It had been an enjoyable ride, because I liked my coworkers, and the free travel was always a bonus. I would have been more than happy to stay on, but the universe had other plans for me.

I was due a raise, and although I had been given a five-star review, the increase they offered was a poor reflection of that. On the train ride home, I stewed in my anger. When I finally reached the front door of the house, the emotions I had been fighting back for hours poured out of me. After a good long cry, the anger returned, hot and bitter.

I was so damn mad, all I could think about was quitting. I knew that would be an irresponsible choice, because I didn't have a job lined up and I had no idea how long it would take to find one. We'd had a rough time in those early years when Robert first lost his job. But we'd made it through, using credit cards and cash advances, when needed.

Robert was still drinking, but his cruelty had softened over the years. I supposed grandchildren did that to you, and he had two firstborn granddaughters, because my sister had had a child, and we were all living under one roof.

Life was stable, and I was worried that my quitting my job would upset that. For my entire life, I had been conditioned to be selfless, to consider other people's feelings, needs, and desires ahead of my own. As soon as I thought about doing something major for myself, I found myself racked with guilt.

But my urging gut wouldn't quit. I tossed and turned all night, and when dawn broke, I laid there staring at the morning light creeping around the edges of the window blinds. While I was in turmoil, my daughter was lying next to me, sleeping comfortably, without a care in the world. In a few weeks she would turn ten years old. What would my decision mean for her quality of life? My mind spun and spun.

I got up and went upstairs to shower. Under the rain of hot water, I closed my eyes and asked the angelcestors for help. "I don't want to make the wrong decision," I uttered aloud. "Please, please help me."

The answer had already been given to me. What I was looking for was a different response, one that could keep me safe, even if that safety meant I remained in a position where I was undervalued and underpaid.

In the end, however, I went with my gut. My worth and happiness was more important to me than a steady paycheck.

Of course, after spending years investigating and thinking about the lives of the family members who came before me, I was acutely aware that walking away from a job without having another in sight was a privilege that they never had.

I also understood that they did not slave and toil expecting that their descendants would have to do the same. I know they wanted better for us. I know that if we were given the chance, they wanted us to live out our wildest dreams.

That morning, when I made the decision to pursue my dreams, I understood I was taking the first steps toward honoring the hopes and desires they held for their descendants.

I typed up my resignation letter, tucked it into my purse, and headed off to work.

My boss was a petite white woman with wild, thick hair. She reminded me of photos I'd seen of hippies in the sixties. After she read the letter, her face turned pink with surprise.

"Um, um . . ." She fumbled, searching frantically for the right words. "Is this about the money?" What a stupid question.

"Yes."

She looked down at the letter again. "Let me talk to the owner."

"Okay," I said, even though my mind was made up. I went to my desk and began my day. An hour later, I looked up from my work and there she was.

"He wants to know what you want."

The *he* was the Greek owner.

"What I want?"

She rubbed her fingers together and mouthed the word: *money*.

I looked her dead in face. "I don't want money; I just want my freedom."

"YOU QUIT YOUR JOB?"

I heard this from Vivian. I heard it from Linford and everyone else I told.

"You quit your job without having another one in the wings? Gurl, you crazy!" My friend Robyn cackled into the phone. "What you going to do?"

"Sell my book."

"Gurl, you better than me!" She laughed. Which is Black-speak for "You are not better than me, but you are crazy."

Some prayed for my success, and others waited for my fall.

I POOLED MY TAX REFUND with the money I'd saved. It wasn't much, but if I was diligent, I could make it stretch for at least six months.

It was nice to see my daughter off to school in the morning and be there to greet her in the afternoons and help her with her home-work, listen to her stories about her day at school. I didn't realize how much I'd missed of her life until I had no other place to be except home with her. While Vivian and Robert did most of the cooking for the family, now that I had time, I contributed as well and found it to be therapeutic and a nice break between writing. I really enjoyed spending all of that time with myself, my daughter, and the characters in my story.

But before I knew it, I looked up and five months had gone by. My savings were nearly depleted, and I hadn't sold my novel. I had enough rejection letters from agents and publishers to paper an en-tire wall in my apartment. I cursed my gut for having deceived me into believing so completely in myself and now I'd have to contend with the I told-you-so's.

Despondent, that Sunday I bought a copy of the *New York Times* and turned to the want-ads section.

I was a good ten pounds heavier than I'd been when I left Sun-burst Holidays. After all, I'd done little more than experiment with recipes and sit at my computer, writing and rewriting while sipping Grand Marnier.

So, when I arrived for my interview for a job as a meeting coor-dinator with Goldman Sachs, I walked into that office wearing an ill-fitted skirt suit. On top of that, I had three inches of new growth because I hadn't dyed my hair for the entirety of the time I'd been on sabbatical from corporate America. Because I was angry that I had to be there at all, I did not grin, pander, shuffle, or jive. I did my absolute best to sabotage any chance of being considered for the position, but it backfired on me.

By the time I returned home, there was a message on my answering machine, offering me the job. I could only assume that my callousness was interpreted as confidence. Or maybe my angelcestors did what they'd always done for me, which, chief among many things, was protecting me from my own foolish self.

The department was new, and the rollout was slow. So slow, that the phones rarely rang. There were two of us in the office, me and a Dominican woman who had been with the company for years. She took a lot of smoke breaks. Long smoke breaks. Which is to say I was left in the office alone for hours at a time. For the first few weeks, I utilized the quiet to read until it dawned on me that I could put that time to better use.

At home I'd been writing on an ancient IBM computer that was on the brink of death. I had a dot matrix printer that was loud and as slow as molasses. But in the office, I had a state-of-the-art computer and a fast laser-jet printer. So I emailed my manuscript to myself at work and got down to business.

By midsummer, things had picked up. There were three new hires, and they were looking for more. The Dominican girl was gone, demoted back to the catering department, where she'd initially started her career with the company. They replaced her with a waif-thin, bright-eyed bubbly white girl whom the Dominican had trained. The white girl didn't smoke, so she was always at her desk, save for the two or three trips a day to the bathroom and her lunch break. She wore Ann Taylor suits, was genteel, and when she spoke, sunshine and rainbows shot out of her mouth—which is to say that she sounded like Glinda the Good Witch from *The Wizard of Oz*.

By September, work had picked up tremendously, which meant the phones rang nonstop. I no longer had time to work on my novel, which was fine, because I had done all that I could do with that book and was already thinking about the next one.

That said, I still printed copies at work to mail to interested parties. And that's how my coworkers discovered that I had written a book.

"Is this yours?"

I looked up into the ruddy face of one of the VPs on the floor. I wasn't a fan of his. I found him patronizing and condescending to the women in the office.

I blinked stupidly at him. "Sorry?"

He waved the stack of white papers at me. It was my manuscript. Of course he knew it belonged to me, because my name was on the title page as well as the upper-far-right corner of every page after that.

"You're writing a book?" he repeated.

We eyed each other. I reached for the pages. "Um, yes, I am."

He smirked at me, uttered a little laugh, and stalked off, shaking his head.

You'll see, I thought to myself.

40

I believe numbers are magical.

Take the number 7 for instance. World round, the number 7 is associated with luck. In Western culture, the number 9 represents the completion of one cycle and preparation for the next. I was born in September, the ninth month of the year. It was in September that I died at age two and came back.

On February 9, 1999, I mailed off a query letter to James Vines, of the Vines Agency. On that day, Alice Walker turned fifty-five and my daughter, Azsá, turned eleven.

A few weeks later, it was March, and James Vines was in my inbox, asking me to send along the first three chapters of *Sugar*, and also asking if I would give him exclusivity until I heard back from him. It wasn't the first time an agent had made this request. It might have been the eighth or tenth time, but it always ended the same: *Thank you but no, thank you.* Close but no cigar.

While I was hopeful, my heart didn't flutter with excitement like it had all those times before. I'd learned to temper my anticipation, because I didn't like the nose dive my emotions took every time I was rejected. It was best to stay grounded, where the fall was short.

I agreed to the exclusivity, mailed off the three chapters to his office, but continued to query agents, because I knew the disappointment of placing all my eggs in one basket.

It was April when I heard back. Daffodils and tulips were everywhere. Spring, the season of new beginnings. He wrote that he'd enjoyed the three chapters and wanted to see the entire manuscript.

"I'll send a messenger to pick it up. What's the address?"

A messenger? Well, this was new. . . . The little bird in my chest chirped and quivered. I placed a calming hand over my heart.

When I started this journey to becoming a writer—a published author—I was just a young mother, still learning about myself, my family, America, and the world.

When I started this journey, I had two grandmothers and great- and grandaunts who were so instrumental in my life that I would spend my career re-creating and reimaging their lives in a litany of novels and short stories I had yet to write.

I had spent the last decade dreaming about publishing *Sugar*, imagining sharing shelf space with books by authors whom I admired, revered, and deified. Sometimes those visualizations felt so real, they took my breath away.

Now, I was thirty-three years old: a fully grown woman, with strands of gray in my hair, the mother of a tween-aged daughter who had changed and enhanced my life in ways I could have never imagined. I'd watched her grow from a baby into a healthy, beautiful young lady, who, similar to me, found joy in reading and was curious and excited about seeing the world.

Reggie had married, and he and his wife had welcomed a son. He was still living in LA, still wowing people with his good looks, charisma, and comedy. The twins were twenty-one years old, legal adults out in the world working and making lives for themselves.

Herzfeld & Stern was bought by Gruntal & Co. and after three decades of dedication, Vivian was laid off. She'd tried to find work elsewhere, but by then companies were requiring applicants to have a high school diploma at minimum. Which Vivian did not have. And there was the matter of her arrest and conviction for theft back when she was fifteen, which made her a felon.

It seemed that she could never win for losing.

The disappointment and rejection were more than she could take, and after a few months she gave up on looking for a job and enrolled in GED classes to, as she is fond saying, "better myself."

Ten years after Robert lost his job, he became eligible to collect his pension and returned to contributing financially to the household. He was still drinking, but not as much as he had in the past, not because he wanted to slow down but because his body was forcing him to slow down, and his heart, weak as it was, was the organ leading the charge.

After several more debilitating strokes, Wilfred became completely bedridden. Family members encouraged Thelma to put him in a nursing home, but she refused. "I will not! They don't treat people good in those places."

Well, we knew that was true, but we also knew that if Wilfred went into a nursing home, his social security check would go there too, and Thelma couldn't have that.

As for me, I'd started this journey with ambivalent feelings about my father and confused feelings about my mother because she had stayed with him for thirty-three miserable years. But I'd matured during this decades-long expedition called life, and with that growth came understanding and compassion and empathy for them both.

I'd started this journey knowing little to nothing about my ancestors, completely oblivious that they had *always* been with me, protecting and guiding.

Flanked by a legion of angelcestors, I'd started this journey with one step and continued placing one foot after the other, walking by closed window after closed window, until I finally stepped over the threshold of the open door into my destiny.

THREE DAYS.

Three days is all it took for my life to completely change.

The number 3 represents the birth, life, and death cycle. The number 3 denotes the mind, body, and soul connection. There are three acts in a story, and now, I am completing the third act of this particular tale.

The call came at work, just before I was preparing to head out to lunch.

"Bernice McFadden?"

I adjusted my headset and glanced at the screen on my desk phone. It wasn't an internal number, but it did have a New York City area code.

"Yes, this is she."

"This is Jimmy Vines, how are you?"

"I'm . . . fine. . . . How are you?" I felt lightheaded. The ringing phones, the clattering of keyboards, my coworkers' voices all faded to a hum.

"I'm good, Bernice, thank you," Jimmy said. "Listen, I read your novel in two sittings, and I just think it's phenomenal. . . ."

And with that, the little bird in my chest broke free.

Breathless, I closed my eyes just in time to see a cardinal as red and as bright as a flame, streaking through the darkness behind my closed lids.

Suddenly all my ancestors were behind me.

Be still, they say. *Watch and listen.*
You are the result of the love of thousands.
—LINDA HOGAN, *DWELLINGS:*
A SPIRITUAL HISTORY OF THE LIVING WORLD

ACKNOWLEDGMENTS

My gratitude starts with my mother, Vivian McFadden, who gave me life, then saved my life, and who was the first person to put a book in my hands.

And to my daughter, Azsá, who made me a mother, which remains a remarkable gift and privilege in my life.

Thanks to my agent, Melissa Danaczko, of the Stuart Krichevsky Literary Agency, Inc., who believed in and rallied for this memoir from its inception.

I'm indebted to my editors, Maya Ziv and Rose Tomaszewska, for their keen eyes, patience, guidance, encouragement, and the copious amounts of time and effort they put into helping me shape and birth the book you hold in your hands today.

To Johnny Temple and Johanna Ingalls and the staff of Akashic Books, who said yes when everyone else said no; and created a safe, welcoming, and nurturing space for me to write and publish at a time when I was in the midst of one of the darkest and most destabilizing periods of my professional and personal life. THANK YOU!!

I'm blessed to have a multitude of family and friends who have loved and supported me from day one. There are too many people to list by name, but they know who they are.

A million and one thank-yous!!!

To my teachers, those authors I read, reread, studied, and read again. I hope my weight on your shoulders ain't too heavy. . . .

It wasn't in my life plan to become a professor of creative writing, but as the saying goes: "You make plans and God laughs. . . ."

I want to thank Tulane University, my colleagues and new friends at that academic institution who have supported and embraced me as one of their own.

Special appreciation to the city of New Orleans, which has become my home away from home. Life for me here is easy in the softest of ways.

Special acknowledgment to Linda Jones, the Writing Doula, who after a decades-long absence, suddenly reappeared in my life during a critical juncture in the writing of this memoir and blessed me with the phrase: "Legacy Literature." The journey after that was golden. Thank you, Linda Jones.

My gratitude to Dutton, who published my debut novel, *Sugar*, in 2000 and then twenty-five years later welcomed me back into the fold to debut this memoir.

Coming full circle has never felt so sweet.

To the *women* who raised the *women* who raised me; you are every beat of my heart.

To my readers, where would I be without you? Thank you! Thank you!

And finally, to my angelcestors, whom I thank in the morning when I wake up, all through the day, and again at night before I go to sleep. I know that you all know how I revere and appreciate your protection and direction. I am so looking forward to being in your company on the other side.

Light.

FINAL AUTHOR'S NOTE

Dear reader, I want you to know that I started writing this book in Brooklyn, New York, in June 2020, during the coronavirus pandemic. I was writing and sheltering in place with my then seventy-seven-year-old mother. At the time, my ninety-four-year-old grandmother was in a nursing home in Queens, and my mother and I were afraid that we would never see her again, because she was a member of that vulnerable community who were dying in droves from the virus.

In May 2020, I watched with the world, in horror, as a white police officer knelt on the neck of a forty-five-year-old Black man named George Perry Floyd Jr. until he was dead.

It was pure fear and anger that compelled me to write this book, and for the next four years, I wrote under duress.

On April 13, 2024, I finished writing this book in New Orleans, Louisiana.

By then, my grandmother had joined the ancestors, but my

mother is still alive and well, and I am still afraid and I am still angry and I am still a Black woman writing under duress in America.

But dear God, I'm here. I'm here!
—CELIE, *THE COLOR PURPLE* BY ALICE WALKER

NOTES

CHAPTER 1

24 **"There has never been"**: "Our Future Citizens," *New York Times*, March 5, 1882, https://timesmachine.nytimes.com/timesmachine/1882/03/05/103405623.html?pageNumber=6.

24 **"Lately the Italian element"**: *Times-Picayune*, December 31, 1890, 3.

24 **"The savages swoon"**: "The Ghost Dance," *Salt Lake Tribune*, November 23, 1890, 1.

24 **"a rather good thing"**: Jennifer Theriault, "A Rather Good Thing," *The American in Italia*, March 29, 2013, https://theamericanmag.com/a-rather-good-thing/.

25 **"just a little worse than"**: Theriault, "Rather Good Thing."

CHAPTER 2

37 **"He had three long gashes"**: Sea Stachura, "Remembering the Augusta Civil Rights Riot, 50 Years Later," *All Things Considered*, NPR, October 1, 2020, https://www.npr.org/2020/10/01/918414307/remembering-the-augusta-civil-rights-riot-50-years-later.

37 **"Oatman was beaten"**: "Ten Years Given in Oatman Death," *Augusta Chronicle*, September 15, 1970, 11.

38 **"The deputies took Oatman"**: "Death of Young Jail Inmate Sparked Rioting in Augusta," *Augusta Chronicle*, May 11, 1980, 49.

39 **That January, a carload:** *Charlotte Observer,* January 18, 1970, 2.

39 **"tapped by destiny":** *Charlotte Observer,* January 18, 1970, 2.

CHAPTER 7

76 **Risk factors for children:** Marilyn A. Mendoza, "Why Do Young Children Commit Suicide?," *Psychology Today,* November 12, 2018, https://www.psychologytoday.com/us/blog/understanding-grief /201811/why-do-young-children-commit-suicide.

78 **Studies show:** Sara West and Mendel Feldsher, "Parricide: Characteristics of Sons and Daughters Who Kill Their Parents," *Current Psychiatry* 9, no. 11 (November 2010): 20–38, https://cdn .mdedge.com/files/s3fs-public/Document/September-2017/0911CP _Article1.pdf.

81 **four in ten Black women:** Susan Green, "Violence Against Black Women—Many Types, Far-Reaching Effects," Institute for Women's Policy Research, July 13, 2017, https://iwpr.org/violence-against-black -women-many-types-far-reaching-effects/.

81 **presence of a gun:** "Firearm Intimate Partner Homicides," Brady Campaign to End Gun Violence, https://www.bradyunited.org/resources /research/analysis-firearm-intimiate-partner-homicides.

83 **"A new speed record":** "Court Breaks Record in Quick Trial," *Daily News,* April 12, 1934, https://www.newspapers.com/article/daily-news /99328277/.

CHAPTER 8

91 **"the island was also densely populated":** Jack D. Warren Jr., "Washington's Journey to Barbados," Mount Vernon Ladies' Association, https://www.mountvernon.org/george-washington /washingtons-youth/journey-to-barbados.

CHAPTER 11

132 **In an interview:** American Heart Association News, "Why Are Black Women at Such High Risk of Dying from Pregnancy Complications?," American Heart Association, February 20, 2019, https://www.heart.org /en/news/2019/02/20/why-are-black-women-at-such-high-risk-of-dying -from-pregnancy-complications.

CHAPTER 14

160 **US Police Have Killed:** Sam Levin, "US Police Have Killed Nearly 600 People in Traffic Stops Since 2017, Data Shows," *The Guardian,* April 21, 2022, https://www.theguardian.com/us-news/2022/apr/21/us-police -violence-traffic-stop-data.

CHAPTER 15

164 **In America, she is legally white:** "Dow v. United States," vLex, https://
case-law.vlex.com/vid/dow-v-united-states-885459875.

166 **In 2018, Father Arthur J. Long:** "Fr. Arthur J. Long—Archdiocese of
Washington," Horowitz Law, June 5, 2019, https://www.adamhorowitz
law.com/blog/2019/06/fr-arthur-j-long-archdiocese-of-washington/.

166 **When confronted, Father Long:** "Fr. Arthur J. Long," Horowitz Law.

167 **In 2004, John Jay College:** "The Nature and Scope of Sexual Abuse of
Minors by Catholic Priests and Deacons in the United States 1950–
2002," study by John Jay College of Criminal Justice for the United
States Conference of Catholic Bishops, June 2004, https://www.usccb
.org/sites/default/files/issues-and-action/child-and-youth-protection
/upload/The-Nature-and-Scope-of-Sexual-Abuse-of-Minors-by
-Catholic-Priests-and-Deacons-in-the-United-States-1950-2002.pdf.

167 **A series published:** "Catholic Church Sex Abuse," AbuseLawsuit.com,
https://www.abuselawsuit.com/church-sex-abuse.

CHAPTER 17

190 **"The bones show the hardships":** Ann Kellan, "Bones Reveal Little-
Known Tale of New York Slaves," CNN, February 12, 1998, http://www
.cnn.com/TECH/9802/12/t_t/burial.ground/.

CHAPTER 21

225 **that the virus had been around since the 1800s:** University of
Arizona, "HIV/AIDS Pandemic Began Around 1900, Earlier Than
Previously Thought; Urbanization in Africa Marked Outbreak,"
ScienceDaily, October 2, 2008, www.sciencedaily.com/releases/2008/10
/081001145024.htm.

CHAPTER 22

228 **"Well, I was a little":** Sal Bono, "How Detectives Caught 'Palm Sunday
Massacre' Gunman, Who Killed 8 Kids and 2 Women: 'Their Faces Still
Haunt Me,'" *Inside Edition*, April 25, 2018, updated May 1, 2018,
https://www.insideedition.com/how-detectives-caught-palm-sunday
-massacre-gunman-who-killed-8-kids-and-2-women-their-faces-still.

228 **East New York was plagued:** Bono, "How Detectives Caught 'Palm
Sunday Massacre' Gunman."

CHAPTER 24

246 **sprinkling pearl dust:** Pearl dust is an ingredient in love potions.

247 **80 percent of Black people:** "Lactose Intolerance," Boston Children's
Hospital, https://www.childrenshospital.org/conditions/lactose
-intolerance.

249 **in Philadelphia, the local police:** "May 13, 1985: Philadelphia Police
Bomb MOVE," Zinn Education Project, https://www.zinnedproject.org
/news/tdih/move-bombing/.

250 **In fact, their remains:** Michelle Watson and Amanda Musa, "Brother
of 1985 MOVE Bombing Victims Sues Philadelphia and UPenn for
Allegedly Mishandling the Black Teens' Remains," CNN, November 10,
2022, https://www.cnn.com/2022/11/10/us/philadelphia-move
-bombing-lawsuit-remains-reaj/index.html.

250 **"There he was stripped":** Lawrence Goldstone, *Inherently Unequal: The
Betrayal of Equal Rights by the Supreme Court, 1865–1903*, quoted in
Library of America, "How Sam Hose's Lynching Became an Awakening
for W.E.B. Du Bois," Reader's Almanac, March 18, 2011, https://blog
.loa.org/2011/03/how-sam-hose-lynching-became-awakening.html.

CHAPTER 25

265 **"A Federal jury today":** Associated Press, "U.S. Jurors Award $7
Million Damages in Slaying by Klan," *New York Times*, February 13,
1987, https://www.nytimes.com/1987/02/13/us/us-jurors-award-7
-million-damages-in-slaying-by-klan.html.

CHAPTER 26

270 **"Barbados was the birthplace":** Sir Hilary Beckles, "On Barbados, the
First Black Slave Society," Black Perspectives, April 8, 2017, https://
www.aaihs.org/on-barbados-the-first-black-slave-society/.

CHAPTER 31

302 **"Central Park Horror":** David Handschun, "Central Park Horror: Wolf
Pack's Prey," *Daily News*, April 21, 1989, https://www.nydailynews.com
/2013/04/09/central-park-jogger-near-death-after-savage-attack
-in-1989.

302 **Black children have been adultified:** Kiara Alfonseca, "Ralph Yarl
Case Highlights 'Adultification' of Black Children, Researchers Say,"
ABC News, April 19, 2023, https://abcnews.go.com/US/ralph-yarl-case
-highlights-adultification-black-children-researchers/story?id
=98662646.

CHAPTER 32

309 **"The 1990s were":** Douglas Coupland, "1990s: The Good Decade,"
History.com, March 17, 2017, updated September 21, 2023, https://
www.history.com/news/1990s-the-good-decade.

312 **even though white women:** Ryan Sit, "Trump Thinks Only Black
People Are on Welfare, but Really, White Americans Receive Most
Benefits," *Newsweek*, January 12, 2018, updated May 25, 2018, https://
www.newsweek.com/donald-trump-welfare-black-white-780252.

CHAPTER 36

338 *Well John:* Harvey Young, "The Black Body as Souvenir in American Lynching," *Theatre Journal* 57, no. 4 (2005): 639–57, https://doi.org /10.1353/tj.2006.0054.

338 **March 16, 1908:** "Negro Woman Shot," *Commercial Appeal*, March 16, 1908, 5.

339 **March 16, 1916:** *The Daily Advocate*, March 16, 1916, 1.

339 **March 16, 1991:** Erika D. Smith, "The Killing of Latasha Harlins Was 30 Years Ago. Not Enough Has Changed," *Los Angeles Times*, March 17, 2021, https://www.latimes.com/california/story/2021-03-17/latasha -harlins-memorial-playground-black-lives-matter-south-los-angeles.

339 **given five years' probation:** Tracy Wilkinson and Frank Clifford, "Korean Grocer Who Killed Black Teen Gets Probation," *Los Angeles Times*, November 16, 1991, https://www.latimes.com/archives/la-xpm -1991-11-16-mn-1402-story.html.

ABOUT THE AUTHOR

Bernice L. McFadden is an Assistant Professor of English at Tulane University and the author of several critically acclaimed novels, including *Sugar*, *The Warmest December*, *Loving Donovan*, *Nowhere Is a Place*, *Glorious*, *Gathering of Waters* (a *New York Times* Editors' Choice and one of the 100 Notable Books of 2012), *The Book of Harlan* (winner of a 2017 American Book Award and the NAACP Image Award for Outstanding Literary Work, Fiction), and *Praise Song for the Butterflies* (long-listed for the 2019 Women's Prize for Fiction). She is a five-time Hurston/Wright Legacy Award finalist, as well as the recipient of three awards from the Black Caucus of the American Library Association.